D1484051

cogito

and

the

unconscious

SIC

A

series

edited

by

Slavoj

Žižek

and

Renata

Salecl

SIC stands for psychoana-
lytic interpretation at its
most elementary: no dis-
covery of deep, hidden
meaning, just the act of
drawing attention to the
litterality [*sic!*] of what precedes it. A "*sic*" reminds
us that what was said, inclusive of its blunders, was
effectively said and cannot
be undone. The series SIC
thus explores different
connections of the Freud-
ian field: each volume provides a bundle of Lacanian
interventions into a specific domain of ongoing
theoretical, cultural, and
ideologico-political battles.
It is neither "pluralist"
nor "socially sensitive":
unabashedly avowing its
exclusive Lacanian orienta-
tion, it disregards any form
of correctness but the
inherent correctness of
theory itself.

cogito

and

the

unconscious

Slavoj Žižek,
editor

sic **2**

DUKE UNIVERSITY PRESS   Durham and London 1998

© 1998 Duke University Press

All rights reserved

Printed in the United States

of America on acid-free paper ∞

Typeset in Sabon by Tseng

Information Systems, Inc.

Library of Congress Cataloging-in-

Publication Data appear on the

last printed page of this book.

Contents

Slavoj Žižek

Introduction:

Cogito as a

Shibboleth

There are two standard ways to approach the relationship between philosophy and psychoanalysis. Philosophers usually search for so-called
"philosophical foundations of psychoanalysis": their premise is that, no
matter how dismissive psychoanalysis is of philosophy, it nonetheless
has to rely on a series of conceptual presuppositions (about the nature
of drives, of reality, etc.) that psychoanalysis itself does not render thematic and that bear witness to the way in which psychoanalysis is only
possible within a certain philosophical horizon. On the other hand,
psychoanalysts at their worst, indulge in so-called "psychoanalyzing of
philosophers," trying to discern pathological psychic motivations beneath fundamental philosophical attitudes (philosophical idealism as the
last vestige of the childish belief in the omnipotency of thoughts; paranoiac systematizing as the foundation of the need to form all-embracing
philosophical systems, etc.). *Both* these approaches are to be rejected.
While the psychoanalytic reduction of philosophy to an expression of
psychic pathology is today, deservedly, no longer taken seriously, it is
much more difficult to counter the seemingly self-evident claim that
psychoanalysis cannot relate anything truly relevant to philosophy, since
psychoanalysis must itself rely on a set of philosophical presuppositions
that it is unable to reflect upon. What if, however, references to the
Freudian subject are not external to philosophy, but can, in fact, tell us
something about the modern, Cartesian subject? What if psychoanalysis renders visible something that the modern philosophy of subjectivity

accomplishes without knowing it, its own grounding gesture, which philosophy has to disavow if it is to assume its place within academic knowledge? To use Lacan's pun, what if psychoanalysis renders visible the ex-timate kernel of modern subjectivity, its innermost core that philosophy is not ready to assume, which it tries to keep at a distance— or, to put it in a more fashionable way, what if psychoanalysis renders visible the constitutive *madness* of modern philosophy? We are thus playing a double strategic game: this ex-timate kernel of philosophy is not directly accessible to the psychoanalysis conceived of as a branch of psychology or psychiatry—what we encounter at this level are, of course, the "naive" pre-philosophical theses. What one has to do, is to bring to light the philosophical implications of psychoanalysis, that is, to retranslate, to transpose psychoanalytic propositions back into philosophy, to "elevate them to the dignity of philosophical propositions": in this way, one is able to discern the ex-timate philosophical kernel of psychoanalysis, since this transposition back into philosophy explodes the standard philosophical frame. This is what Lacan was doing all the time: reading hysteria or obsessional neurosis as a philosophical "attitude of thought towards reality" (the obsessional compulsion to think— "if I stop thinking, I will cease to exist"—as the truth of the Cartesian *cogito ergo sum*), etc., etc.

Are we thus not again engaged in "psychoanalyzing philosophy"? No, since this reference to madness is strictly internal to philosophy—the whole of modern philosophy, from Descartes onward, involves an inherent reference to the threat of madness, and is thus a desperate attempt to draw a clear line that separates the transcendental philosopher from the madman (Descartes: how do I know I'm not hallucinating reality?; Kant: how to delimit metaphysical speculation from Swedenborgian hallucinatory rambling?). This excess of madness against which modern philosophy fights is the very founding gesture of Cartesian subjectivity. . . . At this point, anyone versed in postmodern deconstructionism will utter a sigh of bored recognition: of course, the Cartesian ego, the self-transparent subject of Reason, is an illusion; its truth is the decentered, split, finite subject thrown into a contingent, nontransparent context, and this is what psychoanalysis renders visible. . . . Things, however, are more complicated. The problem with the central Freudian and Lacanian notions (the unconscious, the subject) is that they function as theoretical shibboleths. One knows the story of shibboleth from Judges 12:4–6: the difference is visible only from one side, that is, only the people of Gilead perceive the difference in the pronunciation of the word "shibboleth" — the unfortunate people of Ephraim are unaware of any difference and, consequently, cannot grasp at all what they have said wrong, why they have to die. The supreme case of shibboleth in psychoanalytic theory is the very notion of the unconscious: when Freud proposes his thesis on the unconscious psychic processes, philosophers immediately react to it by saying "Of course! We knew this for a long time — Schopenhauer, *Lebensphilosophie*, the primordial Will . . ."; all of a sudden, the place swarms with hermeneutical and other recuperations that endeavor to (re)integrate psychoanalysis into the standard philosophical problematic (by providing its "philosophical foundation": unconscious is grounded in the opacity of the life-world context, in the latent, nonfulfilled subjective intention, etc.), while the surplus that resists this integration is rejected — for example, in the guise of "Freud's biologism," of his "unacceptable speculations on the death drive," and so on.[1]

It is against this background that one should appreciate the paradoxical achievement of Lacan, which usually passes unnoticed even by his advocates: on the very behalf of psychoanalysis, he returns to the modern rationalist notion of subject. Philosophers and psychoanalysts, of course, promptly exclaim "We are here on our home terrain!" and proceed to reduce the Freudian subject to a psychological subject of introspection, to philosophical self-consciousness, to Nietzschean will to power. . . . Lacan's underlying thesis here is even more radical than with the unconscious: not only has the Freudian subject nothing to do with the self-transparent, unified self-consciousness, it is the Cartesian subject itself (and its radicalization in German Idealism, from Kant's transcendental apperception to self-consciousness from Fichte onward) that is already a shibboleth within the domain of philosophy itself: the standard philosophy of subjectivity, as well as the critics of the notion of "unified transcendental subject," both misrecognize the shibboleth at work here, that is, the gap that separates the Cartesian subject (when it is "brought to its notion" with Kant) from the self-transparent ego, or from man, from the "human person." What they fail to see is that the Cartesian subject emerges precisely out of the "death of man": "transcendental subjectivity" is philosophical antihumanism at its purest.

One can see, now, why, in his seminar on *The Four Fundamental Concepts of Psycho-Analysis,* Lacan asserts that the subject of psychoanalysis is none other than the Cartesian *cogito:* the Freudian unconscious emerges through the very reduction of the "person's" substantial content to the evanescent punctuality of the *cogito.*

In this precise sense, one could say that Martin Luther was the first great antihumanist: modern subjectivity is not announced in the Renaissance humanist celebration of man as the "crown of creation", that is, in the tradition of Erasmus and others (to which Luther cannot but appear as a "barbarian"), but rather in Luther's famous statement that man is the excrement who fell out of the God's anus. Modern subjectivity has nothing to do with the notion of man as the highest creature in the "great chain of being," as the final point of the evolution of the universe: modern subjectivity emerges when the subject perceives himself as "out of joint," as *excluded* from the "order of the things," from the positive order of entities. For that reason, the ontic equivalent of the modern subject is inherently *excremental:* there is no subjectivity proper without the notion that, at a different level, from another perspective, I am a mere piece of shit. For Marx, the emergence of the working-class subjectivity is strictly codependent to the fact that the worker is compelled to sell the very substance of his being (his creative power) as a commodity on the market, that is, to reduce the *agalma,* the treasure, the precious kernel of his being, to an object that can be bought for a piece of money—there is no subjectivity without the reduction of the subject positive-substantial being to a disposable "piece of shit." In this case of the correlation between the Cartesian subjectivity and its excremental objectal counterpart, we are not dealing merely with an example of what Foucault called the empirico-transcendental couple that characterizes modern anthropology, but, rather, with the split between the subject of the enunciation and the subject of the enunciated:[2] if the Cartesian subject is to emerge at the level of the enunciation, he is to be reduced to the "almost-nothing" of a disposable excrement at the level of the enunciated content.

Or, to put it in a slightly different way, the intervention of the subject undermines the standard premodern opposition between the universal order and the hubris of a particular force whose egotistic excess perturbs the balance of the universal order: "subject" is the name for the hubris, the excessive gesture, whose very excess grounds the universal order; it is the name for the pathological abject, *clinamen,* deviation from the universal order, that sustains this very universal order. The transcendental subject is the "ontological scandal," neither phenomenal nor noumenal, but an excess that sticks out from the "great chain of being," a hole, a gap in the order of reality, and, simultaneously, the agent whose "spontaneous" activity constitutes the order of (phenomenal) reality. If, for the traditional ontology, the problem was how to deduce chaotic phenomenal reality from the eternal order of the true reality (how to account for the gradual "degeneration" of the eternal order), the problem of the subject is that of the imbalanced excess, hubris, deviation, that sustains the order itself. The central paradox of the Kantian transcendental constitution is that the subject is not the absolute, the eternal grounding principle of reality, but a finite, temporal entity—precisely as such, it provides the ultimate horizon of reality. The very idea of the universe, of the all of reality, as a totality that exists in itself, is thus rejected as a paralogism: what appears as an *epistemological limitation* of our capacity to grasp reality (the fact that we are forever perceiving reality from our finite, temporal standpoint), is the positive *ontological condition* of reality itself.

Our philosophical and everyday common sense identifies the subject with a series of features: the autonomous source of spontaneous, self-originating activity (what German Idealists called "self-positing"); the capacity of free choice; the presence of some kind of "inner life" (fantasizing); etc. Lacan endorses these features, but with a twist: the autonomous source of activity—yes, but only insofar as the subject displaces onto an Other the fundamental passivity of his being (when I am active, I am simultaneously inter-passive, i.e., there is an Other who is passive for me, in my place, like the weepers, the hired women who cry for me at funerals in so-called "primitive" societies); the free choice—yes, but, at its most radical, the choice is a forced one (i.e., ultimately, I have a freedom of choice only insofar as I make the right choice); the presence of fantasizing—yes, but, far from coinciding with the subject in a direct experience of "inner life," the fundamental fantasy is that which cannot ever be "subjectivized," that which is forever cut off from the subject. . . . What Lacan focuses on is this specific twist, this additional turn of the screw that confronts us with the most radical dimension of subjectivity.

How, then, does this endeavor of ours relate to Heidegger's well-known attempt to "think through" the horizon of subjectivity? From our perspective, the problem with Heidegger is, *in ultima analisi,* the following one: the Lacanian reading enables us to unearth in the Cartesian subjectivity its inherent tension between the moment of excess (the "diabolical Evil" in Kant, the "night of the world" in Hegel) and the subsequent attempts to gentrify-domesticate-normalize this excess. Again and again, post-Cartesian philosophers are compelled, by the inherent logic of their philosophical project, to articulate a certain excessive moment of "madness" inherent to *cogito,* which they then immediately endeavor to "renormalize." And the problem with Heidegger is that his notion of modern subjectivity does not seem to account for this inherent excess — in short, this notion simply does not "cover" that aspect of *cogito* on account of which Lacan claims that *cogito* is the subject of the unconscious.[3]

One of the basic presumptions of contemporary *doxa* is that the Cartesian *cogito* paved the way for the unheard-of progress of modern science that profoundly affected the everyday life of mankind. Today, however, it seems as if the Cartesian *cogito* itself has acquired the status of a prescientific myth, superseded by the very progress of knowledge it unleashed. For that reason, the title *Cogito and the Unconscious* is bound to give rise to two immediate associations: that it is to be understood as designating the *antagonism* between *cogito* (the transparent subject of self-consciousness) and the unconscious, its opaque Other that subverts the certitudes of consciousness; and, consequently, that *cogito* is to be repudiated as the agency of manipulative domination responsible for all present woes, from patriarchal oppression to ecological catastrophes. The specter of the "Cartesian paradigm" roams around, simultaneously proclaimed dead and feared as the ultimate threat to our survival. In clear contrast to this predominant *doxa,* Lacan pleads for a psychoanalytic *return to cogito.*

Today's predominant position involves the assertion of multiple subjectivities against the specter of (transcendental) Subject: the unified Subject, the topic of transcendental philosophy, the constitutive source of all reality, is dead (or so we are told), and the void of its absence is filled in by the liberating proliferation of the multiple forms of subjectivity — feminine, gay, ethnic. . . . One should thus abandon the impossible search for the Subject that is constitutive of reality, and, instead, focus attention on the diverse forms of asserting one's subjectivity in our complex and dispersed postmodern universe. . . . What, however, if we perform the exact opposite of this standard operation, and endeavor to think *a subject bereft of subjectivity* (of the self-experience of a historical agent embedded in a finite horizon of meaning)? What kind of monster remains when we subtract from the subject the wealth of self-experience that constitutes subjectivity? The present volume provides an answer to this question: its underlying premise is that the Cartesian subject *is* this monster, that it emerges precisely when we deprive the subject of all the wealth of the "human person."

Following Lacan's path, this second volume of the SIC series sets out to explore the vicissitudes of the *cogito*. Part 1 (*Cogito as a Freudian Concept*) provides the basics: in his introductory essay, Mladen Dolar explains in detail why, for Lacan, the subject of the unconscious is none other than the Cartesian *cogito,* while Alenka Zupančič, in her reading of Kant, delineates the contours of the ethical attitude that befits the notion of modern subjectivity. Finally, through an analysis of the "larger-than-life" figures in the work of Orson Welles and Ayn Rand, Slavoj Žižek elaborates the four elementary modes of modern subjectivity, as well as their inherent sexualization. Part 2 (*Cogito's Body*) focuses on Nicolas Malebranche, the Cartesian philosopher and theologist who, with an unheard-of-audacity, tackled the deadlocks in which the Cartesian project gets involved apropos of the enigmatic status of the human body (Alain Grosrichard, Miran Božovič). Is the monster with a phallic protuberance above his one eye, analyzed by Grosrichard, not a kind of obscene double of the Cartesian *cogito,* its impossible spectral embodiment? In the concluding essay of this part, Renata Salecl tackles the lethal *jouissance* of the siren's voice. The three essays in part 3 (*Cogito and Its Critics*) deal with three paradigmatic contemporary critiques of the Cartesian subjectivity: Bataille's assertion of the excessive expenditure that allegedly undermines *cogito*'s restrained economy (Marc de Kessel), the Althusserian notion of subject as the effect of ideological interpellation (Robert Pfaller), and Daniel Dennett's dismissal of the Cartesian Theatre from the perspective of cognitive science (Slavoj Žižek).

Notes

1   As it was emphasized by Robert Pfaller (on whom I rely here), the notion of shibboleth enables us also to define in a precise way, the paradoxical relationship between
science and ideology: ideology does not exclude science; rather, it endeavors to *integrate* it into its field, like "clinching" to the opponent in a boxing match instead of
directly fighting him. The point is thus that the difference ideology/science is visible
only from one side, from the side of science. A further example of ideological shibboleth is provided by the way in which dominant ("high") culture relates to counterculture. When members of counterculture are gnawed by the fear of being "integrated"
into or "co-opted" by the official high culture, thus losing their subversive sting, they
thereby commit a grave theoretical mistake: the line of separation that divides high
culture from counterculture is visible only from the side of the counterculture, which
is why high culture is as a rule "open," its members always want to "talk," to establish
a common field of activity. . . . In theology, the exemplary case of the logic of shibboleth is offered by the Jansenist notion of miracle, which also relies on a paradoxical
"nonsymmetrical visibility": for the Jansenists, a miracle does not occur at the direct,
"vulgar" material level, as a proof of the faith for all to see. For those who do not
believe, the miraculous event is part of the simple continuity of the natural course of
things—a miracle can be recognized as such only by those who (already) believe.

2   See Jacques Lacan, *Écrits: A Selection* (New York: Norton, 1977), 300.

3   For a more detailed account of this excess, see, in the present volume, Slavoj Žižek,
"The Cartesian Subject versus the Cartesian Theater."

PART I | **cogito as a freudian concept**

1

Cogito as the

Subject of the

Mladen Dolar | **Unconscious**

In the opening paragraph of one of the earliest pieces in his *Écrits,* the famous paper entitled "The mirror stage as formative of the function of the I as revealed in psychoanalytic experience" (1949, presented in Zürich at the International Congress of Psychoanalysis), Lacan situates his notion of the mirror stage in the following way: "The conception of the mirror stage that I introduced at our last congress, thirteen years ago [that was the congress in Marienbad in 1936, the last one where Freud was present as well], has since become more or less established in the practice of the French group. However, I think it worthwhile to bring it again to your attention, especially today, for the light it sheds on the formation of the *I* as we experience it in psychoanalysis. It is an experience that leads us to oppose any philosophy directly issuing from the *Cogito*" (Lacan 1977, 1; 1966, 93). So in the very first paragraph of the first notorious *écrit,* there is a clear alternative, an emphatic choice that one has to assume: *either the mirror phase or the cogito.* One has to decide one way or the other between psychoanalysis and philosophy, which has, in the past three centuries, largely issued from cogito, despite its variety of forms and despite its often proposed criticism of cogito. Psychoanalysis, on the other hand, if properly understood and practiced, promises to offer a way out of the "age of cogito." The alternative that Lacan has in mind, in this particular strategically situated spot, is the following: the mirror stage, insofar as it is indeed formative of the function of the I, demonstrates that the I, the ego, is a place of an imaginary blinding, a deception; far from being the salutary part of the mind that could serve as a firm support of the psychoanalytic cure, against the vagaries of the id and the superego (such was the argument of ego-psychology), rather, it is itself the source of paranoia, and of all kinds of fantasy formations. If such is the nature of the I, then it must be most sharply opposed to cogito, with its inherent pretension to self-transparency and self-certainty.[1]

But even apart from Lacan's particular theory of the mirror stage, with all its ramifications, the dilemma seems to pertain to psychoanalysis as such, to its "basic insight." For is the discovery of the unconscious not in itself inherently an attack on the very idea of cogito? The self-transparent subjectivity that figures as the foundation of modern philosophy—even in those parts of it that were critical of cogito—seems to be submitted to a decisive blow with the advent of psychoanalysis. Cogito must be seen not only at odds with, but at the opposite end in relation to the unconscious. Such was Freud's own implicit self-understanding (although he didn't deal at any length with Descartes, except for his curious short paper on Descartes's dream, "Über einen Traum des Cartesius," [Freud 1929b]), and this is the spontaneous, seemingly self-evident, and widespread conception of that relation. This view can then be considered alongside other contemporary radical attempts to dismantle cogito, most notably with Heidegger, who was also during that period Lacan's source of inspiration. So both the analysis of the ego and that of the unconscious, although running in different directions, appear to undermine the very idea of cogito.

Yet, Lacan's position in that respect has undergone a far-reaching change. First of all, a clear distinction had to be made, in his further development, between the "I," the ego, on one hand, and the subject on the other. The "I" is not the subject, and the mechanism discovered in the mirror stage, the blinding, the recognition that is intrinsically miscognition, while defining the function of the "I," doesn't apply at all to the function of the subject. If the first one is to be put under the heading of the Imaginary, the second follows an entirely different logic, that of the Symbolic. In this division, cogito, surprisingly for many, figures on the side of the subject.

Lacan's perseverance toward retaining the concept of the subject certainly ran against the grain of the time, especially in the days of a budding and flowering structuralism that seemed to have done away with the subject, inflicting upon it a final mortal blow after its protracted moribund status. The general strategy promoted by structuralism could, in a very simplified manner, be outlined as an attempt to put forward the level of a "nonsubjective" structure as opposed to the subject's self-apprehension. There is a nonsubjective "symbolic" dimension of which the subject is but an effect, an epiphenomenon, and which is necessarily overlooked in the subject's imaginary self-understanding. This basic approach could be realized in a number of different ways: Lévi-Strauss's structure as the matrix of permutations of differential elements regulating mythologies, rituals, beliefs, habits, etcetera, behind the subjects' backs; Foucault's *episteme*, "anonymous" discursive formations and strategies, or later the dispositions of power, etcetera; Althusser's "process without a subject" that science has to unearth behind the ideological interpellation that constitutes subjectivity; Derrida's notion of writing, or *la différance*, as "prior" to any split into subject/object, interior/exterior, space/time, etcetera; Kristeva's opposition between the semiotic and the symbolic. In spite of great differences between those attempts and their sometimes sharply opposed results, there was a common tendency to conceive of a dimension "behind" or "underneath" or "anterior to" the subject, the very notion of the subject thereby falling into a kind of disrepute and becoming synonymous with "self-deception," a necessary illusion, an essential blinding as to the conditions that produced it. The structuralist revolution has thus seen itself as a break away from the humanist tradition centered on the subject (cf. Foucault's ponderous reference to the "death of man"), and particularly as a radical rupture with the philosophical tradition based on cogito.

Lacan's view sharply differed from this model by firmly clinging to the notion of the subject and "rescuing" it all along. His talk about *the subject of the unconscious* was certain to provoke some astonishment.[2] He saw the unconscious, along structuralist lines, as a structure—"structured as a language," as the famous slogan goes—discovering in it the Saussurean and Jakobsonian operations of metaphor and metonymy, etcetera, but as a *structure with a subject,* a subject conceived as opposed to the consciousness and the "I." So for Lacan, on whatever level we look at matters, *there is no process, and no structure, without a subject.* The supposedly "nonsubjective" process overlooked in the constitution of subjectivity, was for Lacan essentially always already "subjectivized," although the subject it implied was a very different entity from the one that the structuralist strategy strove to dismantle. Retaining the concept was for him far more subversive in its effects than simply dismissing it.

In the next step, he went even further with the baffling suggestion that cogito *was* the subject of the unconscious, thus turning against some basic assumptions (shall one say prejudices?) of that period. It was a suggestion that has baffled Lacan's opponents and followers alike. Lacan largely defined his project with the slogan announcing a "return to Freud," but subsequently it turned out that this slogan had to be complemented with a corollary: the return to Freud had to pass by way of a return to Descartes. So there is a huge gap that separates Lacan from the rest of the structuralist generation, which defined itself as basically anti-Cartesian (and also as anti-Hegelian, but that is another story), regardless of many differences between the proposed theories, whereas Lacan saw himself rather as an heir to that tradition. This divide ultimately depends on the different ways of grasping subjectivity.

At the simplest level, one can approach this divide with the notion of recognition, which was largely seen as the necessary and sufficient condition of subjectivity, turning it thus necessarily into an imaginary or "ideological" notion that one has to be rid of. For Lacan, however, *the subject emerges only at the point of a nonrecognition*: all formations of the unconscious have this in common, they are accompanied by a "this is not me," "I was not there," although they were produced by the subject him/herself (or to put it in the terms of cogito: they cannot be followed by a "therefore I am"). They depend on the emergence of an "alien kernel" within subjectivity, an automatism beyond control, a "discourse of the Other," the breakdown, in certain points, of the constituted horizon of recognition and sense. This nonintegration is constitutive for the subject, although it may appear as its limit, reduction, or failure. So Lacan's criticism of the "I," the illusion of autonomous and self-transparent subjectivity, was well embedded in the general structuralist strategy, but the fact that he nevertheless stubbornly espoused the concept of the subject was the mark of his far-reaching dissent and opposition.

How can the subject of the unconscious be possibly conceived of as cogito? How to conceive of cogito after the advent of psychoanalysis? Is there a Freudian cogito? The question should perhaps be reversed: *is there an unconscious outside of cogito?* Lacan's wager is that there is not.

Hence his insistence that the subject that psychoanalysis has to deal with is none other than the subject of modern science, thoroughly dependent on cogito.[3] The Freudian unconscious is the unconscious of cogito, in both senses of the genitive. There is, however, a subplot in this story, for if the subject of psychoanalysis is that of science as well, its object is not. The object that psychoanalysis has to deal with by definition eludes science, it cannot be subjected to scientific scrutiny, it is the evasive singular object that provides *jouissance*. So the tricky problem that the two Lacanian accounts of cogito will attempt to solve is also the following: how does the subject of the unconscious, as cogito, relate to *jouissance*?

One can start with a simple observation about Descartes's own procedure in the *Meditations,* the procedure of a "methodical doubt," which can be seen as a gradual reduction of consciousness, its "evacuation." Consciousness must lose any worldly support, it must be cleansed of any objective counterpart—and the recognition/miscognition, in relation to the object opposed to it, is precisely what defines the meanderings of the Imaginary, which the mirror stage has dealt with at their core. It must also eliminate the support in the signifier, any received truths and certainties, the seemingly evident mathematical laws, etcetera. What eventually remains, is a pure vanishing point without a counterpart, which can only be sustained in a minimal gesture of enunciation. It is questionable whether this yields the subject of thought—Descartes himself considered alternative suggestions of "I doubt, I err, I lie," etcetera, *ergo sum,* the minimal form of which is "I enounce, *ergo sum.*" One has to entrust oneself to the signifier, yet the subject that is at stake has no signifier of its own, it is the subject of enunciation, absent from and underlying what is enunciated: "Note in passing that in avoiding the *I think,* I avoid the discussion that results from the fact that this *I think,* for us, certainly cannot be detached from the fact that he can formulate it only by *saying* it to us, implicitly—a fact that [Descartes] forgets" (Lacan 1986, 36). What remains is purely an empty spot occupied by the subject of enunciation. For being empty, it can be universal, and it can indeed be seen as the form of subjectivity implied by science, a merely formal subjectivity purified of all content and substance. Each proposition of science must display the ability to be posited universally, that is, in such a way that it can be assumed by the empty form of subjectivity epitomized by cogito.

To be sure, this view already departs from Descartes. People as divergent in thought as Kant, Hegel, Husserl, and Lacan all agree that Descartes's "error," if it can be so called, consists in substantializing this empty spot of cogito by turning it into *res cogitans*. Cogito marks a "non-place," a gap, a chasm in the chain of being, it doesn't delineate a certain sphere of being to be placed alongside other spheres, it cannot be situated in some part of reality, yet it is at the same time correlative to reality as such.[4]

Lacan's starting point in this reading of cogito is the assumption that cogito implies, in its pure and minimal form, a non-imaginary subject as a void. This is immediately followed by a tour de force: the coupling of this empty spot with the lack implied by the Symbolic that has been produced in other ways. Lacan has spent much time demonstrating that this second lack can ultimately be deduced from Saussure's algorithm of the signifier and its underlying logic. In a nutshell, it follows from the basic property of the signifier that it can never be counted for one; "one" signifier already counts for two, because the empty place of its absence also counts. Differentiality, the Saussurean definition of the signifier has to be extended to the point where the signifier differs from itself: ultimately, it is the difference between itself and the void of its absence. Once we find ourselves in the realm of the Symbolic, there is never a simple absence or an innocent lack, and this invisible "missing half" that inherently sticks to the signifier is for Lacan precisely the place to which the subject can be "pinned" (hence the notion of *suture*). At a later stage, Lacan extensively uses some devices of set theory (as we shall see), which, in the most rudimentary form, implies (and formalizes) the difference between the set and the element it contains. The empty set, in this entirely formal view, is precisely the place of the subject. Its emptiness and its purely formal character have been designated by Lacan, in his algebra, by the signum $, to be read as *sujet barré*, the barred subject—there is quite literally a bar crossing its S, it is what remains when any S, with any positive feature, has been "crossed over," erased. Nothing remains, but this nothing counts.

To be sure, again, this view can hardly be seen as Cartesian, for Descartes, having produced this vanishing point, didn't allow it to vanish. Quite the opposite, his whole problem was how to proceed from there, and it turned out that this point could only be sustained by being pinned to the Other, the big Other epitomized by God: "When Descartes introduces the concept of a certainty that holds entirely in the *I think* of cogitation . . . one might say that his mistake is to believe that this is knowledge. To say that he knows something of this certainty. Not to make of the *I think* a mere point of fading. . . . He puts the field of this knowledge at the level of this vaster subject, the subject who is supposed to know, God" (Lacan 1986, 224). So the barred subject needs the guarantee of the Other if there is to be any following step, the emergence of any knowledge, and in this way, by this support, it can be rid of its bar. This thesis encroaches upon a notorious controversy concerning the question of whether Descartes has committed a *circulus in demonstrando,* a vicious circle in his argument. The debate started already with the objections to the *Meditations,* and in his response, Descartes had to defend himself against the criticism about *la faute qu'on appelle le cercle.* The debate has a long history and I cannot venture into this difficult matter here. For our present purpose it suffices to say that according to Lacan, Descartes did indeed commit such a fallacy.[5]

The implication of this reading is that the existence of cogito as such cannot be sustained—at least not without reverting to the support of the big Other, the figure of God, the intimidating subject supposed to know. If the cogito is indeed just a pure vanishing point of the subject of enunciation, then its existence doesn't follow from it. It cannot assume an *ergo sum.* All consistence it has is pinned to a signifier—there is no $ without a signifier—but only as a void that sticks to it and cannot be presentified as such. In order to see what this means and how this works, one has to consider the mechanism of alienation, itself a necessary effect of language.

Alienation was for Lacan always essentially connected with the idea of a forced choice, although the terms of this choice and its implications varied at different stages of his teaching. The subject is subject to a choice—this is what makes it a subject in the first place—but this choice is rather the opposite of the free and autonomous choice one is accustomed to associate with the subject. One could say that the very elementary device of psychoanalysis, free associations, spectacularly stages this paradox: one is supposed to freely say anything that passes through one's mind, autonomously choosing whatever one wants, yet the moment one begins, it becomes clear that one is trapped; every free choice, in free associations, turns out to have been a forced one.

There is a mechanism at the bottom of forced choice that Lacan attempts to delineate: the subject can choose only one way, and furthermore, by choosing s/he meets with a loss. This doesn't mean simply that by choosing one side one loses the other, but also that even the side one has chosen is ridden with a loss—one can only get it curtailed, cut off from its part, so that the choice requires a double loss. Lacan has demonstrated this by the famous situation of a *vel,* epitomized by the somewhat drastic example of "your money or your life," *la bourse ou la vie.* The two sides of the choice are not symmetrical: I can only choose to cling to my life, thus losing the money, while clinging to money would entail losing both, the life and the money. The choice is decided in advance, there is no freedom of choice, and the chosen element can only be retained as curtailed, *écorné* (the life minus the money), or else one would lose both.

Here is the next tour de force in Lacan's reading of cogito: there is a way in which cogito has the same structure, it can be taken as a case of "your money or your life." This is the scene of the Lacanian cogito: one is pushed against the wall, the gun pointing at one's head, with an unfathomable voice crying out in the dark: "Your thought or your being! Make up your mind!" One can appreciate the irony of the situation, for the moment one stops to think it over, the choice is already decided, one has lost one's being by thinking. And one can only hold on to being if one doesn't stop to think, but stops thinking.

In 1964, in the seminar on *The Four Fundamental Concepts of Psycho-Analysis,* generally taken as Lacan's "standard account" of cogito, Lacan proposes the cogito as a forced choice between *cogito* and *sum.* There is an alternative: *either to think or to be,* and since there is no freedom of choice, one can only choose one way—but which one? One could assume that, following the model of "your money or your life," one is supposed to cling to one's being at the price of losing thought, but Lacan surprisingly sees the situation in the opposite way: one must choose thought, the thought that makes sense, curtailed of being. More paradoxically still, as we shall see, some years later Lacan espoused the opposite view, that one is forced to opt for being at the expense of thought, eventually yielding a quite different account of cogito.

If I choose *I think,* I lose my being by entrusting myself head over heels to the tricky logic of the signifier. This is the choice that Descartes proposes, making the being of the subject dependent on thought and deducible from it. But Lacan's point, in this forced choice, is that *sum* doesn't follow once one has made the first step. Thought depends on the signifier, which turns the subject into the empty point of enunciation, instead of founding his/her being. In the place of the supposed certainty of the subject's being, there is just a void. *It is not the same subject that thinks and that is; the one that is is not the one that thinks,* even more, the one *that is* is ultimately not a subject at all. One should already mark here that should one choose being, one would have to espouse the object, precisely the object that Lacan has labeled *objet a,* the object that detains being, but a being over which one cannot be master. Choosing being would entail desubjectivation, one would have to give up the status of the subject altogether. But apart from that, from Descartes's own point of view choosing being would be void, it would thrust the subject back into the vagaries of the Imaginary, a confusion without hope for foundation and consistency, the black hole of being outside rationality, briefly, a non-being.

Since the choice of being is an impossible choice, coinciding with the non-being of the subject, one is bound to choose thought insofar as it makes sense (but there is a thought that doesn't, and this will emerge as the unconscious). And although one can make sense only by adopting signifiers, this seals the subject's fate, for s/he becomes merely what "a signifier represents for another signifier," thus essentially chained to it, while gliding along the signifying chain.[6] This is the point of the little scheme that one finds in the English translation (figure 1): "If we choose being, the subject disappears, it eludes us, it falls into non-sense. If we choose sense, the sense survives only deprived of that part of non-sense that is, strictly speaking, that which constitutes in the realization of the subject, the unconscious. In other words, it is of the nature of this sense, as it emerges in the field of the Other, to be in a large part of its field, eclipsed by the disappearance of being, induced by the very function of the signifier" (Lacan 1986, 211; translation modified). There is a choice between being and sense, where one is forced to wind up with sense, but a sense that is necessarily curtailed, cut off from its part, the part of non-sense, and this is precisely the part where one has to place the unconscious. The unconscious is to be situated at the intersection, the lost intersection of being and sense, whereas the part of being, as an impossible choice, is an empty set. It is in the place of the loss—the loss of

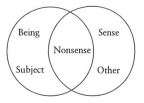

Figure 1

being—in this empty set, that the subject is located. The subject's place is the formal empty set of an impossible choice—for the forced choice is not simply an absence of choice: choice is offered and denied at the same time, but its empty alternative is what counts for the subject. The implication can also be read as follows: one cannot choose oneself as a subject, one can only remain a subject by holding on to something else, a positive element of sense, which, paradoxically, entails *aphanisis*, that is, the disappearance of the subject—but this oscillation between sense and *aphanisis* precisely constitutes the subject: "Alienation consists in this *vel*, which . . . condemns the subject to appearing only in that division . . . , if it appears on one side as sense, produced by the signifier, it appears on the other as *aphanisis*" (Lacan 1986, 210; translation modified). In this scheme Lacan inscribes the subject, superimposed at the void place of being, and the Other, superimposed on sense. The sense one chooses is necessarily entrusted to the Other, it is only by subscribing to the signifiers that are at a disposal in the Other—as the reservoir of signifiers—that one can "make sense" at all.

Perhaps things can be made clearer if we introduce Lacan's later notation, which he developed in the following years in an attempt to be as economical and as clear as possible (figure 2). (Maybe the difficulty in understanding Lacan stems largely from his attempts to be simple, to clarify matters to the utmost.) One necessarily chooses S_2, the signifier of sense and knowledge, which schematically condenses and represents the entire chain of signifiers. But that choice exacts its revenge: we are cut off from an essential signifier, marked by S_1, the signifier without a signified, a senseless signifier, which reemerges as the incomprehensible, nonsensical message of the unconscious—"this is not me," "I was not there."

We can consider separately the left circle and the right circle of this scheme. On the left side, we have $\$/S_1$, which can actually be seen as an interpretation of the slogan "cogito as the subject of the unconscious."

$ is the subject that can be ascribed to the formations of the uncon-
scious, the place where the Freudian subject emerges: "I am not saying
that Freud introduces the subject into the world—the subject as distinct
from psychical function, which is a myth, a confused nebulosity—since
it was Descartes who did this. But I am saying that Freud addresses the
subject in order to say to him the following, which is new—*Here, in the
field of the dream, you are at home. Wo es war, soll Ich werden*" (Lacan
1986, 44).[7] The subject, $, has to be ascribed to S_1 of the unconscious—
but that makes it something very different from the overwhelming talk
about modern subjectivity (Heidegger, etc.). The Lacanian cogito is not
the modern subject that philosophers love to talk about; caught as it is
in the structure of alienation, it cannot found its being in its thought;
rather, the repressed part of thought (the unconscious) comes constantly
to haunt it and dislocate it, and it is maintained only through this repression. It emerges only through the impossibility of integrating this lost
part, the intersection where sense and being would seemingly coincide
and ground the subject. Yet, for not being the modern subject of the
philosophical *doxa,* it is not something else either: it emerges with and
within cogito, as its invisible reverse side. There is a recurring criticism
that Lacan's subject still remains within the framework of cogito[8]—
but this is the whole point. *The Lacanian subject is indeed "structured as
cogito,"* as it were, just as the unconscious is structured as a language.
What was so difficult to swallow with the concept of the unconscious
was its closeness to the "normal" ways of thinking, its being structured
just as the language that we are familiar with, just slightly displaced—
and it goes the same for the subject as the dislocation of cogito.[9]

On the right-hand side, we have the couple of signifiers, S_1/S_2. If one
is forced to choose sense, S_2, this has to be paid for by the loss of an
essential signifier that remains structurally inaccessible—this is what
Freud aims at with *Urverdrängung,* the primary repression as the pre-

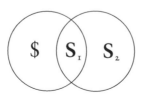

Figure 2

condition of all other repression, and also with *Vorstellungsrepräsentanz*, the representation that is essentially a stand-in for the structurally missing representation. The *urverdrängt* part is a place where signification and being would coincide—and this is indeed the usual understanding of cogito: a sense that immediately involves being and a being that immediately "makes sense," the grounding of being in sense (in thought), and vice versa. For Lacan, this is a mirage, a mythical point of coincidence and transparency that tries to get rid of, or to disavow, the essential disparity of signification and being. Thus the lost part reemerges only as the non-sense of the unconscious, an S_1 to which, to be sure, one can always ascribe a series of S_2, trying to make sense of it. This is the fate of the process of analytical interpretation: it endeavors to reduce the non-sense produced by the formations of the unconscious by adding a series of S_2 that would hopefully shed light on it. Yet, the prolongation of the series, enlightening as it may be, doesn't bring about a final resolution—and the analysis can indeed run into infinity, in a vain search for some ultimate signifier. This is why the business of making sense of non-sense is only the first part of interpretation, a prelude to be followed by its opposite: "The consequence of alienation is that interpretation is not limited to providing us with the meanings of the way taken by the psyche that we have before us. This role is no more than a prelude. Interpretation is directed not so much at sense as towards reducing the signifiers to their non-sense, so that we may rediscover the determinants of the subject's entire behaviour" (Lacan 1986, 212; translation modified). Instead of looking for an ultimate S_2 that could stop the extension of the chain as its final link and thus provide the conclusive interpretation, one has to admit the irreducibility of this structure, the impossibility to catch and grasp S_1 by S_2. And this is what this scheme of alienation tries to pinpoint in the minimal way.

One can also see, on this right-hand side, why Lacan insists that the Other is barred as well, or that there is the lack in the Other. What the other lacks is precisely the S_1 of the intersection, the inaccessible signifier that could found it and complete it, and that can only be represented by a stand-in for the inherently missing part (hence the mechanism of *Vorstellungsrepräsentanz*). This signifier is what Lacan designates by $S(\cancel{A})$, the signifier of the barred Other, and S_1 is nothing but the positivation of this irreparable absence.

But there is a second movement that follows and complements the forced choice of alienation, the step that Lacan calls separation and that forms a conceptual pair with it. In the first step, as we have seen, the intersection was necessarily eluded whatever one chose; now in the second step, the subject is precisely forced to face the intersection.[10] But what is there in this intersection? We have seen in the first part that the subject coincides with its own *aphanisis,* while the Other contains only the signifiers that remain of its disappearance. There is no element of the Other that would intersect with the subject, and vice versa—except the lack as such. The Other and the subject intersect only in the lack. This lack in the Other appears in the very intervals between signifiers, the intervals of discourse, and those intervals present an enigma. The Other cannot simply be reduced to the signifiers it contains, there is a question constantly running in the gaps between them:

> A lack is encountered by the subject in the Other, in the very intimation that the Other makes to him by his discourse. In the intervals of the discourse of the Other, there emerges in the experience of the child something that is radically mappable, namely, *He is saying this to me, but what does he want?*
>
> In this interval intersecting the signifiers, which forms part of the very structure of the signifier, is the locus of what . . . I have called metonymy. It is there that what we call desire crawls, slips, escapes, like the ferret. The desire of the Other is apprehended by the subject in that which does not work, in the lacks of the discourse of the Other. (Lacan 1986, 214)

The subject's response to this inscrutable, unfathomable desire of the Other, emerging in the lacks, is to offer his/her own being as the object of this desire, to offer his/her own loss: "Now, to reply to this hold, the subject . . . brings the answer of the previous lack, of his own disappearance, which he situates here at the point of lack perceived in the Other. The first object he proposes for this parental desire whose object is unknown is his own loss—*Can he lose me?* The phantasy of one's death, of one's disappearance, is the first object that the subject has to bring into play in this dialectic" (Lacan 1986, 214). Two lacks are thus superimposed in the intersection—but what can this yield? Can two lacks produce some "positive" result? In order to deal with the lack in the Other, the subject has to pawn his/her own being, but not the kind of being seemingly implied by cogito. If alienation excluded the choice of being, which would coincide with turning into the object and thus losing subjectivity, then in the second stage the subject seems to be forced to assume precisely that which was excluded: to present itself as the object of the desire of the Other, an object to fill its lack. One pawns one's being by offering one's non-being, in order to find out whether one detains the object of the Other's desire. If alienation forced the subject to hold on to sense in order to retain subjectivity, then it is separation that forces him/her to abandon sense in order to sustain the Other as his/her support. It is when the Other doesn't make sense that its lack and its desire appear, and this is the only foundation for the subject's own desire.[11] So the separation is first the separation from sense, from the realm of signification, and in the same movement the separation from subjectivity, for it demands that the subject separates him/herself from the object.[12] The desire of the Other presents a question—what does he want?—which is countered by another question—do I possess what he wants? What is it in me that could possibly satisfy this desire? So the subject is ultimately put in a position of offering not only what s/he has, but essentially what s/he doesn't possess—and this is precisely Lacan's definition of love: *donner ce qu'on n'a pas,* "to give what one doesn't have."

In alienation, non-sense was placed at the intersection of the subject and the Other, but now it appears that what even more radically doesn't make sense is the lack, the interval between signifiers. "Nonsense" could be dealt with through interpretation, the infinite task of endowing it with sense, adding new signifiers. The lack presents a trickier problem: it can only be "interpreted" by the offer of an object, and the impossible task is now to procure an object that could measure up to it, that would be on the level with the Other's desire.

Lacan's brief mention of metonymy can provide us with another clue: the opposition between alienation and separation can also be read as an elaboration of the difference between metaphor and metonymy in his previous theory (cf. in particular "The agency of the letter in the unconscious or reason since Freud," Lacan 1977, 159–71). The account of the metaphor focused precisely on the elision of a signifier ("one signifier for another") that linked the status of the subject to metaphoricity ("*le métaphore du sujet*", was Lacan's frequent dictum), and this mechanism

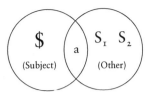

Figure 3

was now formalized in alienation; while metonymy, with its evocation of the "unsayable," its infinite gliding along the signifying chain from one signifier to another (like "the ferret" of the children's game), corresponds to the mechanism of separation. So alienation and separation give a new formalized version of the Lacanian tenet that the "metaphor of the subject" provides the basis of the "metonymy of desire" (figure 3). The covering of two lacks produces something: the very status of the object of desire, which appears precisely where the two lacks coincide — the lack of the subject and the lack of the Other. There is an object involved on both sides, figuring as a pivotal point of fantasy — the object "within the subject" that one tries to present in order to fill the lack in the Other, to deal with its desire; and on the other hand, the object "within the Other," its surmised surplus, the source of its unfathomable *jouissance,* the secret clue to what makes the Other enjoy and that one wants to partake of.[13] Ultimately, what makes the Other the Other, what makes it unfathomable, is what appears in its lack, an object heterogeneous to signification, irreducible to signifiers, which poses the radical problem of desire. What the Other lacks now is not just a signifier — be it $S(\cancel{A})$ — but, more intriguingly, the object. The surplus pairs with the lack, the coincidence of two lacks, and this is the way in which the subject, having lost its being in alienation, nevertheless partakes of it in separation — through the elusive surplus object one can never get hold of.[14]

Indeed, ironically, in separation as the second step, a being does follow from the cogito of alienation, but not the kind of being to rejoice Descartes and to procure any foundational certainty.

This reading of cogito, usually taken as the standard Lacanian view of the matter, has been proposed in the most famous of Lacan's seminars, which also happened to be the first one to be published. However, there is another reading that in a way continues the one briefly presented here, and also gives it some unexpected twists. This second reading was given by Lacan in 1966–67, in the seminar entitled *La logique du fantasme* (The logic of fantasy), which has not yet been published, so that this other approach has rarely attracted proper attention and has not been subjected to much scrutiny. It is still relegated to the somewhat obscure realm of secretly circulated copies that can be highly unreliable, while Lacan himself has written only a frustratingly short and cryptic account of it (Lacan 1984, the summary of the course composed for the *Annuary* of the École pratique des hautes études, the academic institution that provided the formal framework for his seminar at the time).

It seems that this second account of cogito in many respects turns things upside down in relation to the first one.[15] The problem is approached from another angle, that of the logic of fantasy, and fantasy, in Lacan's view, is precisely something that confronts the subject with being—a being heterogeneous to signifiers and their play, their differentiality, etcetera; and on the other hand, a being irreducible to objectivity, to the (imaginary) counterpart of consciousness, the perceived being that one can lay one's hands on and which one can manipulate, or which can be submitted to scientific investigation. Lacan, again trying to simplify matters to the extreme, proposed a rudimentary formula of fantasy, $\$ \lozenge a$—the subject confronted with that being, that bit of the Real, which s/he tries to cope with in fantasy ("there is no other entry for the subject into the real except the fantasy" [Lacan 1984, 16]). So what is at stake in fantasy is a certain "choice of being" that pins down one's *jouissance*. If the chain of signifiers is always prone to extension, without an ultimate signifier that could stop its gliding, without the proper signifier of the subject that could fix it (in both senses of the word), then the object that is at stake in fantasy is something that does stop the endless gliding—but only at the price of not being a signifier. It provides the subject with what Lacan calls its complement of being, *le complément d'être,* but the problem is that the two parts, the lack and the object, never fit or make a whole. And since this object is something nonsignifiable, it also follows that it defies interpretation. Whereas the interpretation of the formations of the unconscious can run into infinity, the fantasy, on the other hand, is not to be interpreted, as Lacan's frequent slogan goes (*on n'interprète pas le fantasme*). It is the halt of any interpretation, the infinity is suspended by the object.

The consideration of fantasy demands a reinterpretation of cogito. In the above account Lacan has used the simple scheme of the intersection of two circles quite innocuously, as a very elementary and generally comprehensible device of set theory. But now, three or four years later, this device has acquired a much more precise and technical meaning; it seems that Lacan has in the meantime devoted much time to studying the set theory and some other mathematical devices (Klein's group, etc.). Lacan's point can be made independently of the technicalities that call for some expert mathematical knowledge.

Cogito aims at the intersection of thought and being, and this intersection is inaccessible, a mirage, as we have seen—this point of the prior analysis retains the same validity. Now according to De Morgan's laws in set theory, the negation of the intersection is equivalent to the conjunction of what remains of the two intersecting circles—that is, of a being without thought and of a thought without being. So one can reformulate the alternative between "I think" and "I am" as the one between "I don't think" and "I am not"—*ou je ne pense pas ou je ne suis pas* (Lacan 1984, 13). Where I am, I don't think, and where I think, I am not.

Our hypothetical situation of cogito as a choice at gunpoint now takes a new turn. As a subject, one has to choose being, but a being devoid of thought. This is the basis of assuming a cogito, while the other alternative, that of thought without being, belongs to the unconscious. What are the compelling reasons for this forced choice, and what does one lose by it in this new constellation? Lacan's considerations can be seen as more elementary than those underlying the previous account, and, further, can be seen actually to produce not the cogito as the subject of the unconscious, but rather the cogito opposed to it.

Let us first consider the second part of the alternative, the thought without being. Is this not a good definition of the unconscious—the place where thinking takes place, but devoid of an "I," and where one can never draw the implication "therefore I am"? It is a thought that cannot be chosen; I cannot choose the unconscious, it always makes its appearance as an intruder that chooses me. And it is a thought that doesn't make sense—if Lacan, in the previous account, tacitly assumed that the choice of thought involved the choice of sense, now he sharply opposes the two. It is also a thought without an "I," and the first question that the analysis of cogito must resolve is on what conditions one can as-

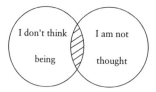

Figure 4

sume an "I" at all. If I am to assume an "I," I cannot choose thought, which pertains to the unconscious, so that I am forced to choose being, thereby giving up thought. The fundamental choice of the subject is the choice of being without thought. *Je ne pense pas, je suis*—I don't think, therefore I am—this is the new version of cogito; furthermore, I don't think in order to be—*je ne pense pas pour être*. In order to be, I have to exclude a knowledge that I don't want to know anything about. The excluded thought emerges in the unconscious, so that cogito, as the choice of being, coincides with the exclusion of thought as unconscious, of the unconscious as thought. If before I couldn't choose being—this choice concurred with non-being—it now appears that I cannot do otherwise but to choose being, yet at the price of an "I don't think" (figure 4).

The choice of being is the choice of a subject without the unconscious, thus the choice of consciousness, the choice of a "normal," a seemingly "natural" form of subjectivity. It is this choice that now constitutes the fundamental alienation of the subject. "[In] 'I don't think,' [the subject] imagines himself to be master over [of] his being, i.e., not to be of language" (Lacan 1984, 14; my translation). The choice endeavors to secure a mastery over one's being and to reject, or disavow, the part where the subject is an effect of language and dependent on the signifier. (There is an untranslatable pun in French that Lacan was very fond of, the homonymy between *maître* and *m'être,* the master and "self-being.") And since this choice involves a basic disavowal, it can only yield a false being, *un faux être,* a "counterfeit" being, a fake, which serves as the support of consciousness. If the subject necessarily chooses being, and avoids thought, the being s/he chooses has to differ from the being of the object; s/he chooses being in such a way so as not to turn into the object. The pit of desubjectivation, of turning into the *objet a,* was what prevented the choice of being in the previous account. Now the same scheme serves another insight: there is a being at stake in consciousness, but which has to remain a "half-being," a false being, given the impossibility to espouse the object *a*. It is this false being that gives support to the "I" and thus enables the mechanism of the Imaginary, providing the ground, as it were, to the vagaries of the mirror. "I," in the gesture of recognition, espouses the false being, accompanied by the corollary "I don't think." It constitutes what Lacan now calls "*moi-je*," based on a rejection of thought, yet experiencing itself precisely as the subject of thought in the usual and accepted sense of the word. So the current notion of "thinking" relies on a tacit choice, a rejection of thought that relegates it to the unconscious.

This is now the basic point of this second reading of cogito: it should be read as *sum, ergo cogito,* the choice of being to found thought, but this is what strikes with inanity the thought produced by this choice. The forced choice of *sum, ergo cogito* is the invisible truth of the Cartesian gesture.

The thought worthy of its name emerges only with the second option, that of the thought without being, but not as what one could possibly choose. Freud insisted that "the unconscious thinks," and Lacan would go even further, adding another twist: *it is only the unconscious that thinks,* with the true dignity of thought that never fails to astonish by its novelty. In the previous account, the necessary choice of thought coincided with the choice of sense, to be paid by the return of non-sense; now the two are opposed—the true thought is separate from sense, cut off from understanding.[16] It is a thought without being or substance— whereas one can make substance of the half-being of *moi-je,* and this is indeed what Descartes did with *res cogitans,* the thinking thing (and perhaps it goes the same for all notion of substance). It is also a thought without an "I," though not without a subject.[17]

Alienation now appears to mean quite the opposite from the previous account: before it meant that the subject had to entrust him/herself to the signifier in order to be a subject at all, alienation was alienation in the signifier, synonymous with the entry into language and its signifying logic. Now alienation figures precisely as the refusal of this logic, the choice of being against the effects of the signifier, the rejection of the signifier. If before one had to entrust oneself to the Other, now the basic gesture is that of the rejection of the Other. One cannot choose oneself as a subject, but the other side of the alternative is that one is forced to choose oneself as an "I," with the false being deprived of thought. Yet, there is a basic postulate of psychoanalysis, an axiom, so to speak, that makes it possible at all: that the "subject" of false being can be induced to be permeable to the effects of the unconscious thought; that the part that one has been forced to choose can be open to the part that one has tried to reject; that the false being can be exposed to (the unconscious) thought. The line connecting the two can be seen as the one that defines transference: "Psychoanalysis postulates that the unconscious, where the 'I am not' of the subject has its substance, can be invoked from the 'I don't think' where he imagines himself to be master of his being, i.e., not to be of language" (Lacan 1984, 14; my translation). The transference is "the diagonal joining the two extremities" (14), thus enabling the "subject" of alienation, with his/her false being, to undergo the effects of truth (the unconscious). Psychoanalysis, ultimately, *is* this connecting line. The hypothetical initial situation was endowed with two vectors: the vector of alienation (being without thought) and the vector Lacan simply called "truth," pointing toward the unconscious. So the transference, joining the two extremities, is the lever to open the alienated subject of forced choice to the effects of the truth of the excluded choice.[18]

The schematic presentation of this choice between "I don't think" and "I am not," the choice between the two circles that are both curtailed at their intersection, was introduced by Lacan also with an additional end in view. There is a huge problem that has been pointed out a number of times since Freud's discovery of psychoanalysis and that Freud himself endeavored to solve in various ways. One could say that the discovery of psychoanalysis seems to involve two different steps, and it is not easy to see how they fit together.

On the one hand, there were the analyses of dreams, of slips of the tongue (parapraxes), and of jokes, which formed the substance of Freud's three separate volumes published between 1900 and 1905. They all dealt with the formations of the unconscious that could be put under the heading of "the unconscious structured as a language." Indeed, it was Lacan's great *tour de force* to have detected in them the very mechanisms that followed from Saussurean linguistics (as read by Jakobson), the mechanisms of the signifier where the Freudian *Verdichtung* and *Verschiebung*, for example, could be read as a paramount version of the great divide between the basic mechanisms of metaphor and metonymy.

The "substance" of the unconscious that comes to light here is manifested in the play of signifiers.

On the other hand, we have Freud's *Three Essays on the Theory of Sexuality,* published in 1905, where the scenery seems to be quite different. The problems there include, among others: the stages in the development of libido; the object around which those stages turn; the partial object epitomized, for instance, by the breast and the feces; the lost object around which the drives circulate; the deviations of the drives as to their goal or their object. And there, surprisingly, we don't find any plays of the signifier, no glittering linguistic metaphors or metonymies. If the unconscious speaks (and Lacan never tired of repeating that in the unconscious, it speaks, *ça parle*), then the drives keep remarkably silent (*le silence des pulsions,* says Lacan). And if the play of the signifiers was the privileged theater of the mechanisms of desire (Freud's basic assumption, in the analysis of dreams, was that the dream was a *Wunscherfüllung,* a fulfillment of desire), then the drive, *la pulsion,* is a rather different matter. Indeed, in *The Four Fundamental Concepts of Psycho-Analysis,* one can see that two of those concepts were precisely the unconscious and the drive, forming a sort of paradigmatic opposition. So how does the "unconscious structured as a language" relate to the dimension of the drives?

Lacan tried to disentangle that problem first by a terminological twist. He took two of the terms proposed by Freud himself, though at different points of his development, namely the unconscious and the id (it, *Es, le ça*). Those two terms were usually taken as largely synonymous, pertaining to different periods of Freud's thought, where the second terminology, that of id-ego-superego, was supposed to have superseded the first one (that of the unconscious-preconscious-consciousness). Lacan's point was to take them together, so that the unconscious would be reserved for the first step, that of "the unconscious structured as a language," while the id would cover the other step, the dimension of the drives. There are two different logics that overlap in certain ways, yet which have to be considered separately.[19] One can already surmise that the two mechanisms of alienation and separation, in the first interpretation of cogito, were among other things also designed to cover those two different logics, the heterogeneous spheres of the subject of the unconscious, $, and that of *jouissance.*

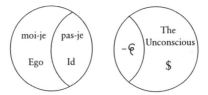

Figure 5

How to situate the two logics on our scheme, designed, as Lacan says, "to open the joint of the id and the unconscious" (Lacan 1984, 14; my translation)? The logic of the drives, the id, always involves the question of being, as well as a dimension of "non-thought"—the drives don't think, the unconscious does. The id should thus be placed on the side of "I don't think, I am," and Lacan proposed the elegant solution that it is to be located in the very part of intersection of which the choice of being has been curtailed. The precarious situation of the "I" was the choice of being while keeping at bay the object, so that the being "I" gets is itself curtailed, cut off from its essential part. And if the part of false being is covered by a *moi-je,* then the supplementary remainder can be labeled as a *pas-je,* a "non-I" (figure 5): "The 'I don't think' which here founds the subject in the option which is for him less bad [*la moins pire*], is curtailed of 'am' [*écorné du 'suis'*] of the intersection negated by his formula. The non-I which can be supposed there, is, although not being, not without being. [*Le pas-je qui s'y suppose, n'est, d'être pas, pas sans être.*] It is well designated by It [*ça*]" (Lacan 1984, 14; my translation). There is a part of "I" that is curtailed from "I," but which nevertheless forms its core, the part where "I" is necessarily based on drives (and Freud spoke precisely of *Ichtriebe,* the ego drives, as well as of an unconscious nucleus of "I").[20] So the two entities proposed in the famous title of Freud's paper, *The Ego and the Id,* find their respective places as two parts of the same circle. The id, although placed on the side of the choice of being, is nevertheless the part to which being cannot simply be ascribed, not in any ordinary sense, not in the sense massively covered by "false being." Yet it is not with-out being, as Lacan says—a paradoxical kind of being that encroaches upon the false being and truncates it, curtails it, pointing toward the object eluded in it. It is the part that cannot be subjectivated, assumed by an "I," but which keeps intruding, returning to the same place.

There is another turn of the screw. Lacan continues the above quotation as follows: "It is well designated by *It,* with an index which points toward the subject by grammar. *It [ça]* is the index carried by *ne,* the knot [*noeud*] which glides along the sentence to assure its unsayable metonymy" (Lacan 1984, 14; my translation). So there is, maybe surprisingly, a grammar involved in the drives. If the signifier is endowed with logic, then the drives are endowed with grammar. "It" (as well as in German, *Es,* and in French, *ça*) is the marker of a grammatical subject, the nonpersonal subject, the one that cannot be assumed by an "I." It is a *pas-je,* non-I, as opposed to *moi-je.* The drives involve the grammatical structure—as opposed to the "I." This is after all not so surprising if we remember some Freudian examples. Consider, for example, Freud's deduction of various forms of paranoia, in Schreber's case, from the grammatical transformations of a single sentence ("I (a man) love him"; Freud 1981, 9:200–204). One can witness the deployment of the whole panoply of quasi-Chomskian syntactic structures. Or consider some of the "vicissitudes of drives" in his famous metapsychological paper (Freud 1983, 11:105ff.), which can be seen as the grammatical passage between the active and the passive voice.[21] The drives may well be silent, but they nevertheless possess a grammar, or more precisely, a syntax. They don't speak, but they are not simply outside language.[22] They aim at, and turn around, what cannot be said in the metonymy of signifiers, what dwells in the intervals between the signifiers—precisely those intervals that the separation had to deal with and that placed separation on par with metonymy. So the grammar, as opposed to the signifying logic, implies the object around which the drives turn. The grammar of the drives is what curtails the "I," thus sustaining the "logic of fantasy."

On the other side, the side of the thought without being, there is also a curtailment encroaching upon the circle of the unconscious. It is there that Lacan placed the castration (designated in his algebra by *minus phi*). For the play of the signifiers that is the stuff of the unconscious thought turns around a lack, the lack of a foundation that could ground signification in being, and that is at the same time the curtailment of *jouissance.* There is the unconscious because this essential part is missing. The two curtailed parts, which together form the intersection, finally go hand in hand, they overlap and form a pair—it is in the place of the lack, the castration, that one can locate the object that the drives aim at and around which they turn. So we ultimately have, at the kernel of our being, the overlapping of castration (*minus phi*) and of the object (*a*), that is, of a being that comes into the place of an inherent lack, and that is nothing but the elusive cover of a void. It is a being over which we are not masters, yet which provides the only elusive bit of *jouissance* accessible to the "speaking being."

We can see that this second account in a way condenses the two schemes of alienation and separation into a single scheme. The unconscious that previously figured in the intersection of alienation is now one of the two curtailed terms, that of an impossible choice. As such it coincides with the impossible choice of the subject, $, and with the Other. So the three terms of previous alienation are now all to be found in the same circle on the right-hand side. Its curtailment is now epitomized by castration, the fundamental loss that condenses both the repression of the primary signifier and the loss of the object, the privation of *jouissance*. The other circle, that of "the ego and the id," suggests that what Lacan now calls alienation is actually much closer to what he previously called separation; one can already see that by the primacy accorded to the choice of being. But the being one chooses now is not the result of the subject's involvement with the Other, but quite the opposite, it results from a refusal: "But the sense of Descartes's cogito is that it substitutes this relation between thought and being [in the line of Aristotelian tradition] with purely and simply the instauration of the being of 'I'. . . . The fact of alienation is not that we are taken, remodeled, represented in the Other, on the contrary, it is essentially founded on the rejection of the Other, insofar as this Other has *replaced* this interrogation of being, around which turns the limit, the surpassing of cogito" (Lacan 1966–67, 11 January 1967; my translation). It is the being that founds the "I" as opposed to the subject and the Other (not the being the subject had to offer to the Other in separation in the aftermath of his alienating entanglement with the Other), a false being cleft from the id that detains its clue. It seems as though Lacan now transformed the programmatic title of "The mirror stage as formative of the function of the "I" into "Cogito as formative of the function of the I." Cogito finds itself on the same side with the "I" and the mirror stage, as its foundation. Alienation as the choice of being involves separation from sense and signification (the rejection of the Other), as well as the separation from the object, now figuring as the separation between the ego and the id, the "I" and the drives that sustain it. The crucial moment is the reversal of succession: there is an alienation that precedes the alienation in the Other, or the first response of the subject in relation to the Other is that of a rejection, an alienation of being prior to signification (with the emergence, on the other side, of the Symbolic prior to subjectivity and meaning). The choice of being relegates the "I" to the underpinnings of the Imaginary (the false being of fantasy) and to the drives, while the emergence of the subject results from the second step, the intrusion of the unconscious. It seems that Lacan, in the second account, goes back to his beginnings and reinterprets them: the primary alienation is not the alienation in the Other, but the espousal of an "imaginary" being of an "I" sustained by the grammar of the drives. The pure vanishing point of the subject of enunciation in cogito is preceded by a choice of *res cogitans,* a false being of the "I" framed by fantasy. So Descartes's indigenous error was to deduce "the thinking being" from what was but a void, but the things have to read in reverse: there is a "stain of being" that forgoes the pure void of the subject, the "stain of *sum*" prior to cogito.[23]

If we put the two circles together, one could venture to interpret this scheme as a disposition of the three basic dimensions that, throughout Lacan's teaching, underlie all human experience: the Real, the Symbolic, and the Imaginary (figure 6). The Real, at the intersection between the Imaginary and the Symbolic, would be thus what holds them together, presenting the two faces of the drives (as pertaining to the "I") and desire (as pertaining to the unconscious). The object *a* (both the object that causes desire and the object around which the drives turn) would thus be the pivotal point between the "I" and the subject of the unconscious. The forced choice in the first instance concerns the imaginary being, which is counteracted by the intrusion of the unconscious, the revenge of the rejected Other, while the Real, the impossible *jouissance,* is always necessarily lost, yet returns as an elusive leftover in the desire and the drives.

One can already see that this scheme is at odds with the notorious

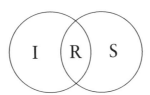

Figure 6

presentation that Lacan gave on the relation between those three dimensions in the Borromean knot. The Borromean knot is the connection of three circles in such a way that any two of them are connected by the third one. So each of the three dimensions, the Real, the Symbolic, and the Imaginary, have been given a separate circle, and they are tied in such a way that each of them holds the other two together. Our scheme looks like a flattened two-dimensional Borromean knot, where the Real is confined to the mere product of the intersection. Lacan, dissatisfied with this scheme, proposed another device, the Borromean knot, which ultimately allowed him to situate the entity that was to become his predominant preoccupation in the later years: the symptom, interpreted in a new light as *sinthome* (an entity different from the formations of the unconscious in the previous accounts). *Sinthome* comes to be placed in the center of the three circles of the Borromean knot, that which actually keeps them together in order to form a knot. And since this elaboration of cogito took form within the framework of "The logic of fantasy," as the title of this seminar goes, *the logic of the symptom* turned out to be something that couldn't be covered by it in a satisfactory way.

So which of these versions is the right one? Are we forced to choose between the two versions of the Lacanian cogito and then the further theory centered on symptom? When faced with our hypothetical villain shouting "your thought or your being," should one cling to thought or to being, or else exclaim "I give up both, only leave me my symptom"? Rather than deciding on some "definitive" account, one should see the progression through the different accounts of cogito as a clue to the general development of Lacan's thought, and, in particular, as a clue to his different ways of conceiving the subject. In the first stage, when his main interest was focused on the Imaginary, cogito was rejected as opposed to the mirror phase—it was seen as the support of an illusory self-transparency that the mirror phase could effectively dismantle. In the second stage, focused on the Symbolic, cogito was taken as the best way to conceive the subject of the signifier, as opposed to the imaginary "I," and its relation to the unconscious. Separation, as the counterpart to the subject's alienation in the signifier, could show how, at the same time, this subject was to figure as the subject of desire. In the third stage, now focused on the Real, the whole problem was shifted toward the realm of drives and fantasy, as opposed to the symbolic logic and the desire. Although drives lack subjectivity (though Lacan occasionally and mysteriously speaks of a "headless subject," *sujet acéphal*, of drives), they sustain the very assumption of an "I" (so that one could even paradoxically maintain that the "I" is the "subject" of drives). Finally, the three heterogeneous dimensions, whose problematic coexistence is at the kernel of Lacan's entire teaching, could be seen to revolve around the nodal point of *sinthome*. Maybe the best way to put it is to claim that cogito itself *is* that symptomatic nodal point around which those three dimensions turn, the point that pushes subjectivity first "beyond" the imaginary "I," then "beyond" the symbolic subject; any ultimate foundation (for example, "the Real of the anonymous drives") turns out to be caught in this circular movement and cannot be grasped as such independently of the other two. For is the impossible coupling of thought and being not at the very core of the symptom upon which any subjectivity depends?

The problem with understanding Lacan stems, among other things, from the fact that one has to follow the logic of the development of his theory and not to take any of its stages for granted, as some definitive shape of truth. While his preoccupations remained remarkably the same and his research presents an exceptional unity, there are at the same time quite baffling differences among the various answers that he proposed at different times. The new answers never simply discarded the previous ones and disclaimed their validity: the preceding steps found their place within the new pictures of growing complexity. Lacan's dogmatic stance goes hand in hand with his most undogmatic demeanor. Only a dogmatist "on the level of his task" can never be afraid of putting into question the previous results, turning them upside down without mercy if the new quests make it necessary, thus turning them into provisional stages of a search. It is the stubborn continuity and the implacable logic of this search that is his main message, rather than any one given result.

Notes

1   Even the best contemporary philosophy—such as the one promoted by Sartre, who is briefly alluded to—remains prey to cogito: "But unfortunately that philosophy [of being and nothingness] grasps negativity only within the limits of a self-sufficiency of consciousness, which, as one of its premises, links to the *méconnaissances* that constitute the ego, the illusion of autonomy to which it entrusts itself. This flight of fancy, for all that it draws . . . on borrowings from psychoanalytic experience, culminates in the pretention of providing an existential psychoanalysis" (Lacan 1977, 6).

2   A formulation like "the subject of the unconscious" (as well as "the subject of sci-

ence") was at that time deemed to be an "idealist reinscription" of Lacan committed by Lacan himself, Lacan supposedly falling back into the traps of superseded ways of thinking, or even failing to understand the significance of his own work. Althusser, for instance, expressly declared that the "process without a subject" was the key to Freud's discovery of the unconscious.

3   "To say that the subject on which we operate in psychoanalysis can be no other than the subject of science, may appear as a paradox" (Lacan 1966, 858; my translation). In what follows I will leave aside the cardinal problem of the relationship of psychoanalysis to science.

4   Cf. "However, by reducing his *cogito* to *res cogitans,* Descartes, as it were, patches up the wound he cut into the texture of reality. Only Kant fully articulates . . . the impossibility of locating the subject in the 'great chain of being', into the Whole of the universe—all those notions of the universe as a harmonious Whole in which every element has its own place. . . . In contrast to it, subject is in the most radical sense 'out of joint'; it constitutively lacks its own place, which is why Lacan designates it by the mathem $\emptyset$, the 'barred' *S*" (Žižek 1993, 12).

5   "Let us go back to our Descartes, and to his subject who is supposed to know. How does he get rid of it? Well, as you know, by his voluntarism, by the primacy given to the will of God. This is certainly one of the most extraordinary sleights of hand that has ever been carried off in the history of the mind" (Lacan 1986, 225).

6   One of the most famous quotations from *Écrits* states the following: "My definition of a signifier (there is no other) is as follows: a signifier is that which represents the subject for another signifier" (Lacan 1977, 316.) Cf.: "The signifier, producing itself in the field of the Other, makes manifest the subject of its signification. But it functions as a signifier only to reduce the subject in question to being no more than a signifier, to petrify the subject in the same movement in which it calls the subject to function, to speak, as subject" (Lacan 1986, 207).

7   "In a precisely similar way, Freud, when he doubts—for they are *his* dreams, and it is he who, at the outset, doubts—is assured that a thought is there, which is unconscious, which means that it reveals itself as absent. . . . [I]t is to this place that he summons the *I think* through which the subject will reveal himself. . . . It is here that the dissymmetry between Freud and Descartes is revealed. It is not in the initial method of certainty grounded on the subject. It stems from the fact that the subject is 'at home' in this field of the unconscious" (Lacan 1986, 36).

8   Cf. Borch-Jacobsen 1991 and Sipos 1994.

9   Cf. "Indeed, this is the essential flaw in philosophical idealism which, in any case, cannot be sustained and has never been radically sustained. There is no subject without, somewhere, *aphanisis* of the subject, and it is in this alienation, in this fundamental division, that the dialectic of the subject is established" (Lacan 1986, 221).

10   There is a technical aspect to it pertaining to the use of set theory. "Whereas the first phase is based on the sub-structure of joining, the second is based on the substructure that is called intersection or product. It is situated precisely in that same lunula in which you find the form of the gap, the rim" (Lacan 1986, 213). It can be given

a more precise formal background with De Morgan's laws, but Lacan inflects those technical aspects for his own purposes.

11   "It is in so far as [the desire of the Other] is beyond or falls short of what [the mother as the first Other] says, of what she hints at, of what she brings out as meaning, it is in so far as her desire is unknown, it is in this point of lack, that the desire of the subject is constituted" (Lacan 1986, 218–19; translation modified).

12   "Through the function of the *objet a,* the subject separates himself off, ceases to be linked to the vacillation of being, in the sense that it forms the essence of alienation" (Lacan 1986, 258).

13   The two sides also appear in the process of transference: the "subject supposed to know" functions on the level of alienation, the supposition of a signifier in possession of the Other, whereas the other slope of transference, its second stage, as it were, transference as love, involves the supposition of a secret object hidden and detained by the other, *agalma,* in relation to which one is prepared to offer everything, including what one doesn't possess, the Lacanian definition of love, and this is where being comes into play.

14   "One lack is superimposed upon the other. The dialectic of the objects of desire, in so far as it creates the link between the desire of the subject and the desire of the Other—I have been telling you for a long time now that it is one and the same—this dialectic now passes through the fact that the desire is not replied to directly. It is a lack engendered from the previous time that serves to reply to the lack raised by the following time" (Lacan 1986, 215).

15   For what follows I am much indebted to the courses given by Jacques-Alain Miller, particularly his seminar entitled *1, 2, 3, 4* given in 1984–85.

16   One is tempted to quote Adorno's dictum from *Minima moralia:* "True are only the thoughts that don't understand themselves."

17   "Without substance, yet as a subject" could be taken as a rephrasing of the Hegelian "not only as a substance, but also as a subject"—for one could say that the subject appears precisely at the point of a "lack in the substance," the failure of substantiality.

18   This doesn't entail that one should become aware of the unconscious as one's truth, but rather the reverse: "the 'I don't think,' as correlative of It [*ça*], is called to join the 'I am not,' as correlative of the unconscious, but in such a way that they eclipse and occult each other in being superimposed. In the place of 'I am not' It [*ça*] will come, giving it a positive form of 'I am It [*ça*]' which is a pure imperative, precisely the imperative which Freud has formulated in *Wo es war, soll Ich werden*" (Lacan 1966–67, 11 January 1967; my translation).

19   One can mention in passing that the famous "graph of desire" (Lacan 1977, 315) displays those two dimensions on two parallel stages, and the graph can be seen as nothing but an attempt to link them, to conceive them together.

20   Cf. "It is certain that much of the ego is itself unconscious, and notably what we may describe as its nucleus; only a small part of it is covered by the term 'preconscious'" ("Beyond the Pleasure Principle" [Freud 1983, 11:289–90]). "We have come upon something in the ego itself which is also unconscious, which behaves exactly like the

repressed—that is, which produces powerful effects without itself being conscious and which requires special work before it can be made conscious. . . . A part of ego, too—and Heaven knows how important a part—may be unconscious, undoubtedly is unconscious" ("The Ego and the Id" [Freud 1983, 11:356]).

21   "As to the relation between the drive and activity/passivity, I think I will be well enough understood if I say that at the level of the drive, it is purely grammatical" (Lacan 1986, 200).

22   "When I say structure, logical structure, you should understand that as grammatical [structure]. It's nothing else but the support of what is at stake in drive . . . a grammatical montage, whose inversions, reversions, complex turnings are regulated in the application of diverse inversions, *Verkehrung,* chosen and partial negations, and there is no other way to make function the relation of I, as a being-in-the-world, but to pass it through this structure which is nothing else but the essence of It [*ça*]" (Lacan 1966–67, 11 January 1967; my translation).

23   Žižek (1993, 59–60) makes an interesting suggestion that the two versions of cogito can be taken as the feminine and the masculine versions: the feminine position would present the choice of thought in the first account, and the masculine one the choice of being in the second. This suggestion is in many ways illuminating and inspiring, but it is hard to reconcile with the detail of Lacan's text.

Works Cited

Baas, Bernard, and Armand Zaloszyc. 1988. *Descartes et le fondement de la psychanalyse.* Paris: Navarin.

Borch-Jacobsen, Mikkel. 1991. *Lacan: The Absolute Master.* Stanford, Calif.: Stanford University Press.

Freud, Sigmund. 1973–85. *The Pelican Freud Library,* 15 vols. London: Penguin.

Lacan, Jacques. 1966. *Écrits.* Paris: Seuil.

———. 1966–67. "La logique du fantasme" (unpublished seminar).

———. 1973. *Le séminaire, livre XI: Les quatre concepts fondamentaux de la psychanalyse.* Ed. J.-A. Miller. Paris: Seuil.

———. 1977. *Écrits: A Selection.* Trans. A. Sheridan. London: Tavistock/Routledge.

———. 1984. "Comptes rendus d'enseignement 1964–1968." *Ornicar?* Vol. 29. Paris: Navarin, 7–25.

———. 1986. *The Four Fundamental Concepts of Psycho-Analysis.* Ed. J.-A. Miller, trans. A. Sheridan. London: Penguin.

Sipos, Joel. 1994. *Lacan et Descartes. La tentation métaphysique.* Paris: P.U.F.

Žižek, Slavoj. 1993. *Tarrying with the Negative.* Durham: Duke University Press.

Alenka Zupančič

Introduction: The Uncommon Good

In relation to the notion of ethics, such as it was shaped through the history of philosophy, psychoanalysis introduces a double "blow of disillusionment": the first one is associated with the name of Sigmund Freud and the second one with that of Jacques Lacan. It is significant that, in both cases, the same philosopher is at the center of discussion: Immanuel Kant.

The "Freudian blow" could be summarized as follows: what philosophy calls the moral law and, more precisely, what Kant calls the categorical imperative, is in fact nothing other than the superego. This judgment provokes an "effect of disenchantment" that calls into doubt any endeavor to base ethics on foundations other than "pathological" ones. At the same time, it places "ethics" at the core of what Freud called "civilization and its discontents." As far as it has its origins in the constitution of the superego, ethics is nothing more than a convenient tool for any ideology that tries to pass off its own commandments as authentic, spontaneous, and "honorable" inclinations of the subject.

The "Lacanian blow" is of a different nature. It is, in fact, a double blow that aims firstly at Freud and only secondly at Kant. Lacan's critique of Freud is related to Freud's discussion of the commandment "Thou shalt love thy neighbor as thyself" in *Civilization and Its Discontents*. Lacan dedicates to this issue one chapter of his seminar *The Ethics of Psychoanalysis,* the chapter that actually begins with Freud and ends with Kant.

First, he defines traditional ethics as the "service of goods" or the "sharing of the good" and points out that, strictly speaking, there is no ethics involved here, because "it is in the nature of the good to be altruistic."[1] The register we are dealing with is that of the imaginary: "It is a fact of experience that what I want is the good of others in the image of my own. That doesn't cost so much. What I want is the good of others provided that it remain in the image of my own."[2] Lacan takes the example of Saint Martin sharing his cloak with a naked beggar and remarks that in this case the philanthropy is strictly correlative to the sharing of the "material" that is, in its very nature, made to be shared and disposed of. Then he invites us to consider a different situation where the naked man begs for something else, namely, that Saint Martin "either kill him or fuck him." This example introduces the difference between philanthropy and love (of our neighbor). And this is precisely what Freud recognizes in the commandment "Thou shalt love thy neighbor as thyself": the invitation to share with one's neighbor something other than one's goods—namely one's *jouissance.*

Freud turns from this with horror, pointing out that we consider our love to be something valuable and that we feel that we ought not throw it away without reflection, giving it to the first stranger that comes along. In the next step, Freud remarks that not only is this stranger generally unworthy of our love but that he has, because of his hostility and aggressiveness, more claim to our hostility and even our hatred: "if he can satisfy any sort of desire by it, he thinks nothing of jeering at me, insulting me, slandering me and showing his superior power."[3] Thus, Freud rejects this commandment together with another one that also "arouses strong opposition" in him, namely, to "Love thine enemies." And yet Freud concludes that it is wrong to see in this second commandment an even greater imposition: "At the bottom, it is the same thing."[4]

Lacan's critical commentary regarding Freud's position apropos of this question does not in any way imply that Freud was wrong (that our neighbor is not necessarily as bad as Freud indicates, or that the greatness of ethics is precisely that we love him in spite of his hostility). On the contrary, it is precisely insofar as everything that Freud says is true that we must examine this eventuality, this hostility that inevitably rises up in our encounter with our neighbor. Lacan argues that precisely in pointing to this aggressiveness and turning away from it, Freud remains within the horizon of the "traditional ethics." What characterizes the latter — in all its different shapes and systems — is a certain definition of the good that can be summarized as follows: the good is that which keeps us away from our *jouissance*. "The whole Aristotelian conception of the good is alive in this man [Freud] who is a true man; he tells us the most sensitive and reasonable things about what it is worth sharing the good that is our love with. But what escapes him is perhaps the fact that precisely because we take that path we miss the opening on to *jouissance*." [5]

One does not have to look very far in order to grasp all the topicality of this issue. Suffice it to recall the modern, profane version of the commandment "Thou shalt love they neighbor as thyself": "Respect the difference of the other," or, "The other has the right to be different." Admittedly, this commandment does not require that we love this other, it is enough that we tolerate him/her. And yet, as Freud would have said, at the core it is the same thing. It raises exactly the same problems: what happens if this other is really the Other, if his/her difference is not only a "cultural," "folkloric" difference, but a fundamental difference? Are we still to respect him/her, to love him/her? Alain Badiou formulated this problem in the following way: "The first suspicion arises when we consider the fact that proclaimed advocates of ethics and of the 'right to be different' are visibly horrified by any important difference. For them the African customs are barbarous, the Islamists are hideous, the Chinese are totalitarian and so on. In fact, this famous 'other' is presentable only if he is a *good* other, that is to say if he is *the same as we are*. . . . Just as there is no freedom for the enemies of freedom, there is no respect for the one whose difference consists precisely in not respecting the differences." [6] It is clear that if the word ethics is to have any serious meaning today, it must be situated at this level and dealt with from the perspective of this hostility and intolerance that inevitably spring up in my encounter with the Other. As is well known, Lacan situates the reasons for this hostility in our encounter with *jouissance*. *Jouissance* is by its very definition "strange," "other," "dissimilar." However, the important point here is that I do not experience *jouissance* as "strange" and "dissimilar" because it is the *jouissance* of the Other, but, on the contrary, that it is because of this *jouissance* that I perceive my neighbor as (radically) Other and "strange." Moreover, it is not simply the *jouissance* of the neighbor, of the other, that is strange to me. The kernel of the problem is that I experience my own *jouissance* as strange, dissimilar, other, and hostile. "Thou shalt love thy neighbor as thyself" compels me to love "that most neighborly of neighbors who is inside me," my *jouissance*. In other terms, one cannot think the radical otherness, the "completely different" (to use the famous Monty Python line) without stumbling against the problem of the *Same* (which has nothing to do with the *semblable*, the fellow men who resemble us). "My neighbor possesses all the evil Freud speaks about, but it is no different from the evil I retreat from in myself. To love him, to love him as myself, is necessarily to move toward some cruelty. His or mine?, you will object. But haven't I just explained to you that nothing indicates that they are distinct? It seems rather that they are the same, on condition that those limits which oblige me to posit myself opposite the other as my fellow man [*mon semblable*] are crossed."[7] In fact, the identity, the resemblance, and the sameness can be situated each in one of the three Lacanian registers: the Symbolic, the Imaginary, and the Real. The Real is not simply something entirely Other, Different, but is essentially linked to the paradoxes of the Same.

If traditional ethics draws its strength from the fact that it defined the good in such a way that it helps the subject to stay away from his *jouissance,* psychoanalysis deals precisely with the ingress, the intrusion of *jouissance* into the subject's universe. Not only can psychoanalysis not ignore or turn away from the paradoxes of *jouissance*, the latter constitutes its pivotal point. This is the precise reason why Lacan speaks of the "ethics of psychoanalysis"—which is not in the least "natural" or "obvious," especially if we bear in mind that what Lacan calls the "ethics of psychoanalysis" has nothing to do with "medical ethics," that is, the code that determines what a doctor can or cannot do with his practice. For Lacan, ethics is not an "annex" to the fundamental (clinical) know-how, but rather concerns the very core of the psychoanalytic practice. Because it deals with *jouissance,* psychoanalysis steps into the field traditionally reserved for ethics (or morality), and it steps into this field at a point "on which that morality turns":[8] the point of the impossible, which was traditionally designated as the Evil. The greatest difficulty, of course, consists in finding the "right" way to reintroduce *jouissance* into the center of the discussion of ethics, to reformulate ethics from its perspective, without adopting the Sadian discourse. For it was precisely Sade who explicitly made *jouissance* a matter of ethics.

It was roughly at the same time that Kant wrote his *Critique of Practical Reason,* the first systematic attempt to base ethics on something that lies "beyond the pleasure principle," and to make the impossible the pivot of the ethics.[9] Kantian ethics is no longer an ethics designed to keep us away from our *jouissance.* In this aspect Kant escapes the criticism that Lacan addresses to Freud; he does not miss "the opening on to *jouissance,*" that is, the Real, and Lacan prizes him for that. However, this prizing is followed by a blow that bears the title "Kant avec Sade." Kant walks on an edge where it is very difficult to maintain balance and not to slip back either to the "traditional morality" or to the Sadian discourse. In fact, according to Lacan, Kant does not succeed in maintaining this balance. On the one hand, he tends to reintroduce, "through the back door," the imaginary dimension; in his examples he "envelops" the moral law in the sympathy for our fellowman, our *semblable.* On the other hand, he makes the Real an object of the will, which brings his ethics close to Sade. The price to pay for this "wanting the Real" is that the subject has to assume the perverse position where he sees himself as the instrument of the Will of the Other.

Sex, Lies, and Executions

Here is Kant's famous "apologue of gallows" to which Lacan often refers:

> Suppose that someone says his lust is irresistible when the desired object and opportunity are present. Ask him whether he would not control his passions if, in front of the house where he has this opportunity, a gallows were erected on which he would be hanged immediately after gratifying his lust. We do not have to guess very long what his answer may be. But ask him whether he thinks it would be possible for him to overcome his love of life, however great it may be, if his sovereign threatened him with the same sudden death unless he made a false deposition against an honorable man whom the ruler wished to destroy under a plausible pretext. Whether he would or not he would perhaps not venture to say; but

that it would be possible for him he would certainly admit without hesitation. He judges, therefore, that he has to do something because he knows that he ought. . . .[10]

Let us put aside for the moment the first part of the apologue, and focus on the second part, which is made to illustrate the way the moral law imposes itself upon the human subject, even if it implies the ultimate sacrifice. What is wrong with Kant's argument in this part? Lacan remarks: "In effect, if an assault on the goods, the life, or the honor of someone else were to become universal rule, that would throw the whole of man's universe into a state of disorder and evil."[11] We must not overlook the irony implied in this remark. Lacan reproaches Kant for introducing a perfectly pathological motive, hidden behind the appearance of a pure moral duty. In other words, Lacan reproaches Kant for cheating ("Kant, our dear Kant, in all his innocence, his innocent subterfuge").[12] Kant deceives his readers by disguising the true stakes and the true impact of the (ethical) choice. In his example, he puts the categorical imperative (our duty) on the same side as the good (the well-being) of our fellowman: the reader will follow Kant without much hesitation when he says that in this case the idea of accepting one's own death is, at least, possible. And the problem resides in the fact that the reader does *not* follow Kant because s/he is convinced of the inexorability of duty as such, but because of the image of the pain inflicted on the other that plays here the role of the counterpoint. Kant's example is destined to produce in us "a certain effect of *a fortiori*" (Lacan), as a result of which we are deceived about the real stakes of the choice. In other words, the reader will agree with Kant for, if we may say so, "nonprincipal reasons," s/he will agree with Kant on the grounds of an *a fortiori* reasoning: not because s/he is convinced of the *a priori* value of the moral law, but on account of a "stronger reason." We accept Kant's argument because we are guided by a certain representation of the good in which we situate our duty — and this is heteronomy in the strictest Kantian sense of the word. If we bear in mind that the crucial novelty of Kantian ethics (*the* point of the "Copernican revolution" in ethics) consists in reversing the hierarchy between the notion of the good and the moral law, then the very least we can say regarding the discussed example is that it obscures this crucial point.

This is why Lacan suggests that we change the example a little, in order to elucidate the real issue: What if I find myself in a situation where my duty and the good of the other are on opposite sides, and where I can accomplish my duty only to the detriment of my fellowman? Will I stop before the evil, the pain that my action would inflict on the other, or will I stick to my duty, despite the consequences? It is only this case that allows us to see whether the issue is the attack on the rights of the other, as far as s/he is my *semblable,* my "fellowman," or, rather if it is a question of the false witness, false testimony as such. Thus, Lacan invites us to consider a case of a true witness, a case of conscience that is raised, for example, if I am summoned to inform on my neighbor or my brother for activities that are prejudicial to the security of the state. This is how Lacan comments on what is at stake in this case: "Must I go toward my duty of truth insofar as it preserves the authentic place of my *jouissance,* even if it is empty? Or must I resign myself to this lie which, by making me substitute forcefully the good for the principle of my *jouissance,* commands me to blow alternatively hot and cold?"[13] Indeed, it is in this alternative that the crucial issue of Kantian ethics is formulated in the clearest way. If the moral law excludes any prior consideration of the good, then it is clear where this ethics stands in relation to the aforementioned alternative. Once the good enters the stage, the question necessarily springs up: *Whose good?* This is what Lacan has in mind with the phrase "blow alternatively hot and cold": if I do not betray my brother or my neighbor, I may betray my other countrymen. Who is to decide whose good is more valuable than the others'? This is the fundamental deadlock of any ethics based on the notion of the good, be it "individualist" or "communitarian." The project of Kantian ethics is precisely to escape this deadlock, and this is the reason why Kantian ethics is not only a version of "traditional ethics," but an irreversible step toward something else. However, as we have seen, Lacan reproaches Kant for not making this point clear enough: Kant seems to have troubles accepting some consequences of his own principal theoretical stand. Therefore Lacan challenges him with this question: Must I go toward my duty of truth insofar as it preserves the authentic place of my *jouissance,* even if it is empty? Or must I resign myself to this lie, which, by making me substitute forcefully the good for the principle of my *jouissance,* commands me to blow alternatively hot and cold?

What is most striking about this "transtemporal" debate between Lacan and Kant is that Kant actually did answer Lacan; he answered him in his (in)famous reply to Benjamin Constant, *On a Supposed Right to Lie because of Philanthropic Concerns* (*Über ein vermeintes Recht aus Menschenliebe zu lügen*, 1797). Kant begins this brief essay by quoting Benjamin Constant, who wrote: "The moral principle, 'It is a duty to tell the truth' would make any society impossible if it were taken singly and unconditionally. We have proof of this in the very direct consequence which a German philosopher has drawn from this principle. This philosopher goes so far as to assert that it would be a crime to lie to a murderer who asked whether our friend who is pursued by him had taken refuge in our house."[14] Constant's text *Des réactions politiques,* in which we find the quoted passage, was translated in German by a professor Franz Cramer who lived in Paris. In the German translation, the passage where Constant speaks of a "German philosopher" is accompanied by a footnote in which the publisher states that Constant told him that the "German philosopher" he had in mind was Kant. What is especially interesting about this case is that, in the work of Kant, we do not find the example to which Constant refers. However, Kant immediately replied to Constant with *On a Supposed Right to Lie because of Philanthropic Concerns.* After quoting Constant (the above passage), Kant adds a footnote saying that he remembers stating somewhere what Constant suggests, but that he does not remember where. The whole affair is quite amusing, because Kant recognizes himself in something that he—at least with these words—never actually wrote. This, of course, becomes irrelevant the moment when Kant takes this position as his own and engages himself in defending it. He states that, even in this particular case, it would be wrong to lie. If there is no other way out, we must tell the murderer who is pursuing our friend the truth.

It is probably not necessary to point out that Kant's position in this case did not meet with much approval from his critics. On the contrary, it still remains the most "abjected" part of Kant's philosophy. There were some attempts to save Kant by shifting the issue from moral to political philosophy.[15] Yet, this does not resolve the problem and the discomfort that it generates, it merely sidesteps it by driving our attention to something else. On the other hand, among those who consider it an ethical issue, it is clearly an object of loathing and rejection. Herbert J.

Paton, for instance, takes "this mistaken essay" as "illustrating the way in which an old man [Kant was seventy-three when he wrote it] . . . can push his central conviction to unjustified extremes under the influence of his early training [namely Kant's mother who supposedly severely condemned lying]."[16] Paton suggests that we dismiss this essay as a "temporary aberration" that has no impact on the basic principles of Kantian ethics.

However, this attitude is quite problematic in that the issue involved in the discussed example brings into play nothing less than the basic principles of Kantian ethics. If the moral law is indeed unconditional, if it does not follow from any notion of the good, but is itself the ground for any possible definition of the good, then it is clear why Kant cannot accept that the good of our fellowman might serve us as an excuse for not doing our duty. Those who are not willing to accept this aspect of Kant's position in the discussed example but reject it, are also rejecting the entire edifice of Kantian ethics that hangs precisely upon this point.

If, however, we accept Kant's position, there is yet another trap to be avoided, namely the "Sadian trap." The Kantian subject cannot escape the Real involved in the unconditional duty by hiding himself behind the image of his fellowman — but neither can this subject hide behind his duty and use the duty as an *excuse* for his actions. As Slavoj Žižek has pointed out, as an ethical subject I cannot say: "Sorry, I know it was unpleasant, but I couldn't help it, the moral law imposed that act on me as my unconditional duty!" On the contrary, the subject is fully responsible for what he refers to as his duty.[17] The type of discourse where I use my duty as an excuse for my actions is perverse in the strictest sense of the word. Here, the subject attributes to the Other (to the duty or to the Law), the surplus enjoyment that he finds in his actions: "I am sorry if my actions hurt you, but I only did what the Other wanted me to do, so go and see Him if you have any objections." In this case, the subject hides behind the law.

In order to illustrate this, let us take an example suggested by Henry E. Allison.[18] Suppose that I have a violent dislike for someone and have come into possession of a piece of information about him, which I know will cause him great pain if he learns of it. With the intent of doing so, I decide to inform him of the matter, but I justify the action on the grounds of his right to know. Accordingly, rather than being a vicious act of causing unnecessary pain, I represent it to myself (and perhaps to others) as a laudable act of truth telling. I might even convince myself that it is a sacred duty. Allison uses this example to illustrate what he calls the "self-deception," by means of which we are able to ignore "the morally salient factor(s)" of a situation. However, we will take this example as an illustration of something else, namely the perverse attitude that consists in presenting our duty as an excuse for our actions. In other words, we are dealing here with two "self-deceptions" and not just one. The first is the one pointed out by Allison: we deceive ourselves as to our actual intention, which is to hurt our fellow man. But this deception is only possible on the basis of another, more fundamental one. It is possible only insofar as we take (the "content" of) our duty to be "ready-made," preexisting our involvement in the situation. This is why we will not expose the hypocrite in question by saying to him "we know that your real intention was to hurt the other person." He could go on asserting hypocritically that he had to muster up all his forces in order to tell the truth to the other, that he himself suffered enormously when hurting the other, yet could not avoid it, because it was his duty to do so. . . . The only way to unmask this kind of hypocrite is to ask him: "And where is it written that it is your duty to tell the other what you know? What makes you believe this is your duty? Are you ready to answer for your duty?"

According to the fundamental principles of Kantian ethics, duty is only that which the subject makes his duty, it does not exist somewhere "outside" like the Ten Commandments. It is the subject who makes something his duty and has to answer for it. The categorical imperative is not a test that would enable us to make a list (however inexhaustible) of ethical deeds, a sort of "catechism of pure reason," behind which we could hide the surplus enjoyment that we find in our acts.[19]

At this point we can return to Kant's essay *On a Supposed Right to Lie from Altruistic Motives*. It is now clear what makes Kant's position unbearable: not the fact that my duty does not necessarily coincide with the good of my fellowman (this is something that we have to admit as possible), but the fact that Kant takes, in this case, the duty to tell the truth as a ready-made duty that passed, once and for all, the test of the categorical imperative and could thus be written on the list of commandments for, so to speak, all the generations to come. It is precisely this gesture that makes it possible for the subject to assume a perverse attitude, to justify his actions by saying that they were imposed upon him by unconditional duty, to hide behind the moral law and present himself as the "mere instrument" of its will. Indeed, Kant goes so far as to claim that the subject who tells the murderer the truth is not responsible for the consequences of this action, whereas the subject who tells a lie is fully responsible for the outcome of the situation. Consequently, instead of illustrating the fact that duty is founded only in itself and that it is precisely this point that allows for the freedom and responsibility of the moral subject, this notorious example illustrates rather the case of a pervert who hides the enjoyment that he finds in the betrayal behind the Law. However, let us stress once again that this itself does not diminish the value of the other aspect of the example. It is *possible* that someone would make it his duty to tell the murderer the truth: as paradoxical as it may sound, this *could be an ethical act*. What is inadmissible is that the subject claims that this duty was imposed upon him, that he could not do otherwise, that he only followed the commandment of the Law. . . .

This brings us to the core of the relation between the subject and the law. Why is it inadmissible to fulfill, once and for all, the enigmatic enunciation of the categorical imperative with a statement (i.e., "Tell the truth!"), which reduces the law to the list of already established commandments? Not simply, as we might suppose, because in this case we neglect all the particular circumstances that may occur in a concrete situation; not simply because one case is never identical to another, so that in any given situation we can come across a factor that we have to take into account when making our decision. The situation is a much more radical one: even if it were possible — by means of some supercomputer — to simulate all possible situations, this still would not imply that we could put together a list of ethical decisions corresponding to the given situations. The crucial problem of the moral law is not the variability of situations to which we "apply" it, but the place or the role of the subject in its very constitution, and thus in the constitution of the universal. The reason why the subject cannot be effaced from the "structure" of the ethical (by means of making a list of duties that would absolve the subject of his responsibility and freedom) is not the particular, the singular, the specific, but the universal. That which can in no way be reduced without abolishing the ethics as such, is not the colorfulness and variability of every given situation, but the gesture by which every subject, by means of his action, posits the universal, performs a certain operation of universalization. The ethical subject is not an *agent* of the universal, he does not act in the name of the universal or with its authorization—if this were the case, the subject would be an unnecessary, dispensable "element" of ethics. The subject is not the agent of the universal, but its *agens*. This does not mean simply that the universal is always "subjectively mediated," that the law is always "subjective" (partial, selective, prejudicial), it does not point toward a certain definition of the universal, but rather toward a definition of the subject: it means that the subject is nothing other than this moment of universalization, of the constitution or determination of the law. The ethical subject is not a subject who brings into a given (moral) situation all the subjective baggage and affects with it (i.e., formulates a maxim that corresponds to his personal inclinations), but a subject who is, strictly speaking, born from this situation, who only emerges from it. The ethical subject is the point where the universal comes to itself and achieves its determination. As Kant knew very well, we are all pathological subjects, and this is what eventually led him to the conclusion that no ethical act is really possible in this world. What he did not see—or rather, what he saw but did not actually conceptualize[20]—is that the subject who enters an (ethical) act is not necessarily the same as the one who emerges from it.

Here we come across one of the most significant questions of Kant's practical philosophy, namely the question of the possibility of (performing) an ethical act. Is it at all possible for a human subject to accomplish an ethical act? This question can be situated in the context of yet another debate: the debate that concerns the Kantian notion of "diabolical evil" and the exclusion of the latter as impossible.

Like Angel like Devil

In *Religion Within the Limits of Reason Alone* Kant identifies several different modes of evil. Let us reiterate them briefly.

1. The *frailty* of human nature, on account of which we yield to pathological motives *in spite of* our will to do the good. The will is good, we wanted the good, but the realization of this good failed.

2. The *impurity* of the human will. Here the problem is not a discrepancy between the maxim and its realization. The maxim is good in

respect to its object, and we are also strong enough to "practice" it, but we do not do so from the respect for the moral law but, for example, out of our self-love, out of some personal interests, because we think this will be useful for us. . . .

3. The *wickedness* (*Bösartigkeit*) or "radical evil" is structured somewhat differently: Its foundation is a (free, although nontemporal) act in which we make the incentives of self-love the *condition* of obedience to the moral law. In other words, "radical evil" reverses the hierarchy of (pathological) incentives and the law: it makes the former the condition of the latter, whereas the latter (i.e., the law) ought to be the supreme condition or the "criterion" for the satisfaction of the incentives. We obey the moral law only "by accident," when it suits us or when it is compatible with our pathological inclinations. "Radical evil" is in fact that which explains the possibility of the first two modes of evil.

To these three "degrees" of evil Kant adds a fourth, the "diabolical evil," which he excludes at the same time as a case that could not apply to men. "Diabolical evil" would occur if we were to elevate the opposition to the moral law to the level of the maxim. In this case the maxim would be opposed to the law not just "negatively" (as it is in the case of radical evil), but directly. This would imply, for instance, that we would be ready to act contrary to the moral law even if this meant acting contrary to our self-interest and to our well-being. We would make it a principle to act against the moral law, and we would stick to this principle no matter what (i.e., even if it meant our death).

The first difficulty that occurs in this conceptualization of diabolical evil lies in its very definition: namely, that diabolical evil would occur if we elevated the opposition to the moral law to the level of a maxim (a principle, a law). What is wrong with this definition? Given the Kantian concept of the moral law—which is not a law that says "do this" or "do that," but an enigmatic law that only commands us to do our duty, without ever naming it—the following objection arises: if the opposition to the moral law were elevated to the maxim or principle, it would no longer be an opposition to the moral law, it would be the moral law itself. At this level, there is no opposition possible. It is not possible to oppose oneself to the moral law at the level of the (moral) law. Nothing can oppose itself to the moral law *on principle* (i.e., because of nonpathological reasons) without itself becoming a moral law. To act without allowing the pathological incentives to influence our actions is good. In relation to this definition of the good, (diabolical) evil would have to be defined as follows: it is evil to oppose oneself, without allowing the pathological incentives to influence one's actions, to actions that do not allow any pathological incentives to influence one's actions—which is absurd. Within the context of Kantian ethics it makes no sense to speak of the *opposition* to the moral law: one may speak of frailty or impurity of the human will (which imply a failure to make the law the only incentive of our actions), but not of the opposition to the moral law. The opposition to the moral law would itself be a moral law, there is no way to introduce any distinction between them at this level. In other words, "diabolical evil" inevitably coincides with the "highest good," introduced by Kant in the *Critique of Practical Reason* as the "necessary object of the will." The way in which Kant introduces diabolical evil is strictly symmetrical to his introduction of the highest good: they are both positioned as the "ideals" in which the will would entirely coincide with the Law, and they are both excluded as cases that cannot apply to human agents. There is only one difference: Kant gives to the highest good the support in the postulate of the immortality of the soul. But we must not forget that the immortal soul could as well function as the postulate of diabolical evil. We could very well transcribe the first paragraph of the chapter "The Immortality of the Soul as a Postulate of Pure Practical Reason" as follows: "The achievement of the highest evil in the world is the necessary object of a will determinable by moral law. In such will, however, the complete fitness of disposition to the moral law is the supreme condition of the highest evil. However, the perfect fit of the will to the moral law is the diabolical, which is a perfection of which no rational being of this world of sense is at any time capable. But since it is required as practically necessary, it can be found only in an endless progression to that perfect fitness. This infinite progress is possible only under the presupposition of the immortality of the soul. Thus the highest evil is practically possible only on the supposition of the immortality of the soul."

In this paraphrase we only had to invent one term, namely the "highest evil." This brings us to another interesting point: In the *Critique of Practical Reason*, Kant distinguishes between, on the one hand, the objects of pure practical reason and, on the other hand, the will. He affirms that "the sole objects of practical reason are those of *the good* and *the evil*." [21] At the same time, he defines a complete fitness of the will to the moral law as holiness. Thus we have, on the one side, the *highest good* as the object of practical reason and, on the other side, the *holy will* as its supreme condition. However, when we move from good to evil, this distinction seems to be abolished, the will and the object to be fused together. This is quite manifest in the expression "diabolical evil," where "diabolical" refers to the will and "evil" to the object. It must be stressed though, that Kant himself never used the expression "diabolical evil": his terms are "*devilish* being" and "that is diabolical"—namely "a disposition (the subjective *principle* of the maxims) to adopt evil *as evil* into our maxim as our incentives." [22] Therefore, instead of speaking of "diabolical evil," we should rather speak of the "highest evil" and "diabolical will." It is precisely in light of this difference that we can fully grasp the importance of the postulate of the immortality of the soul, which is not as innocent as it might appear. The basic operation introduced by this postulate consists in linking the *object* of practical reason (the highest good) to the *will*, in making it an object of the will and positing that the "realization" of this object is only possible under the supposition of the holy will. It is precisely this operation that, on the one hand, brings Kant close to Sade and his *volonté de jouissance*, "the will for enjoyment," and, on the other hand, makes it necessary for Kant (who does not want to be Sade) to exclude the highest good/evil as impossible for human agents. So as to avoid this impasse of Kantian ethics, it would be necessary to separate these two things (the object and the will) and to affirm, at the same time:

1. That the diabolical or highest evil is identical to the highest good and that they are nothing other than the definition of an accomplished (ethical) act. In other words, at the level of the structure of ethical act, the difference between the good and the evil does not exist. The evil is formally indistinguishable from the good.

2. That the "highest evil" and the "highest good" as defined above do exist, or rather, they do occur—what does not exist is holy or diabolical will.

As to the first point, it should be stressed that many critics have already pointed out that virtually any maxim, if suitably formulated, can be made to pass the universalizability test. In other words, Kant was often attacked on the grounds that his conceptualization of the moral law is too "formalistic," which allows for the fact that even the most "evil" actions can pass the test. However, our point is that this supposed weakness of Kantian ethics is in fact its strongest point and that we should accept it as such. If we tried to avoid it, we would be forced to reintroduce some a priori notion of the good and deduce the moral law from it. The fundamental paradox of ethics lies in the fact that in order to found an ethics, we already have to presuppose a certain ethics (a certain notion of the good). The whole project of Kantian ethics is to avoid this paradox: the moral law is founded only on itself, and the good is good only "*after*" the moral law. This demands a certain price, namely that, *on the level of the law*, the evil is formally indistinguishable from the good. Yet this is a price that we have to accept, otherwise we fall into the classical ideological trap. This is what happens to Allison when he tries to save Kant from the attacks that we mentioned above. His argument runs as follows: first, he introduces the notion of self-deception as one of the most important notions of Kant's ethics. Then, he claims that "it is precisely the testing of maxims that provides the major occasion for self-deception, which here takes the form of disguising from ourselves the true nature of the principles upon which we act. In short, immoral maxims appear to pass the universalizability test only because they ignore or obscure morally salient features of a situation." [23] The problem with this argument is, of course, the conceptual weakness of the notion of "morally salient features of a situation." As we know from Althusser on, the salient or the obvious, which is supposed to protect us from self-deception, can be the most refined form of self-deception. Every ideology works hard to make certain things "obvious," and the more we find these things obvious, self-evident, unquestionable, the more successfully the ideology has carried out its job. If we accept what Allison suggests, namely that *there is something in reality on which we can rely* when testing the maxims, then we also accept the logic that underlies the following maxim: "Act in such a way that the *Führer*, if he knew your action, would approve it." We can replace *Führer* with God and we will get a categorical imperative that is far more acceptable in our culture: "Act in such a way that God, if he knew your action, would approve it." But we must not forget that the logic and the structure of these two imperatives is exactly the same. We test our maxims against something that is "external" to the moral law and that determines the horizon of what is generally acceptable and what is not. This is why we have to maintain that there is absolutely nothing in reality that could help us "guess" what our duty is and that could deliver a guarantee against misjudging our duty. At the same time, this theoretical stance has the advantage of making it impossible for the subject to assume the perverse attitude that we discussed in the previous section: the subject cannot hide behind his duty—he is responsible for what he refers to as his duty.

Let us now examine more closely the logic that underlies Kant's exclusion of "diabolical evil" (and of the highest good). The exclusion in question seems to correspond to this common wisdom: a man is only a man, he is finite, divided in himself—and therein resides his uniqueness, his tragic greatness. A man is not a god and he should not try to be one, because if he does, he will inevitably cause evil. The problem with this stance is that it fails to recognize the real source of evil (in the common sense of the word). To take the example that is most frequently used, namely the Holocaust: what made it possible for the Nazis to torture and kill millions of Jews is not simply that they thought they were gods and could therefore decide who would live and who would die, but the fact that they saw themselves as *instruments* of God (or some other Idea), who had already decided who could live and who must die. Indeed, what is most dangerous is not an insignificant bureaucrat who thinks he is God, but rather the God who pretends to be an insignificant bureaucrat. One could even say that for the subject the most difficult thing is to accept that, in a certain sense, he is "God," that he has a choice. The right answer to the religious promise of immortality is not the pathos of the finite; the basis of ethics cannot be an imperative that commands us to endorse our finitude and renounce ourselves to "higher," "impossible" aspirations, but rather an imperative that invites us to recognize as our own the "impossible" that can occur as the "essential by-product" of our actions.

What the advocates of the Kantian exclusion of "diabolical evil" do not see or pass over in silence, is the symmetry of the (highest) good and the (highest) evil. In excluding the possibility of "diabolical evil" we also exclude the possibility of the good, we exclude the possibility of ethics as such or, more precisely, we posit the ethical act as something that is in itself impossible and that exists only in its perpetual failure to "fully" realize itself.

Thus, our reproach to Kant concerning this matter is not that he did not have enough "courage" to accept something as radical and extreme as diabolical evil. On the contrary, the problem is that this extremity (which calls for exclusion) is in itself already a result of a certain Kantian conceptualization of ethics. This is seen most clearly in the first part of Kant's apologue of gallows, which we left aside at the beginning of this discussion. Kant invents two stories that are supposed, first, to "prove" the existence of the moral law and, second, to demonstrate that the subject cannot act contrary to his pathological interests for any other reason than the moral law. The first story concerns a man who is placed in the situation of being executed on his way out of the bedroom if he wants to spend the night with the lady he desires. The other story, which we have already discussed, concerns a man who is put in the position of either bearing false witness against someone who, as a result, will lose his life or of being put to death himself if he does not do it. As a comment to the first alternative Kant simply affirms: "We do not have to guess very long what his [the man's in question] answer would be." As to the second story, Kant claims that it is at least possible to imagine that a man would rather die than tell a lie and send another man to death. As follows from these two comments, apart from the moral law there is no other "force" that could make us act against our well-being and our "pathological interests." To this Lacan raises the following objection: such "force" does exist, namely *jouissance* (as different from pleasure): "The striking significance of the first example resides in the fact that the night spent with the lady is paradoxically presented to us as a pleasure that is weighed against a punishment to be undergone . . . but one only has to make a conceptual shift and move the night spent with the lady from the category of pleasure to that of *jouissance,* given that *jouissance* implies precisely the acceptance of death . . . for the example to be ruined."[24] Lacan's argument is even more subtle. He does not posit *jouissance* as some diabolical force that is capable of opposing itself to the law. On the contrary, he recognizes in *jouissance* the very kernel of the law: it is enough, he states, for *jouissance* to be a form of suffering, for the whole thing to change its character completely, and for the meaning of the moral law itself to be completely changed. "Anyone can see that if the moral law is, in effect, capable of playing some role here, it is precisely as a support for the *jouissance* involved."[25] In other words, if, as Kant claims, no other thing but the moral law can induce us to put aside all our pathological interests and accept our death, then the case of someone who spends a night with a lady even though he knows that he will pay for it with his life, *is the case of the moral law.* It is the case of the moral law, an ethical act, without being "diabolical" (or "holy"). This is the crucial point of Lacan's argument: there are acts that perfectly fit Kant's criteria for an (ethical) act, without being either "angelic" or "diabolical." *It happens* to the subject to perform an act, *whether he wants it or not.* It is precisely this point that excludes the voluntarism that would lead to the romanticization of a diabolic (or angelic) creature. *Jouissance* (as the real kernel of the law) is not a matter of the will. Or, more precisely, if it is a matter of the will, it is insofar as it always appears as something that the subject does not want. That which, according to Lacan, brings Kant close to Sade, is the fact that he introduces a "wanting of *jouissance*" (the highest good), that is, that he makes the Real an *object of the will.* This then necessarily leads to the exclusion of (the possibility of) this object (the highest good or "diabolical evil"), the exclusion that, in turn, supports the fantasy of its realization (the immortality of the soul). For Kant it is unimaginable that someone would *want* his own destruction—this would be diabolical. And Lacan's answer is not that this is nevertheless imaginable, and that even such extreme cases exist, but that there is nothing extreme in this: on a certain level every subject, as average as he might very well be, wants his destruction, *whether he wants it or not.* It is this level that Lacan calls the death drive, and it is here that he situates *jouissance.*

In other words, the "angelization" of the good and the "diabolization" of the evil is the (conceptual) price to pay for making the Real an object of the will, that is, for making the coincidence of the will with the Law the condition of an ethical act. This means nothing other than claiming that the "hero" of the act exists. In the first step, Kant links the ethical dimension of the act to the will of the subject. From there it follows that if the subject were to (successfully) accomplish an ethical act, he would have to be either an angelic or a diabolical subject. But neither of these cases can apply to men, and Kant excludes them as impossible (in this world). From this exclusion of angels and devils then follows a perpetual diaeresis that operates in what is left. The subject is "handed over" to the irreducible doubt that manifests itself in the persistence of guilt: he has to separate himself from his pathology *in indefinitum.* In other words, the (internal) division of the will, its alienation from itself, which many critics prize as the most valuable point of Kantian ethics, is in fact already a consequence of the fact that Kant failed to recognize some more fundamental alienation: the alienation of the subject in the act, an alienation that implies that the subject is not necessarily the *hero* of "his" act. If Kant had recognized this fundamental alienation or division, a "successful" act would not necessitate either a holy or a diabolical will.

In "Kant with Sade," Lacan states: "It is thus indeed the Kantian will which is encountered in the place of this will which can be called the will-to-*jouissance* only to explain that it is the subject reconstituted from alienation at the price of being no more than the instrument of *jouissance*."[26] What exactly does this mean? We have a perfect example of this "subjective position" in Choderlos de Laclos's novel *Les Liaisons Dangereuses*. The only way that Valmont can satisfy his "will for enjoyment" is to become the instrument of the enjoyment (of the Other). The alienation, the split he tries to escape from, is the split between *jouissance* and the consciousness or awareness (of *jouissance*). He endeavors to abolish the split, the alienation between the two, by staging their encounter in the place of the Other. For this purpose, the Other must necessarily become a subject, and the Other can only become a subject by undergoing a division. The subject (Valmont) has to become the object that will cause the division of the Other, his subjectivation. This is the nature of Valmont's seduction of Mme de Tourvel. First, he has to awake a passionate desire in her. But, at the same time, this passion must not make her blind (i.e., unaware) of what she is doing. When she is to make the decisive step (i.e., betray all her principles and beliefs and sleep with Valmont), this step has to be accompanied by the clear *awareness* of what she is doing and what the consequences of her act may be. Her act must not be "pathological" (i.e., carried out in a moment of "blind passion"): before doing it, she must, in a way, state that she *wants* it. That is why Valmont twice refuses to take advantage of an opportunity that is offered to him. He writes, "My plan, on the contrary, is to make her perfectly aware of the value and extent of each one of the sacrifices she makes me; not to proceed so fast with her that the remorse is unable to catch up; it is to show her virtue breathing its last in long-protracted agonies; to keep that somber spectacle ceaselessly before her eyes."[27] Valmont leads Mme de Tourvel to make a certain step, then he stops, pulls himself back and waits for her to become fully aware of the implications of this step, to realize fully the significance of her position. The basic fantasy that underlies Valmont's actions is best expressed in his triumphal exclamation: *la pauvre femme, elle se voit mourrir,* "the poor woman, she is watching herself dying." We must not miss what Valmont is actually saying here, namely: *l'heureuse femme, elle se voit jouir,* "the fortunate woman, she is watching herself enjoying." In this scene, which utterly fascinates Valmont, he is "reconstituted from alienation at the price of being no more than the instrument of *jouissance*" of the Other.[28]

Now, how does all this apply to Kant, what exactly is the "fundamental alienation" that Kant refuses to acknowledge and how is this refusal visible? Once again in "Kantian tales" (i.e., examples that he invites us to consider in order to prove his theoretical stances), in the famous example of the false promise, for instance, or in the even more famous example of the deposit: "I have, for example, made it my maxim to augment my property by every safe means. Now I have in my possession a deposit, the owner of which has died without leaving any record of it. Naturally, this case falls under my maxim. Now I want to know whether this maxim can hold as a universal law. I apply it, therefore, to the present case. . . . I immediately realize that taking such principle as a law would annihilate itself, because its result would be that no one would make a deposit."[29] What exactly is Kant saying here? He is saying that, to use Lacan's words, there is no deposit *without a depository who is equal to his task.* There is no deposit without a depository who wholly coincides with and is entirely reducible to the notion of depository. With this claim Kant actually sets as a condition of an (ethical) act nothing less than the holiness of the will (the complete fitness of the will to the moral law—this is implied in the "equal to his task"). This could be formulated more generally: there is no (ethical) act without a subject who is equal to this act. This implies the effacement of the difference between the level of the enunciation and the level of the statement: the subject of the statement has to coincide with the subject of the enunciation or, more precisely, the subject of enunciation has to be entirely reducible to the subject of the statement.

From this perspective it is probably not a coincidence if the lie or lying is the most "neuralgic" point of Kantian ethics. The problem we are dealing with is precisely the problem of the paradox of the liar. If the liar is equal to his task, he can never say "I am lying" (because he would be telling the truth, etc.). Or, as Kant would have said, because this would make lying impossible. However, as Lacan justly remarked, this is simply not true. We know from our ordinary experience that we have no problem accepting and "understanding" such a statement. Lacan designates this paradox as apparent and resolves it precisely with the conceptualization of the difference between the subject of the enunciation and the subject of the statement.[30] The *am lying* is a signifier that forms part, in the Other, of the treasury of vocabulary. This "vocabulary" is something that I can use as a tool or that can use me as a "talking machine." As subject, I emerge on the other level, on the level of enunciation, and this level is irreducible. Here we come, once again, to the point that explains why the subject cannot "hide behind" the Law, presenting himself as its mere instrument: what is suspended by this gesture is precisely the level of the enunciation.

"There is no deposit without the depository who is equal to his task," or, "there is no (ethical) act without the subject who is equal to his act," implies that we set as the criterion or the condition of the "realization" of an act the abolishment of the difference, of the split between the statement and the enunciation. This abolishment is then posited as impossible (for men) and at the same time (in interpretations of Kant) as forbidden: if we set off to accomplish it, we will inevitably cause evil.

But the crucial question is *why* should the abolishment of this difference be the criterion or the necessary condition of an act? Why claim that the accomplishment of an act presupposes the abolishment of this split? It would be possible to situate the act in another, inverse perspective: it is precisely the act, the ("successful") act, that fully discloses this split, makes it present. From this perspective, the definition of a successful act would be that it has precisely the structure of the paradox of the liar, the structure of a liar who utters "I am lying," who utters "the impossible" and thus fully displays the split between the level of the statement and the level of the enunciation, between the shifter "I" and the signifier "am lying." To say that there is no subject or "hero" of the act means that at the level of "am lying," the subject is always pathological (in the Kantian sense of the word), determined by the Other, by the signifiers that precede him. At this level, the subject is reducible, "dispensable." But this is not all. Whereas the "subject" of the statement is determined in advance (he can only use the given signifiers), the (shifter) "I" is determined *retroactively:* it "becomes a signification, engendered at the level of the statement, of what it produces at the level of the enunciation."[31] It is at this level that we have to situate the ethical subject: at the level of something that only *becomes* what "it is" in the act (here a "speech act") engendered, so to speak, by another subject.[32]

It is also from this perspective that we can understand the claim, "There is no ethic beside that of the Well-spoken."[33] What is the "Well-spoken," *le bien-dire?* It is a statement that produces some unfamiliar, usually surprising effect in which a (new) subject can be discerned. This, of course, presupposes a difference between the "ethics of desire" and the "ethics of drive." The latter is not so much a heroic subjective position as something, precisely that which, gives rise to a subject. This is why Lacan, when speaking about the drive, introduces the term "headless subjectivation" or "subjectivation without subject."[34]

The Quantum of Affect

In Kantian theory, the moral law and the (ethical) subject "meet" at two different levels. One is the level of the signifier (i.e., the level of the categorical imperative), of the "formulation" of the moral law. So far, we have primarily been interrogating this aspect of Kantian ethics and the role that the subject plays in the "formulation" (and "realization") of the moral law. The other level of the encounter between the subject and the moral law is of a very different nature: it is the level of the "affect." The moral law "affects" the subject, and this results in a very singular feeling that Kant calls the "respect" (*Achtung*). Kant's theory of the respect displays in its own way the fundamental ambiguities of his ethics, especially Kant's oscillation between two different "portraits" of the moral law: the unconditional and yet "void" moral law and the somehow "subjectivized" law of the superego.

Kant examines the unique feeling that he calls *Achtung* in the third chapter of the *Critique of Practical Reason,* "Of the Drives of Pure Practical Reason." Respect is the only feeling that characterizes the relation of the subject to the moral law. Kant proposes a very elaborate conceptualization of this feeling, which has nothing to do with our ordinary use of the term "respect." "Respect for the moral law" does not mean "respecting the law," nor does it mean "to have respect" for the moral law. Rather, it indicates that the law is "nearby," it indicates the "presence" of the moral law, the "close encounter" of the subject with the (moral) law. Kant detaches respect from some other feelings that resemble it but are in fact of a very different nature. These feelings are inclination, love, fear, admiration, wonder, and awe.

It has already been suggested that the Kantian notion of respect might be situated in the same register as the psychoanalytic (or rather Lacanian) notion of anguish.[35] In fact, if we examine Kant's developments concerning the feeling of respect, this kinship is quite striking.

The starting point of Kant's developments in the discussed chapter are the following questions: How is it possible for the moral law to be the direct incentive of the will? How is it possible that something that cannot be an object of representation (*Vorstellung*) determines our will and becomes the drive of our actions? Kant replies that this "is an insoluble problem for the human reason."[36] However, Kant proceeds to say that, if it is not possible to show *how* such a thing is possible, we can at least prove that it exists, that it *happens* that the moral law determines our will directly. We can "prove" it because this case produces a certain *effect,* and it is this effect that Kant conceptualizes in terms of (the feeling of) the respect. The feeling of respect demonstrates that something that is not an object of representation can nevertheless determine the will.

According to Kant, respect is a "singular feeling, which cannot be compared with any pathological feeling. It is of such a peculiar kind that it seems to be at the disposal only of reason, and indeed only of pure practical reason."[37] The feeling of respect is not a pathological but a *practical* feeling; it is not of empirical origin but is known a priori; it "is not the drive to morality, it is morality itself."[38]

In order to fully grasp what is at stake here and to understand what impels Kant to call respect an "a priori" and "nonpathological" feeling, we must bear in mind Kant's theory of what causes and how something causes our actions. This theory is best summarized in the following passage: "*Life* is the faculty of a being by which it acts according to the laws of the faculty of desire. The *faculty of desire* is the faculty such a being has of causing, through its representations [*Vorstellungen*] the reality of the objects of these representations."[39] In other words, human actions are governed by the law of the faculty of desire. This faculty implies a representation of a certain object (which might very well be "abstract"—things such as "shame," "honor," "fame," "approval (of others)" are all objects of representation). The subject is "affected" by a certain representation and this "affection" is the cause of his actions and, at the same time, the reason why his actions are determined "pathologically." Now, the problem is that this does not leave any ground for morality, since the latter excludes, by its very definition, all pathological motives for our actions, even the most noble ones. The difficulty—which Kant tries to resolve in the chapter entitled "Of the Drives of Pure Practical Reason"—thus consists in detecting and conceptualizing some other type of causality that is foreign to the mode of representation. As we saw, Kant finds this problem to be an "insoluble problem of the human reason," and yet the problem that is some way always already "solved" in any ethical action. The answer resides in what Kant names respect as the only drive of pure practical reason.

The *avant la lettre* Lacanian intent of Kant's conceptualization of the difference between desire (*Begehrung*) and drive (*Triebfeder*) is striking. Whereas desire belongs, essentially, to the mode of representation (the metonymy of the signifier on the one hand, and fantasy on the other hand), the logic of drive is quite different. When Lacan asserts that drive "attains its satisfaction without attaining its goal," this means precisely that the object of drive is not the object of representation. It is not the object that we aim at, the object that we want to obtain (our "goal"). The object of drive *coincides with the itinerary of the drive*[40] and is not something that this itinerary "intends" to attain. This, as we saw, is exactly how Kant defines respect: it "is not the drive to morality, it is morality itself."

At first sight, this seems to imply that the respect is linked to the lack of representation (i.e., to the fact that the moral law as noumenal cannot become an object of representation), and that it is this lack or void that causes respect. Yet, if we examine the situation more closely, we realize that it is not simply the absence of representation that gives rise to the feeling of respect, but rather the absence of something that is constitutive of the subject of representation. In Kantian theory, the constitution of the subject of representation coincides with a certain loss. The subject loses, so to speak, that which he never had, namely a direct, immediate access to himself. This is the whole point of Kant's critique of Descartes's *cogito.* The subject who coincides entirely with himself is not yet a subject, and once he becomes a subject he no longer coincides with himself, but can only speak of himself as of an "object." The subject's relation to himself does not allow any "shortcut," but is of the same nature as the subject's relation to all other objects (of representation). The "I" is just a thought, a representation as any other representation. This fundamental loss or "alienation" is the condition of the thinking subject, the subject who has thoughts and representations. It is this loss that opens up the "objective reality" (the reality of the phenomena) and allows the subject to conceive himself as subject. In Lacanian terms, there is a bit of the Real that necessarily falls out in the constitution of the subject.

Thus, the cause of the singular feeling that Kant calls respect, is not simply the absence of representation, but the absence of this absence, of this lack that is the support of any subject of representation. The representation itself is founded on a certain lack or loss, and it is this lack that runs short. The situation we are dealing with is that of the "lack which lacks"—and this is exactly Lacan's definition of the cause of the anguish: *le manque vient à manquer.*[41]

In the same way that respect is defined in Kantian theory, anguish is defined in Lacanian theory as an "affect" or "feeling" that is very different from any other feeling. Lacan opposes himself to the theory that claims that anguish differs from fear in that it does not have an object. According to this theory, we always have fear of *something,* whereas in anguish there is no object that we could point to and say "this is the object of my anguish." Lacan claims that, on the contrary, it is in anguish that the subject comes the closest to the object (i.e., to the Real of his/her *jouissance*) and that it is precisely the proximity of the object that is at the origin of anguish. This claim could not be explained only by the specific Lacanian use of the term "object"; one should rather say that it is Lacan's conceptualization of anguish that explains the specific sense that the word *object* has in the Lacanian vocabulary. In this distinction between fear and anguish, Lacan basically agrees with Kant: fear is a feeling as any other feeling, it is "subjective" and "pathological." The fact that we fear some object tells us nothing of this object, it does not mean that this object is "in itself" (i.e., as object of representation) horrible. Or, as Kant puts it, a feeling (*Gefühl*) "designates nothing whatsoever in the object."[42] There is no feeling without a representation (i.e., representation is a necessary condition of feeling), although feeling itself is not a representation of an object. The feeling is the way "the subject feels himself, [namely] how he is affected by the representation."[43] Lacan would say that feeling tells us nothing of the object, but tells us something about the subject's "window of fantasy" in the frame of which a certain object appears as terrifying.

Now, as with respect in Kantian theory, anguish is not, in Lacanian theory, a "subjective" but an "objective feeling." It is a *feeling which does not deceive*" (Lacan) and which indicates that we have come near the "object" (designating the ex-timate place of our *jouissance*). If we do not bear in mind this "objective," "objectal" character of a certain subjective experience, we may find ourselves in the position of the analyst from the well-known joke: A patient comes to see him complaining that a crocodile is hiding under his bed. During several sessions the analyst tries to persuade the patient that this is all in his imagination. In other words, he tries to persuade him that it is all about a purely "subjective" feeling. The patient stops seeing the analyst, who believes that he cured him. A month later the analyst meets a friend, who is also a friend of his ex-patient, and asks him how the latter feels. The friend answers: "You mean the one who was eaten by a crocodile?" The lesson of this story is profoundly Lacanian. If we start from the idea that the anguish does not have any object, how are we to call this thing that killed, that "ate" the subject? What is the subject telling the analyst in this joke? Nothing other than: "I have the *objet petit a* under my bed, I came too close to it."

In his theory of respect, Kant remarks that we tend to "defend" ourselves from this feeing and to "lighten the burden"[44] that it lays upon us. Yet, the question arises as to whether Kant's conceptualization of respect does not, at a certain moment, take precisely the path that already represents a certain "defense" against the real dimension of respect. As a matter of fact, Kant reintroduces the dimension of representation, which allows the subject to "recover," to "regain conscience."

This other path of Kantian conceptualization of respect consists in conceiving it in terms of "*consciousness* of free submission of the will to the law."[45] A new representation enters the stage, and respect becomes the respect *for* the moral law as it is presented in this representation. Respect is no longer the effect/affect that produces in us the moral law *directly* determining our will, rather it becomes a representation of this effect: "The thing, *the representation of which,* as determining principle of our will, humiliates us in our self-consciousness, provokes . . . respect."[46] In other words, what now arouses the feeling of respect is the fact that the subject *sees* himself being subjected to the law, and *observes* himself being humiliated and terrified. Kant writes: "In the boundless esteem for the pure moral law . . . whose *voice* makes even the boldest sinner tremble and forces him to hide himself from its *gaze,* there is something so singular that we cannot wonder at finding this influence of a merely intellectual Idea on feeling to be inexplicable to speculative reason."[47] Here, respect is (re)formulated in terms of "boundless esteem" for the moral law, linked to the fear and horror that "makes even the boldest sinner tremble." We are far from respect as a priori feeling. Instead, we are dealing with a law that observes and speaks. It is difficult to understand how it happened that Kant did not see that, with this conceptualization, the feeling of respect turns into pure and simple *Ehrfurcht,* wonder (defined by Kant as "respect linked to fear"), thus becoming a perfectly pathological motive. It cannot surprise us that there are precisely voice and gaze—the two Lacanian objects par excellence—that spring up in the middle of the Law, transforming it to something frightening, and yet familiar. And the trembling of someone who finds himself in the cross fire of the gaze and the voice of the Law must not bedazzle us—here, the trembling is already a relief. Compared to respect—linked to anguish—fear is already a relief.

If we ask ourselves which is the law that speaks and observes, there is only one possible answer: the superego. In the quoted passage from *Critique of Practical Reason* we see clearly how the moral law transforms itself into the superego. It is the superego that, by definition, sees everything and does not cease to speak, to produce one commandment after another. This also explains another expression that Kant often uses, but that is not entirely compatible with the strict conception of the moral law, namely that it "humiliates" us and that "the effect of this law on feeling is humiliation alone."[48] One could say in fact that in the discussed chapter Kant actually introduces two different feelings linked to two different conceptions of the moral law: respect and humiliation. Or, more precisely, respect as a priori feeling and respect that springs up from the consciousness that we are being humiliated; respect as a mode of anguish and respect as the mode of fantasy (where we observe ourselves being humiliated by the moral law).

This shift of the moral law toward the superego is not without consequences. It governs the whole dialectic of the sublime, and it also explains why Kant, who previously established a clear distinction between respect and other feelings such as wonder and awe, can conclude the second *Critique* with the famous phrase: "Two things fill the mind with ever new and increasing wonder and awe, the oftener and the more steadily we reflect on them: the starry heavens above me and the moral law within me."[49]

In fact, in the *Critique of Judgement* Kant repeatedly links the feeling of respect to the feeling of the sublime.[50] But what exactly is the feeling of the sublime? "An abyss," an "exiting liking," an "agitation that can be compared with a vibration, i.e. a rapid alternation of repulsion from, and attraction to, one and the same object," "a momentary inhibition of the vital forces." These descriptions could easily be taken for extracts from some erotic novel, describing an orgasm, for instance. Yet, they are all Kant's descriptions of the feeling of the sublime, or rather, of the first moment of the sublime. For the feeling of the sublime is a feeling that presupposes a certain temporal dimension. It is composed of two different moments and actually describes the movement from one to the other. In the first moment we (as subjects and spectators) are fascinated by a spectacle in which nature exhibits its might (and magnitude), compared to which we are utterly insignificant and impotent. In the second moment we experience a kind of a triumph, a "self-estimation" (Kant): we become aware of the superiority of our "suprasensible vocation" to even the greatest power of nature. What makes this shift from the first to the second moment possible, "is that the subject's own inability [*Unvermögen*] uncovers in him the consciousness of an unlimited ability which is also his."[51] Kant links this unlimited ability to our suprasensible vocation, and the latter to our moral disposition. In other words, the devastating force *above us* "reminds" us of some even more devastating force *within us:* "The object of a pure and unconditional intellectual liking is the moral law in its might, the *might that it exerts in us over any and all of those incentives of the mind that precede it.*"[52] From there it follows a complete shift of perspective: it is in fact the moral law (or the "suprasensible power") in us that makes it possible for us to find nature sublime. The true sublimity must be sought only in the mind of the judging person, and not in the natural object. The feeling of the sublime in nature is in fact nothing other than the "*respect* for our own vocation. But by a certain subreption . . . this respect is accorded an object of nature that, as it were, makes intuitable for us the superiority of the rational vocation of our cognitive powers over the greatest power of sensibility."[53] In other words, the sublime is a spectacle in which nature stages (i.e., makes "intuitable," "representable" for us) that which escapes intuition and representation. While watching "thunderclouds piling up in the sky and moving about accompanied by lightning and thunderclaps," we actually see the moral law moving about in us, striking with lightning and thunderclaps (i.e., gazes and voices) "any and all of those (pathological) incentives of our mind that precede it."

It could be said that the feeling of the sublime is the way in which the subject who came too close to the moral law (and who experiences a "momentary inhibition of his vital forces"), saves himself from its mortifying proximity by introducing a certain distance between himself and the law. This distance is, of course, nothing other than the intervention of a representation.

It has often been stressed that the sublime is linked to the breakdown of representation. But we must not forget that this is true only insofar as the sublime is, at the same time, a "*representation* of the unrepresentable," and this is precisely that which links it to what Lacan calls "the logic of fantasy."

Kant tells us that there is one necessary condition for the feeling of the sublime: as spectators of some fascinating spectacle of nature we have to be placed somewhere *safe,* that is, outside the immediate danger. The view of the hurricane is sublime. However, if the hurricane sweeps along our house, we will not perceive this as something sublime, we will simply be scared and horrified. In order for the feeling of the sublime to emerge, our (sensible) powerlessness and mortality have to be staged "down there," in such a way that we can observe them quietly. The necessary condition of the feeling of the sublime is that we watch the hurricane "through the window," which is nothing other than what Lacan calls "the window of fantasy": "thunderclouds piling up in the sky and moving about accompanied by lightning and thunderclaps, volcanos with all their destructive power, hurricanes with all the devastation they leave behind . . . compared to the might of any of these, our ability to resist becomes an insignificant trifle. Yet the sight of them becomes all the more attractive the more fearful it is, *provided we are in a safe place.*"[54]

This constellation where we are at the same time "inside" and "outside," where we are at the same time the "insignificant trifle," the grain of sand that the wild forces play with, and the observer of this spectacle, is strictly correlative to that which becomes, in Kantian theory, the feeling of respect. As we already indicated, what provokes the sentiment of respect is now the fact that the subject *watches* himself being subjected to the law, that he watches himself being humiliated and terrified by it.

Notes

1 Jacques Lacan, *The Ethics of Psychoanalysis*, trans. Dennis Porter (London: Routledge, 1992), 186.

2 Ibid., 187.

3 Sigmund Freud, *Civilization and its Discontents*, in *The Pelican Freud Library* (Harmondsworth, England: Penguin, 1972–86), 12:300.

4 Ibid., 12:299.

5 Lacan, *Ethics of Psychoanalysis*, 186.

6 Alain Badiou, *L'éthique* (Paris: Hatier, 1993), 24.

7 Lacan, *Ethics of Psychoanalysis*, 198.

8 Ibid., 325.

9 "A decisive step is taken here. Traditional morality concerned itself with what one was supposed to do 'insofar as it is possible,' as we say, and as we are forced to say. What needs to be unmasked here is the point on which that morality turns. And that is nothing less than the impossible in which we recognize the topology of our desire. The breakthrough is achieved by Kant when he posits that the moral imperative is not concerned with what may or may not be done. To the extent that it imposes the necessity of a practical reason, obligation affirms an unconditional 'Thou shalt.' The importance of this field derives from the void that the strict application of the Kantian definition leaves there" (Lacan, *Ethics of Psychoanalysis*, 315–16).

10 Immanuel Kant, *Critique of Practical Reason*, trans. Lewis White Beck (New York: Macmillan, 1993), 30.

11 Lacan, *Ethics of Psychoanalysis*, 189.

12 Ibid.

13 Ibid., 190.

14 Immanuel Kant, *Ethical Philosophy* (Indianapolis: Hackett, 1978), 428.

15 Cf. François Boituzat, *Un droit de mentir? Constant ou Kant* (Paris: PUF, 1993) and Hans Wagner, "Kant gegen 'ein vermeintes Recht, aus Menschenliebe zu Lügen'," in *Kant und das Recht der Lüge*, ed. G. Geisman and H. Oberer (Würzburg: Königshausen and Neuman, 1986).

16 Herbert J. Paton, "An alleged right to lie. A problem in Kantian ethics," in Geismand and Oberer, *Kant und das Recht der Lüge*, 59.

17 Slavoj Žižek, *The Indivisible Remainder* (London and New York: Verso, 1996), 170.

18 Henry E. Allison, *Idealism and Freedom* (Cambridge: Cambridge University Press, 1996), 181.

19 Cf.: "It is therefore wrong to conceive the Kantian categorical imperative as a kind of formal mould whose application to a concrete case relieves the moral subject of the responsibility for a decision: I am not sure if to accomplish the act X is my duty. No problem—I test it by submitting it to the double formal criterion implied by the categorical imperative . . . and if the act X stands the test, I know where my duty lies. . . . The whole point of Kantian argumentation is the exact opposite of this automatic procedure of verification: the fact that the categorical imperative is an empty form means precisely that it can deliver no guarantee against misjudging our duty. The structure of the categorical imperative is tautological in the Hegelian sense of the repetition of the same that fills up and simultaneously announces an abyss that gives rise to unbearable anxiety; 'Your duty is . . . (to do your duty)!'" (Žižek, *The Indivisible Remainder*, 170).

20 Cf.: "But if a man is to become . . . one who, knowing something to be his duty, requires no incentive other than this representation of duty itself, *this* cannot be brought about through gradual *reformation* so long as the basis of the maxims remains impure, but must be effected through a *revolution* in the man's disposition. . . . He can become a new man only by a kind of rebirth, as it were a new creation" Immanuel Kant, *Religion Within the Limits of Reason Alone* (New York: Harper Torchbooks, 1960), 43.

21 Kant, *Critique of Practical Reason*, 60.

22 Kant, *Religion Within the Limits of Reason Alone*, 32.

23 Allison, *Idealism and Freedom*, 181.

24 Lacan, *Ethics of Psychoanalysis*, 189.

25 Ibid., 189.

26 Jacques Lacan, "Kant with Sade," *October* 51 (winter 1989): 63.

27 Choderlos de Laclos, *Les Liaisons Dangereuses* (Harmondsworth, England: Penguin, 1961), 150.

28 Lacan, "Kant with Sade," 63.

29 Kant, *Critique of Practical Reason*, 27.

30 Cf. Jacques Lacan, *The Four Fundamental Concepts of Psycho-Analysis*, trans. Alan Sheridan (Harmondsworth, England: Penguin, 1979), 139: "Indeed, the *I* of the enunciation is not the same as the *I* of the statement, that is to say, the shifter which, in the statement designates him. So, from the point at which I state, it is quite possible for me to formulate in a valid way that the *I*—the *I* who, at the moment, formulates the statement—is lying, that he lied a little before, that he is lying afterwards, or even, that in saying *I am lying*, he declares that he has the intention of deceiving."

31 Lacan, *Four Fundamental Concepts of Psycho-Analysis*, 138.

32 In his latter work Lacan formulates this same split in terms of another difference: Other/*jouissance*. In regard to the Other, I am not the author of my acts (i.e., the Other "speaks/acts through me"), and thus I may not be held responsible for them. How-

ever, there is something else that "grows" from this act, namely some *jouissance*. It is in this fragment of *jouissance* that we must situate the subject and his responsibility. For a detailed elaboration of this point see Žižek, *The Indivisible Remainder*, 93.

33 Jacques Lacan, *Television*, trans. Denis Hollier, Rosalind Krauss, and Annette Michelson, ed. by Joan Copjec (New York and London: W. W. Norton, 1990), 22.

34 Cf. Lacan, *Four Fundamental Concepts of Psycho-Analysis*, 184.

35 Cf. Jacques-Alain Miller, "L'Extimité" (unpublished seminar), lecture from 8 January 1986.

36 Kant, *Critique of Practical Reason*, 75.

37 Ibid., 79–80.

38 Ibid., 79.

39 Ibid., 9–10 n; translation modified.

40 Cf. Lacan's schema of the drive, in *Four Fundamental Concepts of Psycho-Analysis*, 178.

41 Cf. Jacques Lacan, "L'Angoisse" (unpublished seminar), lecture from 28 November 1962.

42 Immanuel Kant, *Critique of Judgement*, trans. Werner S. Pluhar (Indianapolis: Hackett, 1987), 44.

43 Ibid., 44.

44 Kant, *Critique of Practical Reason*, 81.

45 Ibid., 84; emphasis added.

46 Ibid., 78; translation modified; emphasis added.

47 Ibid., 83; translation modified; emphasis added.

48 Ibid., 82.

49 Ibid., 169.

50 Cf. Kant, *Critique of Judgement*, 98, 114, 132.

51 Ibid., 116.

52 Ibid., 131; emphasis added.

53 Ibid., 114.

54 Ibid., 120; emphasis added.

Slavoj Žižek

A signifier is that which "represents the subject for another signifier"—how are we to read Lacan's classic definition of signifier? The old-style hospital bed has at its feet, out of the patient's sight, a small display board on which different charts and documents are stuck specifying the patient's temperature, blood pressure, medicaments, and so on. This display represents the patient—for whom? Not simply and directly for other subjects (say, for the nurses and doctors who regularly check this panel), but primarily for *other signifiers,* for the symbolic network of medical knowledge in which the data on the panel have to be inserted in order to obtain their meaning. One can easily imagine a computerized system where the reading of the data on the panel proceeds automatically, so that what the doctor obtains and reads are not these data but directly the conclusions that, according to the system of medical knowledge, follow from these and other data. . . . The conclusion to be drawn from this definition of the signifier is that, in what I say, in my symbolic representation, there is always a kind of surplus with regard to the concrete, flesh-and-blood addressee(s) of my speech, which is why even a letter that fails to reach its concrete addressee in a way *does* arrive at its true destination, which is the big Other, the symbolic system of "other signifiers." One of the direct materializations of this excess is the *symptom:* a cyphered message whose addressee is not another human being (when I inscribe into my body a symptom that divulges the innermost secret of my desire, no human being is intended to directly read it), and

$$\frac{\text{agent}}{\text{truth}} \quad \frac{\text{other}}{\text{production}}$$

S$_1$= master-signifier

S$_2$= knowledge

$ = subject

a = surplus-enjoyment

Figure 1

which nonetheless has accomplished its function the moment it was produced, since it did reach the big Other, its true addressee.

Lacan's scheme of the four discourses articulates the four subjective
positions within a discursive social link,[1] which logically follow from
the formula of the signifier. The whole construction is based on the fact
of symbolic *reduplicatio*, the redoubling of an entity into itself and the
place it occupies in the structure. For that reason, the discourse of the
Master is the necessary starting point, insofar as in it, an entity and its
place coincide (figure 1): the Master-Signifier effectively occupies the
place of the "agent," which is that of the Master; the object *a* occupies
the place of "production," which is that of the unassimilable excess,
and so on. On the basis of the discourse of the Master, one can then
proceed to generate the three other discourses by way of successively
putting the other three elements at the place of the Master: in the university discourse, it is Knowledge that occupies the agent's (Master's)
place, turning the subject ($) into that which is "produced," into its un-
assimilable excess-remainder; in hysteria, the true "master," the agent
who effectively terrorizes the Master himself, is the hysterical subject
with her incessant questioning of the Master's position; and so on.

First, the discourse of the Master provides the basic matrix (figure 2):
a subject is represented by the signifier for another signifier (for the
chain or the field of "ordinary" signifiers); the remainder—the "bone
in the throat"—that resists this symbolic representation, emerges (is
"produced") as *objet petit a*, and the subject endeavors to "normalize"
his relationship toward this excess via fantasmatic formations (which is

$$\underline{\text{Master}} \\ \frac{S_1 \longrightarrow S_2}{\$ \longleftarrow a}$$

Figure 2

why the lower level of the formula of the Master's discourse renders the matheme of fantasy $\$ \lozenge a$). In an apparent contradiction to this determination, Lacan often claims that the discourse of the Master is the only discourse that excludes the dimension of fantasy—how are we to understand this? The illusion of the gesture of the Master is the complete coincidence between the level of the enunciation (the subjective position from which I am speaking) and the level of the enunciated content, that is, what characterizes the Master is a speech-act that wholly absorbs me, in which "I am what I say," in short, a fully realized, self-contained performative. Such an ideal coincidence, of course, precludes the dimension of fantasy, since fantasy emerges precisely in order to fill in the gap between the enunciated content and its underlying position of enunciation: fantasy is an answer to the question "You are telling me all this, but why? What do you really want by telling me this?" The fact that the dimension of fantasy nonetheless persists thus simply signals the ultimate unavoidable failure of the Master's discourse. Suffice it to recall the proverbial high manager who, from time to time, feels compelled to visit prostitutes in order to be engaged in masochist rituals where he is "treated as a mere object": the semblance of his active public existence in which he gives orders to his subordinated and runs their lives (the upper level of the Master's discourse: S_1-S_2) is sustained by the fantasies of being turned into a passive object of others' enjoyment (the lower level: $\$$-a).

What is a Master-Signifier? In the very last pages of his monumental *Second World War,* Winston Churchill ponders the enigma of a political *decision:* after the specialists (economic and military analysts, psychologists, meteorologists . . .) propose their multiple, elaborated, and refined analyses, somebody must assume the simple and for that very reason most difficult act of transposing this complex multitude—where for every reason *for* there are two reasons *against,* and vice versa—into a simple "Yes" or "No"—we shall attack, we continue to wait. . . . This gesture that can never be fully grounded in reasons, is that of a Master. The Master's discourse thus relies on the gap between S_2 and S_1, between the chain of "ordinary" signifiers and the "excessive" Master-Signifier. Suffice it to recall military *ranks,* namely the curious fact that they do not overlap with the position within the military hierarchy of command: from the rank of an officer—lieutenant, colonel, general, and so on—one cannot directly derive his place in the hierarchical chain of command (a batallion commander, commander of an army group). Originally, of course, ranks were directly grounded in a certain position of command—however, the curious fact is precisely the way they came to redouble the designation of this position, so that today one says "*General* Michael Rose, *commander* of the UNPROFOR forces in Bosnia." Why this redoubling, why do we not abolish ranks and simply designate an officer by his position in the chain of command? Only the Chinese army in the heyday of the Cultural Revolution abolished ranks and used only the position in the chain of command. This necessity of redoubling is the very necessity of adding a Master-Signifier to the "ordinary" signifier that designates one's place in the social hierarchy.[2]

One can see, now, in what precise sense one is to conceive of Lacan's thesis according to which, what is "primordially repressed" is the binary signifier (that of *Vorstellungs-Repräsentanz*): what the symbolic order precludes is the full harmonious presence of the *couple* of Master-Signifiers, S_1-S_2 as *yin-yang* or any other two symmetrical "fundamental principles." The fact that "there is no sexual relationship" means precisely that the secondary signifier (that of the Woman) is "primordially repressed," and what we get in the place of this repression, what fills in its gap, is the multitude of the "returns of the repressed," the series of the "ordinary" signifiers. In Woody Allen's Tolstoy parody *War and Love*, the first association that automatically pops up, of course, is: "If Tolstoy, where is then Dostoyevsky?" In the film, Dostoyevsky (the "binary signifier" to Tolstoy) remains "repressed"—however, the price paid for it is that a conversation in the middle of the film, as it were, accidentally includes the titles of all Dostoyevsky's main novels: "Is that man still in the underground?" "You mean one of the Karamazov brothers?" "Yes, that idiot!" "Well, he did commit his crime and was punished for it!" "I know, he was a gambler who always risked too much!" and so on. Here we encounter the "return of the repressed," that is, the series of signifiers that fills in the gap of the repressed binary signifier "Dostoyevsky."

There is thus no reason to be dismissive of the discourse of the Master, to identify it too hastily with "authoritarian repression": the Master's gesture is the founding gesture of every social link. Let us imagine a confused situation of social disintegration, in which the cohesive power of ideology loses its efficiency: in such a situation, the Master is the one who invents a new signifier, the famous "quilting point," which again

$$\begin{array}{ccc} & \text{University} & \\ S_2 & \longrightarrow & a \\ S_1 & \longleftarrow & \$ \end{array}$$

Figure 3

stabilizes the situation and makes it readable; the university discourse that then elaborates the network of Knowledge that sustains this readability by definition presupposes and relies on the initial gesture of the Master.[3] The Master adds no new positive content—he merely adds a *signifier*, which all of a sudden turns disorder into order, into "new harmony," as Rimbaud would have put it. Therein resides the magic of a Master: although there is nothing new at the level of positive content, "nothing is quite the same" after he pronounces his Word. . . .

The university discourse is enunciated from the position of "neutral" Knowledge (figure 3); it addresses the remainder of the real (say, in the case of pedagogical knowledge, the "raw, uncultivated child"), turning it into the subject ($). The "truth" of the university discourse, hidden beneath the bar, of course, is power (i.e., the Master-Signifier): the constitutive lie of the university discourse is that it disavows its performative dimension, presenting what effectively amounts to a political decision based on power as a simple insight into the factual state of things. What one should avoid here is the Foucauldian misreading: the produced subject is not simply the subjectivity that arises as the result of the disciplinary application of knowledge-power, but its *remainder,* that which eludes the grasp of knowledge-power. "Production" (the fourth term in the matrix of discourses) does not stand simply for the result of the discursive operation, but rather for its "indivisible remainder," for the excess that resists being included in the discursive network (i.e., for what the discourse itself produces as the foreign body in its very heart).

Perhaps the exemplary case of the Master's position that underlies the university discourse is the way in which *medical discourse* functions in our everyday lives: at the surface level, we are dealing with pure objective knowledge that desubjectivizes the subject-patient, reducing him to an object of research, of diagnosis and treatment; however, beneath it, one can easily discern a worried hystericized subject, obsessed with anxiety, addressing the doctor as his Master and asking for reassurance

Hysteria

$$\frac{\$ \xrightarrow{} S_1}{a \xleftarrow{} S_2}$$

Figure 4

from him. At a more common level, suffice it to recall the market expert who advocates strong budgetary measures (cutting welfare expenses, etc.) as a necessity imposed by his neutral expertise devoid of any ideological biases: what he conceals is the series of power-relations (from the active role of state apparatuses to ideological beliefs) that sustain the "neutral" functioning of the market mechanism.

In the hysterical link, the $\$$ over a stands for the subject who is divided, traumatized, by what an object she is for the Other, what role she plays in Other's desire (figure 4): "Why am I what you're saying that I am?" or, to quote Shakespeare's Juliet, "Why am I that name?" What she expects from the Other-Master is knowledge about what she is as object (the lower level of the formula). Racine's Phèdre is hysterical insofar as she resists the role of the object of exchange between men by way of incestuously violating the proper order of generations (falling in love with her stepson). Her passion for Hippolyte does not aim at its direct realization/satisfaction, but rather at the very act of its confession to Hippolyte, who is thus forced to play the double role of Phèdre's object of desire and of her symbolic Other (the addressee to whom she confesses her desire). When Hippolyte learns from Phèdre that he is the cause of her consuming passion, he is shocked—this knowledge possesses a clear "castrating" dimension, it hystericizes him: "Why me? What for an object am I so that I have this effect on her? What does she see in me?"[4] What produces the unbearable castrating effect is not the fact of being deprived of "it," but, on the contrary, the fact of clearly "possessing it": the hysteric is horrified at being "reduced to an object," that is to say, at being invested with the *agalma* that makes him or her the object of other's desire.[5]

In contrast to hysteria, the pervert knows perfectly what he is for the Other: a knowledge supports his position as the object of Other's (divided subject's) *jouissance*. For that reason, the matheme of the discourse

$$\frac{\begin{matrix} & \text{Analyst} & \\ a & \longrightarrow & \$ \end{matrix}}{\begin{matrix} S_2 & \longleftarrow & S_1 \end{matrix}}$$

Figure 5

of perversion is the same as that of the analyst's discourse (figure 5): Lacan defines perversion as the inverted fantasy (i.e., his matheme of perversion is *a-$*), which is precisely the upper level of the analyst's discourse. The difference between the social link of perversion and that of analysis is grounded in the radical ambiguity of *object petit a* in Lacan, which stands simultaneously for the imaginary fantasmatic lure/screen *and* for that which this lure is obfuscating, for the void behind the lure. So, when we pass from perversion to the analytic social link, the agent (analyst) reduces himself to the void that provokes the subject into confronting the truth of his desire. Knowledge in the position of "truth" below the bar under the "agent," of course, refers to the supposed knowledge of the analyst, and, simultaneously, signals that the knowledge gained here will not be the neutral "objective" knowledge of scientific adequacy, but the knowledge that concerns the subject (analysand) in the truth of his subjective position. What this discourse "produces" is then the Master-Signifier (i.e., the unconscious "sinthome"), the cipher of enjoyment, to which the subject was unknowingly subjected.[6]

So, if a political Leader says "I am your Master, let my will be done!" this direct assertion of authority is hystericized when the subject starts to doubt his qualification to act as a Leader ("Am I really their Master? What is in me that legitimizes me to act like that?"); it can be masked in the guise of the university discourse ("In asking you to do this, I merely follow the insight into objective historical necessity, so I am not your Leader, but merely your servant who enables you to act for your own good. . . ."); or, the subject can act as a blank, suspending his symbolic efficiency and thus compelling his Other to become aware of how he was experiencing another subject as a Leader only because he was treating him as one. It should be clear, from this brief description, how the position of the "agent" in each of the four discourses involves a specific mode of subjectivity: the Master is the subject who is fully engaged in his (speech) act, who, in a way, "is his word," whose word displays an immediate performative efficiency; the agent of the university discourse is, on the contrary, fundamentally *disengaged:* he posits himself as the self-erasing observer (and executor) of "objective laws" accessible to neutral knowledge (in clinical terms, his position is closest to that of the pervert). The hysterical subject is the subject whose very existence involves radical doubt and questioning, his entire being is sustained by the uncertainty as to what he is for the Other; insofar as the subject exists only as an answer to the enigma of the Other's desire, the hysterical subject is the subject par excellence. Again, in clear contrast to it, the analyst stands for the paradox of the desubjectivized subject, of the subject who fully assumed what Lacan calls "subjective destitution," that is, who breaks out of the vicious cycle of intersubjective dialectics of desire and turns into an acephalous being of pure drive.

One of the crucial differences between psychoanalysis and philosophy concerns the status of sexual difference: for philosophy, the subject is not inherently sexualized, sexualization only occurs at the contingent, empirical level, whereas psychoanalysis promulgates sexuation into a kind of formal, a priori, condition of the very emergence of the subject.[7] For that precise reason, the Lacanian problematic of *sexual difference*—of the unavoidability of sexuation for human beings ("beings of language")—has to be strictly distinguished from the (de)constructionist problematic of the "social construction of gender," of the contingent discursive formation of gender identities that emerge by way of being performatively enacted.[8] In order to grasp this crucial distinction, the analogy with class antagonism may be of some help: class antagonism (the unavoidability of the individual's "class inscription" in a class society, the impossibility to stay beyond, to remain unmarked by the class antagonism) also cannot be reduced to the notion of the "social construction of class identity," since every determinate "construction of class identity" is already a "reactive" or "defense" formation, an attempt to "cope with" (to come to terms with, to pacify . . .) the trauma of class antagonism. Every symbolic "class identity" already displaces the class antagonism by way of translating it into a positive set of symbolic features: the conservative organicist notion of society as a collective body, with different classes as bodily organs (the ruling class as the benevolent and wiser "head," workers as "hands," etc.) is only the most obvious case of it. And, for Lacan, things are the same with sexuation: it is impossible to "stay outside," the subject is always already marked by it, it always already "takes sides," it is always already "partial" with regard to it. The paradox of the problematic of the "social construction of gender" is that, although it presents itself as a breakout of the "meta-physical" and/or essentialist constraints, it implicitly accomplishes the return to the pre-Freudian philosophical (i.e., nonsexualized) subject: the problematic of the "social construction of gender" presupposes the space of contingent symbolization, while for Lacan, "sexuation" is the price to be paid for the very constitution of the subject, for its entry into the space of symbolization.

When Lacan claims that sexual difference is "real," he is therefore far from elevating a historical, contingent form of sexuation into a trans-historical norm ("if you do not occupy your proper preordained place in the heterosexual order, as either man or woman, you are excluded, exiled into a psychotic abyss outside the symbolic domain"): the claim that sexual difference is "real" equals the claim that it is "impossible": impossible to symbolize, to formulate as a symbolic norm. In other words, it is not that we have homosexuals, fetishists, and other per-verts, *in spite* of the normative fact of sexual difference (i.e., as proofs of the failure of sexual difference to impose its norm); it is not that sexual difference is the ultimate point of reference that anchors the contingent drifting of sexuality; it is, on the contrary, on account of the gap that forever persists between the real of sexual difference and the determi-nate forms of heterosexual symbolic norms, that we have the multitude of "perverse" forms of sexuality. Therein also resides the problem with the accusation that sexual difference involves "binary logic": insofar as sexual difference is real/impossible, it is precisely *not* "binary," but, again, that on account of which every "binary" account of it (every translation of sexual difference into a couple of opposed symbolic fea-tures: reason versus emotion, active versus passive . . .) always fails.[9]

How, then, is sexual difference, this fundamental Real of human exis-tence, inscribed into the matrix of four discourses? How, if at all, are the four discourses sexualized? The notion of sexual difference we are referring to is, of course, the one elaborated by Lacan in his other great matrix, that of the "formulas of sexuation," where the masculine side is defined by the universal function and its constitutive exception, and the feminine side by the paradox of "non-all [*pas-tout*]" (there is no exception, and for that very reason, the set is non-all, non-totalized). Let us recall the shifting status of the ineffable in Wittgenstein: the passage from early to late Wittgenstein is the passage from *tout* (the order of the universal all grounded in its constitutive exception) to *pas-tout* (the order without exception and for that reason non-universal, non-all). That is to say, in the early Wittgenstein of *Tractatus*, the world is comprehended as a self-enclosed, limited, bounded whole of "facts," which precisely as such presupposes an exception: the ineffable mystical that functions as its limit. In late Wittgenstein, on the contrary, the problematic of the ineffable disappears, yet for that very reason the universe is no longer comprehended as a whole regulated by the universal conditions of language: all that remains are lateral connections between partial domains. The notion of language as the system defined by a set of universal features is replaced by the notion of language as a multitude of dispersed practices loosely interconnected by "family resemblances."

A certain type of ethnic joke renders perfectly this paradox of the non-all: the narratives of the origin in which a nation posits itself as "more X than X itself," where X stands for another nation that is commonly regarded as the paradigmatic case of some property. The myth of Island is that Island became inhabited when those who found Norway, the most free land in the world, too oppressive, flew to Island: the myth of Slovenes as miserly claims that Scotland (the proverbial land of misers) became populated when Slovenes expelled to Scotland one of them who spent too much money. The point is *not* that Slovenes are *the most* avaricious or Islanders *the most* freedom-loving—Scots remain *the most* miserly, yet Slovenes are *even more* miserly; the people of Norway remain *the most* freedom-loving, yet Islanders are *even more* freedom-loving. This is the paradox of "non-all": if we totalize all nations, Scots are *the most* miserly, yet if we compare them one by one, as "non-all," Slovenes are *more* miserly. . . .[10] A variation on the same motif is provided by Rossini's famous statement on the difference between Beethoven and Mozart: when asked "Who is the greatest composer?" Rossini answered "Beethoven"; when asked the additional question "What about Mozart?" he added "Mozart is not the greatest, he is the *only* composer. . . ." This opposition between Beethoven ("the greatest" of them all, since he fought out his compositions with a titanic effort, overcoming the resistance of the musical material) and Mozart (who freely floated in the musical stuff and composed with spontaneous grace) points toward the well-known opposition between the two notions of God: God who is "the greatest," at the top of creation, the ruler of the world, and God who is not the greatest but simply *the only* reality, that is, who does not relate at all to the finite reality as separated from Him, since he is "all there is," the immanent principle of all reality.[11]

In short, what sustains the difference between the two sexes is not the direct reference to the series of symbolic oppositions (masculine reason versus feminine emotion, masculine activity versus feminine passivity, etc.), but a different way of coping with the necessary inconsistency involved in the act of assuming one and the same universal symbolic feature (ultimately that of "castration"). It is not that man stands for logos as opposed to the feminine emphasis on emotions; it is rather that, for man, logos as the consistent and coherent universal principle of all reality relies on the constitutive exception of some mystical, ineffable X ("there are things one should not talk about"), while, in the case of a woman, there is no exception, "one can talk about everything," and, for that very reason, the universe of logos becomes inconsistent, incoherent, dispersed, "non-all." Or, with regard to the assumption of a symbolic title, a man who tends to identify with his title absolutely, to put everything at stake for it (to die for his cause), nonetheless relies on the myth that he is not only his title, the "social mask" he is wearing, that there is something beneath it, a "real person"; in the case of a woman, on the contrary, there is no firm, unconditional commitment, everything is ultimately a mask, but, for that very reason, there is nothing "behind the mask." Or, with regard to love: a man in love is ready to give everything for it, the beloved is elevated into the absolute, unconditional object, but, for that very reason, he is compelled to sacrifice her for the sake of his public or professional cause; a woman is entirely, without restraint and reserve, immersed in love, there is no dimension of her being that is not permeated by love—but, for that very reason, "love is not all" for her, it is forever accompanied by an uncanny, fundamental *indifference*.

So, how does all this relate to (our "concrete", "lived" experience of) sexual difference? Let us begin with one of the archetypal melodramatic scenes, that of a woman writing a letter explaining things to her lover, and then, after oscillation, tearing it apart, throwing it away, and (usually) going *herself* to him, that is, offering herself, in flesh, in her love, instead of the letter. The content of this letter is strictly codified: as a rule, it explains to the beloved why the woman he fell in love with is not the one he thinks she is, and, consequently, why, precisely because she loves him, she must drop him in order not to deceive him. The tearing-up of the letter then serves as a retreat: the woman cannot go to the end and tell the truth, she prefers to go on with her deception. This gesture is fundamentally false: the presence is offered as the false screen of love destined to repress the traumatic truth that was to be articulated in the letter—as in the transference in psychoanalytic treatment where the patient offers herself to the analyst as the ultimate measure of defense, in order to block the emergence of truth.[12] That is to say, love emerges when the analysis comes too close to the unconscious traumatic truth: at this point, the analysand offers herself to the analyst as the object of love, instead of the authentic letter to the analyst that would articulate the traumatic truth. In transferential love, I offer myself as object instead of knowledge: "here you have me (so that you will no longer probe into me)." (In this sense, love is the "interpretation of the other's desire": by way of offering myself to the other, I interpret his desire as the desire for myself and thereby obfuscate the enigma of the other's desire.)[13] This, however, is only one of the ways to interpret the enigma of a letter that was written but not posted. In his *Why Do Women Write More Letters Than They Post?*, Darian Leader proposes a series of answers to this question;[14] one is tempted to systematize them by way of grouping them into two couples:

—As to its addressee, the true addressee of a woman's love letter is the Man, the absent symbolic fiction, its ideal reader, the "third" in the scene, not the flesh-and-blood man to whom it is addressed; or, its true addressee is the gap of absence itself, that is, the letter functions as an object, it is its very play with absence (of the addressee) that provides *jouissance,* since *jouissance* is contained in its act of writing itself, and since its true addressee is thus the writer herself.

—As to the way it relates to its author, the letter remains unposted because it did not say all (the author was unable to put in circulation some crucial trauma that would account for her true subjective position); or, it remains in itself forever unfinished, that is, there is always something more to say, since — like modernity for Habermas — woman is in herself an "unfinished project," and the non-posting of the letter acknowledges this fact that woman, like truth, cannot be "told all," that this is, as Lacan put it, "materially impossible."

Do we not encounter here the split between the phallic economy and the nonphallic domain? Not posting a letter as a false act of "repression" (of suppressing the truth put on paper and offering oneself as a love object in order to maintain the lie) is clearly correlated to the split between man, its flesh-and-blood addressee, and some third Man, the bearer of phallic power, its true addressee. In a homologous way, not posting a letter because the letter is an object that contains its own *jouissance,* is correlated to the non-all of feminine *jouissance,* to the *jouissance* that can never be "said" in its entirety.

The direct sexualization of the gap itself that characterizes feminine sexuality — the fact that, in it, much stronger than in man, the absence as such (the withdrawal, the non-act) is sexualized[15] — also accounts for the gesture of feminine withdrawal at the very moment when "she could have it all (the longed-for partner)" in a series of novels from Madame de Lafayette's *Princesse de Clèves* to Goethe's *Elective Affinities* (or, the obverse/complementary case, the woman's non-withdrawal, her inexplicable perseverance in the unhappy marriage, or with a no longer loved partner, even when the possibility arises to get out of it, as in James's *The Portrait of a Lady*).[16] Although ideology gets invested in this gesture of renunciation, the gesture itself is nonideological. The reading of this gesture to be rejected is the standard psychoanalytic one according to which, we are dealing with the hysterical logic of the object of love (the lover) who is desired only insofar as he is prohibited, only insofar as there is an obstacle in the guise of the husband — the moment the obstacle disappears, the woman loses interest in this love object. In addition to the hysterical economy of being able to enjoy the object only insofar as it remains illicit/prohibited, insofar as it maintains a potential status (i.e., in the guise of fantasies about what "might have" happened), this withdrawal (or insistence) can also be interpreted in a multitude of other ways: as the expression of so-called feminine masochism (which can be further read as an expression of the eternal feminine nature, or as the internalization of the patriarchal pressure) preventing a woman to fully "seize the day"; as a protofeminist gesture of stepping out of the confines of phallic economy, which posits as the woman's ultimate goal her happiness in a relationship with a man; and so on. However, all these interpretations seem to miss the point that consists in the absolutely fundamental nature of the gesture of withdrawal/substitution as constitutive of the subject herself. If, following the great German Idealists, we equate subject with freedom and autonomy, is such a gesture of withdrawal—not as a sacrificial gesture addressed at some version of the big Other, but as a gesture that provides its own satisfaction, as a gesture of finding *jouissance* in the very gap that separates me from the object—not the ultimate form of *autonomy?* [17]

With regard to the way sexual difference affects the role of the third who mediates the constitution of the couple, it would be interesting to compare two classic Hollywood melodramas, Rudolph Mate's supreme *No Sad Songs for Me* (1950) and *A Guy Named Joe* (1944, remade by Steven Spielberg as *Always* in 1989). *No Sad Songs for Me* is the story of a terminally ill woman (played by Margaret Sullavan, who was effectively dying while the film was being shot) who takes care that her family (husband and daughter) will be emotionally provided for after her death: she tacitly approves her husband to marry a younger woman (his junior business collaborator with whom he is already in love), and then spends the last weeks of her life at a holiday resort alone with her husband, convinced that whatever happens, nobody can take these last days of happiness from them. . . . The structure is here fantasmatic, that is, the repressed question of the film's narrative is: what would happen, whom would the husband choose, if the wife were *not* terminally ill? The properly melodramatic fantasmatic coincidence thus consists in the mysterious concord between the two catastrophes: one can say that the other, younger woman emerges to fill in the gap of the wife's decease, yet one can also say that the wife's terminal illness materializes the fact that she is no longer loved by her husband. The symbolic sleight of hand on which the film relies is thus the act of magically combining and transforming *two* catastrophes (her terminal illness and her husband's love for another, younger woman) into a *single* triumph: the wife accomplishes the basic symbolic gesture of *freely assuming what will occur inevitably* (her death and the loss of her husband): she presents her death and the fact that, afterward, her husband will start a new happy life with his new wife, as her own free act of withdrawing and delivering her husband and daughter to another woman.

In contrast to *No Sad Songs for Me*, the mediating third in *A Guy Named Joe* is a man: the dead husband who turns into a guardian angel, a properly phallic paternal figure wisely steering his widow toward a new man he considers appropriate for her. The first, obvious difference between the two films is that the male mediator is *already dead*—he intervenes as the benevolent ghost—while the feminine mediator is *still alive* and presents her very decease as the highest sacrifice, as the parting gift to the future new couple. The feminine mediator died so that the new couple could be happy, her death was *pregnant with meaning*, it echoed the marriage crisis that was already lurking (the husband's love for another woman), while the male mediator died in a pure, *meaningless* accident, interrupting a marital bliss with no shadow of discord. In other words, the dying wife in *No Sad Songs for Me* withdraws in order to enable the future marital bliss of her husband with another woman, while the new male partner of the widow in *A Guy Named Joe* will forever remain the second-best, living in the shadow of the deceased first husband. Or, to put it in yet another way, the libidinal economy of the male mediator is *perverse* (he remains present as a pure gaze, as an instrument of the new couple's *jouissance*),[18] while the feminine mediator is focused on the gesture of sacrificial self-withdrawal in the face of the new idealized couple.

The conclusion to be drawn from this is that it is wrong to contrast man and woman in an immediate way, as if man directly desires an object, while woman's desire is a "desire to desire," the desire for Other's desire. We are dealing here with sexual difference as real, which means that the opposite also holds, albeit in a slightly displaced way. True, a man directly desires a woman who fits the frame of his fantasy, while a woman alienates much more thoroughly her desire in man (i.e., her desire is to be the object desired by man) to fit the frame of his fantasy, which is why she endeavors to look at herself through the other's eyes and is permanently bothered by the question "What do others see in her (or me)?" However, a woman is simultaneously much *less* dependent on her partner, since her ultimate partner is not the other human being, her object of desire (as in man), but the gap itself, the distance from her partner in which is located the *jouissance feminine*. *Vulgari eloquentia*, in order to cheat a woman, a man needs a (real or imagined) partner, while a woman can cheat a man even when she is alone, since her ultimate partner is the solitude itself as the locus of *jouissance feminine* beyond the phallus.

Sexual difference is thus real also in the sense that no symbolic opposition can directly and adequately render it. A woman is essential to man's sexual life, while woman's sexuality involves much more than the presence of man; however, the opposite also holds—precisely because she is "all to him," man is always ready to sacrifice the woman for his career or for some other public-professional requirement (i.e., he has a domain outside his love life), while love life is of much more central concern to a woman. The point, of course, is that this reversal is not purely symmetrical, but slightly displaced—and it is this displacement that points toward the Real of sexual difference. (Another example: men do not mind wearing uniforms, whereas women want to dress uniquely, not to look like other women—yet men usually finish by not minding about fashion, while women are much more keen in following fashion.) The actual difference is thus not the difference between the opposed symbolic features, but the difference between two types of opposition: a woman is essential to man's sexual life, *yet for that very reason he has a domain outside sexual life that matters more to him;* to a woman, sexuality tends to be the feature that permeates her entire life, there is nothing that—potentially, at least—is not sexualized, *yet for that very reason woman's sexuality involves much more than the presence of man.* . . . Again, is the underlying structure here not that of Lacan's formulas of sexuation, the universality (a woman who is essential, all . . .) with an exception (career, public life) in man's case, the non-universality (a man is not all in woman's sexual life) with no exception (there is nothing that is not sexualized) in woman's case? This paradox of the feminine position is captured by the ambiguity of Emily Dickinson's celebrated poem 732:[19]

> She rose to His Requirement—dropt
> The Playthings of Her Life
> To take the honorable Work
> Of Woman, and of Wife—If ought she missed in Her new Day,
> Of Amplitude, or Awe—
> Or first Prospective—Or the Gold

In using, wear away, It lay unmentioned—as the Sea
Develop Pearl, and Weed,
But only to Himself—be known
The Fathoms they abide— [20]

This poem, of course, can be read as alluding to the sacrifice of the *agalma—objet petit a,* the "playthings" of *feminine jouissance—*which occurs when she becomes a Woman (i.e., assumes the subordinate role of Wife): underneath, inaccessible to the male gaze, the part of "she" that doesn't fit her role of "Woman" (which is why, in the last stanza, she refers to herself as "Himself") continues to lead its secret, "unmentioned" existence. However, it can also be read in a far more uncanny *opposite* way: what if the status of this "secret treasure" sacrificed when she becomes a Wife is purely fantasmatic? What if she evokes this secret in order to fascinate *His* (her husband's, male) gaze? Is it not also possible to read "but only to Himself" in the sense that the notion of the feminine treasure sacrificed when a woman enters sexual liaison with a man is a semblance intended to fascinate *His* gaze, and thus stands for the loss of something that was never present, never possessed? (The very definition of *objet a* is: an object that emerges in the very gesture of its loss.) In short, does this "lost treasure" not enter the line of the male fantasy about the feminine secret beyond the confines of the symbolic order, beyond its reach? Or, in Hegelese: the feminine In-itself, out of reach of the male gaze, is already "for the Other," the inaccessible mystery imagined by this very male gaze.

We can see, now, why any reference to pre-symbolic "feminine substance" is misleading. According to a recently popular theory, (the biological) male is just a (falsely emancipated) detour in the female self-reproduction that, in principle, is possible also without men. Elisabeth Badinter claims that biologically, we are all essentially feminine (the X chromosome is the pattern for all humanity, the Y chromosome an addition, not a mutation);[21] for that reason, development into a male implies a labor of differentiation spared female embryos. Furthermore, also concerning social life, males start off as citizens of female homeland (the uterus) before being forced to emigrate and live their lives as homesick exiles. That is to say, since men were originally created female, they must have become differentiated from women by way of social and cultural processes—so it is man, not woman, who is the culturally formed "second sex." [22] This theory can be insightful and useful as a kind of political myth to account for the contemporary insecurity of *male* identity: Badinter is at a certain level right to point out that the true social crisis today is the crisis of male identity, of "what it means to be a man": women are more or less successfully invading the territory of man, assuming functions in social life, without losing their feminine identity, while the obverse process, the male (re)conquest of the "feminine" territory of intimacy, is far more traumatic. While the figure of publicly successful woman is already part of our "social imaginary," problems with a "gentle man" are far more unsettling. However, this theory, while it seems to assert, in a "feminist" way, the primacy of the feminine, reproduces the fundamental metaphysical premises on the relationship between the masculine and the feminine; Badinter herself associates the male position with the values of risking into the exile, out of the safe haven of home, and the need to create one's identity through labor and cultural mediation—is this not the pseudo-Hegelian theory of the social relationship between the two sexes, a theory that, on account of the fact that labor and mediation are on the male side, clearly privileges man? In short, the notion that woman is the base and man the secondary mediation/deviation with no proper/natural identity, lays ground for the antifeminist argument par excellence, since, as Hegel never tires in repeating, Spirit itself is from the standpoint of nature "secondary," a pathological deviation, "nature sick unto death," and the power of spirit resides in the very fact that a marginal/secondary phenomenon, "in itself" a mere detour within some larger natural process, can, through the labor of mediation, elevate itself into an End-in-itself, which subjects to itself its own natural presupposition and "posits" it as part of its own "spiritual" totality. On that account, the apparently "depreciating" notions of femininity as mere masquerade, lacking any substantial identity and inner shape, of woman as a "castrated," deprived, degenerated, incomplete man, are of far greater use for feminism than the ethical elevation of femininity—in short, Otto Weininger is far better than Carol Gilligan.

So, back to our main topic: how is this notion of sexual difference to be connected to the matrix of four discourses? Let us begin with an author whose entire work is focused on the inherent deadlock of *male* subjectivity: Orson Welles. As it was shown by James Naremore,[23] the trajectory of a typical Welles film runs from the initial "realist," ironic, sociocritical depiction of a social milieu, to focusing on the tragic fate of a larger-than-life central character (Kane, Falstaff, etc.). This shift from a social-realist commentary (the liberal, gently critical, "social democratic," depiction of everyday life) to a morbid obsession with its Gothic excess, the prodigious individual and the tragic outcome of his *hubris* (which, incidentally, provides also the background for the shift from Marion to Norman in Hitchcock's *Psycho*), is the central unresolved antagonism of the Welles universe, and, as Adorno would have put it, Welles's greatness resides in the fact that he does not resolve or dissimulate this antagonism.

The first thing to take note of here, is the allegorical character of Welles's obsession with such larger-than-life characters: their ultimate failure is clearly a stand-in, within the diegetic space of his films, of Welles himself, of the *hubris* of his own artistic procedure and its ultimate failure. The second thing to take note of, is the way in which these excessive characters unite two opposite features: they are simultaneously aggressive, protofascist, permeated by a ruthless lust for power, and quixotic, ridiculous, out of contact with real social life, living in their dream world. This ambiguity is grounded in the fact that they are figures of "vanishing mediators": they clearly undermine the old balanced universe for which Welles has such a nostalgic fondness (the old small-town idyll of the Ambersons destroyed by industrial progress, etc.), yet they unknowingly lay the ground for their own demise (i.e., there is no place for them in the new world they helped to create). Moreover, this tension between realist social satire and the *hubris* of the larger-than-life character, is materialized in the radical ambiguity of the Wellesian trademark formal procedure, his manipulation of deep focus, achieved by a wide-angle lens. On the one hand, the depth of field, of course, perfectly renders the immersion of the individual into a wider social field—individuals are reduced to one of the many focal points in a paratactic social reality; on the other hand, however, deep focus "subjectively" distorts the proper perspective by way of "curving" the space and thus confers on it the dreamlike "pathological" quality—in short, deep focus registers at the formal level the split between the excessive main figure and the "ordinary" people in the background:

while there has been a great deal of theoretical discussion about depth of field in the film [*Citizen Kane*], rather little has been said about forced depth of perspective. . . . Again and again Welles uses deep focus not as a "realistic" mode of perception, but as a way of suggesting a conflict between the characters' instinctual needs and the social or material world that determines their fate. . . . The short focal-length of the lens enables him to express the psychology of his characters, to comment upon the relation between character and environment, and also to create a sense of barely contained, almost manic energy, as if the camera, like one of his heroes, were overreaching.[24]

The wide-angle lens thus produces the effect that is the exact opposite of what was celebrated by Andre Bazin (i.e., the harmonious realist immersion of the main character into his environs) as one of the focal points of the multilayered reality: the wide lens rather emphasizes the gap between the hero and his environs, simultaneously rendering visible the way in which the hero's excessive libidinal force almost anamorphicly distorts reality. The depth of field—which, by way of the wide-angle lens, distorts reality, curves its space by pathologically exaggerating the close-up of the main character, and bestows on the reality that stretches behind a strange, dreamlike quality—thus accentuates the gap that separates the main character from social reality; as such, it directly materializes the Wellesian "larger than life" subjectivity in all its ambiguity, oscillating between excessive, superman power and pathological ridicule. One can thus see how the Bazinian notion of the use of the depth of field is not simply wrong: it is as if the very distance between the two uses of the depth of field in Welles—the Bazinian-realist, in which the individual is embedded in the multilayered social reality, and the "excessive," which emphasizes the rift between the individual and his social background—articulates the tension in Welles's work between the liberal-progressive collectivist attitude, and the focus on the larger-than-life individual.[25] Welles's basic motif—the rise and fall of the larger-than-life character, who finally gets his "comeuppance"—allows for different readings. One is the Truffaut reading:

As [Welles] himself is a poet, a humanist, a liberal, one can see that this good and non-violent man was caught in a contradiction between his own personal feelings and those he has to portray in the parts given him because of his physique. He has resolved the contradiction by becoming a moralistic director, always showing the angel within the beast, the heart in the monster, the secret of the tyrant. This has led him to invent an acting style revealing the fragility behind power, the sensitivity behind strength. . . . The weakness of the strong, this is the subject that all of Orson Welles's films have in common.[26]

The obvious problem with this reading is that it romanticizes the monster who is discovered, deep in his heart, to have a fragile, gentle nature — the standard ideological legitimization up to Lenin who, in Stalinist hagiography, was always depicted as deeply moved by cats and children and brought to tears by Beethoven's *Appassionata*. (The ultimate version of this procedure is to feminize masculinity: a true man is in a passive-feminized relationship toward the divine Absolute whose will he actualizes. . . .) However, Welles does not fall into this ideological trap: for him, the essential "immoral" goodness (life-giving exuberance) of his larger-than-life characters is cosubstantial with what their environs perceive as their threatening, "evil," "monstrous" dimension. The other, opposite reading is the Nietzschean one: the larger-than-life hero is "beyond good and evil" and as such, essentially good, life-giving; he is broken by the narrowness and constraints of the self-culpablizing morality that cannot stand life-asserting Will. The fragility and vulnerability of the Wellesian hero directly follows from his absolute innocence, which remains blind to the twisted ways, by means of which, morality strives to corrupt and destroy life. (Is not another aspect of this Nietzscheanism also Welles's growing fascination with the status of semblance, of a "fake," of the truth of the fake as such, etc.?) This larger-than-life character is exuberant with his generosity, "beyond pleasure-principle" and utilitarian considerations. . . . One is thus tempted to repeat again, apropos of Welles, Adorno's thesis according to which the truth of the Freudian theory resides in the very unresolved contradictions of his theoretical edifice: the inner contradiction of the Wellesian subjectivity is irreducible, one cannot assert one side of it as the "truth" of the other side and, say, posit the generous life-substance as authentic, disclaiming the moral person as an expression of the mediocre crowd intended to suffocate the primordial goodness beyond good and evil; or, on the contrary, conceive the primordial life-substance as something that has to be gentrified through the intervention of *logos,* in order to prevent it from turning into a destructive unruliness. Welles himself was clearly aware of this undecidability: "All the characters I've played are various forms of Faust. I hate all forms of Faust, because I believe it's impossible for man to be great without admitting there is something greater than himself— either the law or God or art—but there must be something greater than man. I have sympathy for those characters—humanly but not morally." [27]

Welles's terms here are misleading: his larger-than-life figures are in no way "more human" but on the contrary *inhuman,* foreign to "humanity" in terms of the standard meaning of mediocre human existence with its petty joys, sorrows, and weaknesses. . . . Furthermore, these larger-than-life figures are distributed along the axis that reaches from Falstaff, for Welles the embodiment of essential goodness and life-giving generosity, to Kindler in *The Stranger,* a cruel, murderous Nazi (not to mention Harry Lime in Carol Reed's *The Third Man*)—in one of his interviews to *Cahiers du Cinema,* Welles includes in this series even Goering, as opposed to the bureaucratic-mediocre Himmler. How these larger-than-life figures subvert the standard ethico-political oppositions is clear from Thompson's description of Kane to the reporter, included in the final script but not in the film itself: "He was the most honest man who ever lived, with a streak of crookedness a yard wide. He was a liberal and a reactionary. He was a loving husband—and both wives left him. He had a gift of friendship such as few men have—and he broke his oldest friend's heart like you'd throw away a cigarette you were through with. Outside of that . . ." [28]

A simplified Heideggerian reading, which would conceive the Wellesian larger-than-life figure as the purest exemplification of the *hubris* of modern subjectivity, is also out of place here: the problem is that if subjectivity is to assert itself fully, this excess has to be suppressed, "sacrificed." We are dealing here with the *inner split of subjectivity* into the larger-than-life excess and its subsequent "normalization," which subordinates it to cold power calculation—it is only by means of this self-suppression or, rather, self-renunciation, this self-imposed limitation, that the *hubris* of subjectivity loses its utmost vulnerability. Only as such, by means of this self-limitation, can it elude the "comeuppance" waiting for it at the end of the road, and thus truly take over the rule — the move from Falstaff to Prince Hal. Another way to put it is to say that this Faustian larger-than-life figure is a kind of "vanishing mediator" of modern subjectivity, its founding gesture that has to withdraw in its result. (A raw and massive historical homology to this withdrawal is the way the Renaissance larger-than-life character, with his attitude of excessive generosity and free expenditure, acts as a necessary mediator between hierarchized medieval society and the calculating utilitarian attitude of the modern "disenchanted" world; in this precise sense, Welles himself is a "Renaissance figure.")

The Wellesian antagonism between "normal" and "larger-than-life" characters thus cannot be directly translated into a symbolic opposition: the only way to render it is by means of a repetitive self-referential procedure in which the "higher" pole of the first determination changes its place and becomes the "lower" pole of the next determination. On account of his generosity and life-asserting attitude, the larger-than-life figure is "human," in contrast to the stiff "normal" figure, yet he is simultaneously monstrously excessive with regard to the "humanity" of ordinary men and women. In its self-referential repetition, the "higher" symbolic feature is self-negated: the Wellesian hero is "more human" than ordinary people, yet this very excess of humanity makes him no longer properly "human"—the same as with Kierkegaard, in whose oeuvre the ethical is the truth of the aesthetical, yet the very dimension of the ethical, brought to its extreme, involves its own religious suspension. Welles's ultimate topic, which he approaches again and again from different perspectives, is thus the Real, the impossible kernel, the antagonistic tension, in the very heart of modern subjectivity. This same undecidability is also at work in the Wellesian formal tension between the realistic depiction of community-life, and the "expressionistic" excesses of the depth-of-field: these "expressionistic" excesses (uncanny camera angles, play with lights and shadows, etc.) are simultaneously a self-referential excess of form, with regard to the calm and transparent rendering of "social reality," *and* much closer to the true impetuses and generative forces of social life than the stiff conventions of realism. It is thus not merely that Welles's formal excesses and inconsistencies render or stage the inherent inconsistencies of the depicted content; rather, they function as the "return of the repressed" of the depicted content (i.e., their excess is correlative to a hole in the depicted content). The point is not only that the ambiguous use of the deep focus and depth-of-field indexes the ambiguity of the Wellesian ideological project, that is, Welles's ambivalent attitude toward the larger-than-life Faustian figures that are simultaneously condemned from the liberal-humanist progressive standpoint and function as the obvious object of fascination—if this were the fact, we would have a simple relation of reflection/mirroring between the formal excess and the content's ideological inconsistency. The point is rather that the formal excess reveals the "repressed" truth of the ideological project: Welles's libidinal *identification* with what his official liberal-democratic view rejects.

In this sense, one is tempted to speak about the Wellesian *obscenity of form*. That is to say, insofar as the autonomized form is to be conceived as the index of some traumatic repressed content, it is easy to identify the repressed content that emerges in the guise of Welles's formal extravaganzas and the excesses that draw attention to themselves (in *Citizen Kane*, in *Touch of Evil* . . .): the obscene, self-destructive *jouissance* of the non-castrated "larger-than-life" figure. When, in Welles's later films (exemplarily in *Chimes at Midnight*, although this tendency is already discernible in *Ambersons*), this excess of the form largely disappears in favor of a more balanced and transparent narrative, this change bears witness to a shift of accent in the structural ambiguity of the larger-than-life figure from its destructive and evil aspect (Quinlan in *Touch of Evil*), to its aspect of pacifying, life-giving goodness (Falstaff in *Chimes*)—the Wellesian formal extravaganzas are at their strongest when the larger-than-life figure is perceived in its destructive aspect.

The central necessity around which the tragic dimension of this Wellesian larger-than-life hero turns, is his necessary *betrayal* by his most devoted friend or successor, who can save his legacy and become "the one who will follow you" only by organizing his downfall. The exemplary case of this fidelity-through-betrayal occurs when the only way for a son to remain faithful to his obscene father is to betray him, as in the turbulent relationship between Falstaff and Prince Hal in Welles's *Chimes at Midnight*, where Falstaff is clearly the obscene shadowy double of Hal's official father (King Henry IV).[29] In *Chimes at Midnight*, the most poignant scene is undoubtedly that of renunciation, when Prince Hal, now the newly invested King Henry V, banishes Falstaff: the intense exchange of gazes belies the explicit content of the king's words, and bears witness to a kind of telepathic link between the two, to an almost unbearable compassion and solidarity—the implicit message delivered by the king's desperate gaze is "Please, understand me, I am doing this on behalf of my fidelity to you!"[30] Prince Hal's betrayal of Falstaff as the supreme act of fidelity, is furthermore grounded in the concrete political stance of the new king: as is well known, Henry V was a kind of royal counterpoint to Joan of Arc, the first "patriotic" protobourgeois king to use wars to forge national unity, appealing to the national pride of ordinary people in order to mobilize them—his wars were no longer the conventional feudal games fought with mercenaries. One could thus claim that Prince Hal "sublated" (in the precise Hegelian sense of *Aufhebung*) his socializing with Falstaff, his mixing with lower classes, his feeling the pulse of the ordinary people with their "vulgar" amusements: his message to Falstaff is thus, "only by betraying you, can I transpose/integrate what I got from you into my function of the king." (It is the same with the betrayal of the father: only by betraying him can one assume the paternal symbolic function.)

This trauma of the excessively enjoying father who must be betrayed is at the very root of neurosis: neurosis always involves a perturbed, traumatic, relationship to the father: in neurosis, the "sublation" of the Father-Enjoyment into the paternal Name fails, the figure of the Father remains marked with a traumatic stain of *jouissance,* and one of the traumatic scenes that brings such a distasteful *jouissance* to the neurotic is the scene of the father either caught "with his pants down" (i.e., in an act of excessive, obscene enjoyment), or being humiliated (in both cases, the father is not "at the level of his symbolic mandate"). Such a scene transfixes the hysteric's gaze, it paralyzes him: the encounter with the real of the paternal *jouissance,* turns the hysteric into an immobilized, frozen gaze, like Medusa's head. In Dostoyevsky's *Karamazov Brothers,* we find both versions of this trauma: the Karamazov father himself is the obscene father, an embarrassing figure indulging in excessive enjoyment; furthermore, we have a scene in which, after Dimitri attacks a poor man, his son, observing them, approaches Dimitri, pulls his sleeve to divert his attention from beating his father and gently asks him "Please, do not beat my father. . . ." This is how one is to read the triad of Real-Symbolic-

Imaginary with regard to the father: symbolic father is the Name of the Father; imaginary father is the (respectful, dignified . . .) "self-image" of the father; real father is the excess of enjoyment whose perception traumatically disturbs this "self-image." The encounter with this trauma can set in motion different strategies to cope with it: the death wish (should the father die, to stop being such an embarrassment to me—the ultimate source of embarrassment is the very fact that the father is alive . . .); assuming the guilt (i.e., sacrificing myself in order to save the father); and so on. The hysterical subject tries to locate the lack in the father that would weaken him, while the obsessional neurotic who perceives the father's weakness and feels guilty for it, is ready to sacrifice himself for him (and thus to obfuscate his desire to humiliate the father).

Do we not encounter both versions of the obscene father in Wagner? Let us recall the traumatic relationship between Amfortas and Titurel, a true counterpart to the dialogue between Alberich and Hagen from *The Twilight of Gods*. The contrast between the two confrontations of father and son is clear: in *The Twilight,* the dynamics (nervous agitation, most of the talking) is on the side of the father, with Hagen for the most part merely listening to this obscene apparition; in *Parsifal,* Titurel is an immobile oppressive presence who barely breaks his silence with the superego-injunction "Reveal the Grail!" whereas Amfortas is the dynamical agent giving voice to his refusal to perform the ritual. . . . Is it not clear, if one listens very closely to this dialogue from *Parsifal,* that the truly obscene presence in *Parsifal,* the ultimate cause of the decay of the Grail community, is not Klingsor, who is evidently a mere small-time crook, but rather Titurel himself, an obscene undead apparition, a dirty old man who is so immersed in the enjoyment of the Grail that he perturbs the regular rhythm of its disclosure? The opposition between Alberich and Titurel is thus not the opposition between obscene humiliation and dignity, but rather *between the two modes of obscenity itself,* between the strong, oppressive, father-*jouissance* (Titurel) and the humiliated, agitated, weak father (Alberich).

Is the ultimate example of the obscene father not provided by the Bible itself?:

Noah, a man of the soil, proceeded to plant a vineyard. When he drank some of its wine, he became drunk and lay uncovered inside his tent. Ham, the father of Canaan, saw his father's nakedness and told his two brothers outside. But Shem and Japheth took a garment and laid it across their shoulders; then they walked in backwards and covered their father's nakedness. Their faces were turned the other way, so that they would not see their father's nakedness.

When Noah awoke from his wine and found out what his youngest son had done to him, he said, "Cursed be Canaan! The lowest of slaves / will he be to his brothers." (Genesis 9:20–26)[31]

Apart from the enigmatic fact that Noah did not curse Ham directly, but rather Ham's offspring (his son), used by some interpretations as the legitimization of slavery (Canaan is often referred to as "black"), the key point is that this scene clearly stages the confrontation with the helpless obscene *Père-Jouissance:* the proper sons respectfully look aside, cover up their father, and thus protect his dignity, while the evil son maliciously trumpets forth father's helpless obscenity. Symbolic authority is thus grounded in voluntary blindness, it involves a kind of will-*not*-to-know, the attitude of *je n'en veux rien savoir*—that is to say, about the obscene side of the father.

What we find in Welles is thus the fundamental tension of the male subjectivity, its constitutive oscillation between the Master's excessive expenditure and the subject's attempt to "economize" this excess, to normalize it, to contain it, to inscribe it into the circuit of social exchange, the oscillation best rendered by Bataille's opposition of autonomous sovereignty and economizing heteronomy. It is also easy to discern how this tension refers to the two Lacanian matrices: with regard to the matrix of the four discourses, we are clearly dealing with its upper level, with the shift from the Master to the university discourse; with regard to the formulas of sexuation, we are dealing with the masculine side, with the tension between the universal function (epitomized by the "knowledge" embodied in the agent of the university discourse) and its constitutive exception (the Master's excess). In what, then, would consist the feminine counterpoint to this tension of the male subjectivity? Let us elaborate this point apropos of an author who is all too easily dismissed as "phallocratic," Ayn Rand. Rand, who wrote the two absolute best-sellers of our century, *The Fountainhead* (1943) and *Atlas Shrugged* (1957), yet was (deservedly) ignored and ridiculed as a philosopher, shared with Welles the obsession with larger-than-life figures: her fascination for male figures displaying absolute, unswayable determination of their Will, seems to offer the best imaginable confirmation of Sylvia Plath's famous line, "every woman adores a Fascist." Although it is easy to dismiss the very mention of Rand alongside Welles as an obscene extravaganza—artistically, she is, of course, worthless—the properly subversive dimension of her ideological procedure is not to be underestimated: Rand fits into the line of "overconformist" authors who undermine the ruling ideological edifice by their very excessive identification with it. Her over-orthodoxy was directed at capitalism itself, as the title of one of her books (*Capitalism, the Unknown Ideal*) tells us; according to her, the truly heretic thing today is to embrace the basic premise of capitalism without its communitarian, collectivist, welfare sugar-coating. So what Pascal and Racine were to Jansenism, what Kleist was to German nationalist militarism, what Brecht was to Communism, Rand is to American capitalism.

It was perhaps her Russian origins and upbringing that enabled her to formulate directly the fantasmatic kernel of American capitalist ideology. The elementary ideological axis of her work consists in the opposition between the prime movers, "men of mind," and second handers, "mass men." The Kantian opposition between ethical autonomy and heteronomy is here brought to extreme: the "mass man" is searching for recognition outside himself, his self-confidence and assurance depend on how he is perceived by others, while the prime mover is fully reconciled with himself, relying on his creativity, selfish in the sense that his satisfaction does not depend on getting recognition from others or on sacrificing himself, his innermost drives, for the benefit of others. The prime mover is innocent, delivered from the fear of others, and for that reason without hatred even for his worst enemies (Roark, the "prime mover" in *The Fountainhead*, doesn't actively hate Toohey, his great opponent, he simply doesn't care about him—here is the famous dialogue between the two: "Mr. Roark, we're alone here. Why don't you tell me what you think of me? In any words you wish. No one will hear us." "But I don't think of you.") On the basis of this opposition, Rand elaborates her radically atheist, life-assertive, "selfish" ethics: the "prime mover" is capable of the love for others, this love is even crucial for him since it does not express his contempt for himself, his self-denial, but, on the contrary, the highest self-assertion—love for others is the highest form of the properly understood "selfishness" (i.e., of my capacity to realize through my relationship with others my own innermost drives). On the basis of this opposition, *Atlas Shrugged* constructs a purely fantasmatic scenario: John Galt, the novel's mysterious hero, assembles all prime movers and organizes their strike—they withdraw from the collectivist oppression of the bureaucratized public life. As a result of their withdrawal, social life loses its impetus, social services, from stores to railroads, no longer function, global disintegration sets in, and the desperate society calls the prime movers back—they accept it, but under their own terms. . . . What we have here is the fantasy of a man finding the answer to the eternal question "What moves the world?"—the prime movers—and then being able to "stop the motor of the world" by organizing the prime movers' retreat. John Galt succeeds in suspending the very circuit of the universe, the "run of things," causing its symbolic death and the subsequent rebirth of the New World. The ideological gain of this operation resides in the reversal of roles with regard to our everyday experience of strike: it is not workers but the capitalists who go on strike, thus proving that they are the truly productive members of society who do not need others to survive.[32] The hideout to which the prime movers retreat, a secret place in the midst of the Colorado mountains accessible only via a dangerous narrow passage, is a kind of negative version of Shangri-la, a "utopia of greed": a small town in which unbridled market relations reign, in which the very word "help" is prohibited, in which every service has to be reimbursed by true (gold-covered) money, in which there is no need for pity and self-sacrifice for others.

The Fountainhead gives us a clue as to the matrix of intersubjective relations that sustains this myth of prime movers. Its four main male characters constitute a kind of Greimasian semiotic square: the architect Howard Roark is the autonomous creative hero; Wynand, the newspaper tycoon, is the failed hero, a man who could have been a "prime mover"—deeply akin to Roark, he got caught in the trap of crowd manipulation (he is not aware of how his media manipulation of the crowd actually makes him a slave who follows the crowd's whims); Keating is a simple conformist, a wholly externalized, "other-oriented" subject; Toohey, Roark's true opponent, is the figure of diabolical evil, a man who never could have been *and who knows it*—he turned his awareness of his worthlessness into the self-conscious hatred of prime movers (i.e., he becomes an evil Master who feeds the crowd with this hatred). Paradoxically, Toohey is the point of self-consciousness: he is the only one who knows it all, who, even more than Roark, who simply follows his drive, is fully aware of the true state of things. We thus have Roark as the being of pure drive in no need of symbolic recognition (and as such uncannily close to the Lacanian saint—only an invisible line of separation distinguishes them), and the three ways to compromise one's drive: Wynand, Keating, Toohey. The underlying opposition is here that of desire and drive, as exemplified in the tense relationship between Roark and Dominique, his sexual partner. Roark displays the perfect indifference toward the Other characteristic of drive, while Dominique remains caught in the dialectic of desire that is the desire of the Other: she is gnawed by the Other's gaze—by the fact that others, the common people totally insensitive to Roark's achievement, are allowed to stare at it and thus spoil its sublime quality. The only way for her to break out of this deadlock of Other's desire is to *destroy* the sublime object in order to save it from becoming the object of the ignorant gaze of others: "You want a thing and it's precious to you. Do you know who is standing ready to tear it out of your hands? You can't know, it may be so involved and so far away, but someone is ready, and you're afraid of them all. . . . I never open again any great book I've read and loved. It hurts me to think of the other eyes that have read it and of what they were." [33]

These "other eyes" are the evil gaze at its purest, which grounds the paradox of property: if, within a social field, I am to possess an object, this possession must be socially acknowledged, which means that the big Other who vouchsafes this possession of mine must in a way possess it in advance in order to let me have it. I thus never relate directly to the object of my desire: when I cast a desiring glance at the object, I am always already gazed at by the Other (not only the imaginary other, the competitive-envious double, but primarily the big Other of the symbolic institution that guarantees property), and this gaze of the Other that oversees me in my desiring capacity is in its very essence "castrative," threatening.[34] Therein consists the elementary castrative matrix of the dialectics of possession: if I am truly to possess an object, I have first to lose it, that is, to concede that its primordial owner is the big Other. In traditional monarchies, this place of the big Other is occupied by the king who in principle owns the entire land, so that whatever individual landowners possess was given, bequeathed, to them by the king; this castrative dialectic reaches its extreme in the case of the totalitarian leader who, on the one hand, emphasizes again and again how he is nothing in himself, how he only embodies and expresses the will, the creativity of the people, but, on the other hand, he gives us everything we have, so we have to be grateful to him for everything we have, up to our meager daily bread and health. At the level of drive, however, immediate possession *is* possible, one can dispose of the Other, in contrast to the everyday order of desire in which the only way to remain free is to sacrifice everything one cares for, to destroy it, to never have a job one wants and enjoys, to marry a man one absolutely despises. . . . So, for Dominique, the greatest sacrilege is to throw pearls to swines: to create a precious object and then to expose it to the Other's evil gaze (i.e., to let it be shared with the crowd). And she treats *herself* in precisely the same way: she tries to resolve the deadlock of her position as a desired object by way of willingly embracing, even searching for, the utmost humiliation—she marries the person she most despises and tries to ruin the career of Roark, the true object of her love and admiration.[35] Roark, of course, is well aware of how her attempts to ruin him result from her desperate strategy to cope with her unconditional love for him, to inscribe this love in the field of the big Other; so, when she offers herself to him, he repeatedly rejects her and tells her that the time is not yet ripe for it: she will become his true partner only when her desire for him will no longer be bothered by the Other's gaze—in short, when she will accomplish the shift from desire to drive. The (self-)destructive dialectics of Dominique, as well as of Wynand, bears witness to the fact that they are fully aware of the terrifying challenge of Roark's position of pure drive: they want to break him down in order to deliver him from the clutches of his drive.

This dialectics provides the key to what is perhaps the crucial scene in *The Fountainhead*: Dominique, while riding a horse, encounters on a lone country road Roark, working as a simple stonecutter in her father's mine; unable to endure the insolent way he looks back at her, the look that attests to his awareness of her inability to resist being attracted to him, Dominique furiously whips him (in the film version, this violent encounter is rendered as the archetypal scene of the mighty landlord's lady or daughter secretly observing the attractive slave: unable to admit to herself that she is irresistibly attracted to him, she acts out her embarrassment in a furious whipping of the slave). She whips him, she is his Master confronting a slave, but her whipping is an act of despair, an awareness of *his* hold over her, of her inability to resist him—as such, it's already an invitation to brutal rape. So the first act of love between Dominique and Roark is a brutal rape done with no compassion: "He did it as an act of scorn. Not as love, but as defilement. And this made her lie still and submit. One gesture of tenderness from him—and she would have remained cold, untouched by the thing done to her body. But the act of a master taking shameful, contemptuous possession of her was the kind of rapture she had wanted" (217). This scorn is paralleled by Dominique's unconditional willingness to destroy Roark—the willingness that is the strongest expression of her love for him; the following quote bears witness to the fact that Rand is effectively a kind of feminine version of Otto Weininger:

> "I'm going to fight you—and I'm going to destroy you—and I tell you this as calmly as I told you that I'm a begging animal. I'm going to pray that you can't be destroyed—I tell you this, too— even though I believe in nothing and have nothing to pray to. But I will fight to block every step you take. I will fight to tear away every chance you want away from you. I will hurt you through the only thing that can hurt you—through your work. I will fight to starve you, to strangle you on the things you won't be able to reach. I have done it to you today—and that is why I shall sleep with you tonight. . . . I'll come to you whenever I have beaten you—when- ever I know that I have hurt you—and I'll let you own me. I want to be owned, not by a lover, but by an adversary who will destroy my victory over him, not with honorable blows, but with the touch of his body on mine." (272-73)

The woman strives to destroy the precious *agalma*, which is what she doesn't possess in her beloved man, the spark of his excessive autono- mous creativity: she is aware that only in this way, by destroying his *agalma* (or, rather, by making *him* renounce it), she will own him, only in this way will the two of them form an ordinary couple; yet she is also aware that in this way, he will become worthless—therein resides her tragic predicament. Is then, *in ultima analisi*, the scenario of *The Fountainhead* not that of Wagner's *Parsifal?* Roark is Parsifal the saint, the being of pure drive; Dominique is Kundry in search of her delivery;

Wynand is Amfortas, the failed saint; Toohey is Klingsor, the impotent evil magician. Like Dominique, Kundry wants to destroy Parsifal, since she has a foreboding of his purity; like Dominique, Kundry simultaneously wants Parsifal not to give way, to endure the ordeal, since she is aware that her only chance of redemption resides in Parsifal's resistance to her seductive charms.[36]

The true conflict in the universe of Rand's two novels is thus not between the prime movers and the crowd of second handers who parasitize on the prime movers' productive genius, with the tension between the prime mover and his feminine sexual partner being a mere secondary subplot of this principal conflict. The true conflict runs within the prime movers themselves: it resides in the (sexualized) tension between the prime mover, the being of pure drive, and his hysterical partner, the potential prime mover who remains caught in the deadly self-destructive dialectic (between Roark and Dominique in *The Fountainhead,* between John Galt and Dagny in *Atlas Shrugged*). When, in *Atlas Shrugged,* one of the prime mover figures tells Dagny, who unconditionally wants to pursue her work and keep the transcontinental railroad company running, that the prime movers' true enemy is not the crowd of second handers, but *herself,* this is to be taken literally. Dagny herself is aware of it: when prime movers start to disappear from public productive life, she suspects a dark conspiracy, a "destroyer" who forces them to withdraw and thus gradually brings the entire social life to a standstill; what she does not yet see is that the figure of "destroyer" that she identifies as the ultimate enemy, is the figure of her true redeemer. The solution occurs when the hysterical subject finally gets rid of her enslavement and recognizes in the figure of the "destroyer" her savior—why?

Second handers possess no ontological consistency of their own, which is why the key to the solution is not to break *them,* but to break the chain that forces the creative prime movers to work for them—when this chain is broken, the second handers' power will dissolve by itself. The chain that links a prime mover to the perverted existing order is none other than her attachment to her productive genius: a prime mover is ready to pay any price, up to the utter humiliation of feeding the very force that works against him—that is, which parasitizes on the activity it officially endeavors to suppress—just to be able to continue to create. What the hystericized prime mover must accept is thus the fundamental existential *indifference:* she must no longer be willing to remain the hostage of the second handers' blackmail ("We will let you work and realize your creative potential, on condition that you accept our terms"), she must be ready to give up the very kernel of her being, that which means everything to her, and to accept the "end of the world," the (temporary) suspension of the very flow of energy that keeps the world running. In order to gain everything, she must be ready to go through the zero-point of losing everything. And, far from signaling the "end of subjectivity," this act of assuming existential indifference is, perhaps, the very gesture of absolute negativity that gives birth to the subject. What Lacan calls "subjective destitution" is thus, paradoxically, another name for the subject itself (i.e., for the void beyond the theater of hysterical subjectivizations).

The reference to *Parsifal* brings us back to the matrix of the four discourses: Wynand, the failed Master; Toohey, the corrupted agent of Knowledge; the hysterical Dominique; Roark the analyst (i.e., the subject who assumed subjective destitution). This matrix provides the two versions of everyday subjectivity, the subject of the university discourse (the "instrumental reason," the self-effacing manipulator)[37] and the hysterical subject (the subject engaged in the permanent questioning of her being), as well as the two versions of the "larger-than-life" subjectivity: the (masculine) Master who finds fulfillment in gestures of excessive expenditure, and the (feminine) desubjectivized being of pure drive. One can also see, now, how the matrix of the four discourses is to be sexualized: its upper level (Master-university) reproduces the constitutive tension of masculine subjectivity, while its lower level (hysteric-analyst) reproduces the constitutive tension of the feminine subjectivity. Welles's films focus on the shift from Master to University, from the constitutive excess to the series this excess grounds—that is, on the traumatic necessity of the Master's betrayal[38]—while Rand's universe is centered on the shift from the hysterical ambivalence of desire (the need to destroy what one loves, etc.), to the self-contained circuit of drive. The hysteric's logic is that of the non-all (for a hysteric, the set is never complete—there is always something missing, although one can never pinpoint what, exactly, is missing . . .), while drive involves the closure of a circular movement with no exception (the space of drive is like that of the universe in the relativity theory: it is finite, although it has no external boundary).

The matrix of the four discourses thus contains two radically different narratives that are not to be confused: the standard masculine narrative of the struggle between the exceptional One (Master, Creator) and the "crowd" that follows the universal norm, as well as the feminine narrative of the shift from desire to drive — from the hysteric's entanglement in the deadlocks of the Other's desire to the fundamental indifference of the desubjectivized being of drive. For that reason, the Randian hero is *not* "phallocratic" — phallocratic is rather the figure of the failed Master (Wynand in *The Fountainhead*, Stadler in *Atlas Shrugged*): paradoxical as it may sound, with regard to the formulas of sexuation, the being of pure drive that emerges once the subject "goes through the fantasy" and assumes the attitude of indifference toward the enigma of the Other's desire, is a *feminine* figure. What Rand was not aware of was that the upright, uncompromising masculine figures with a will of steel that she was so fascinated with, are effectively figures of the *feminine subject liberated from the deadlocks of hysteria*.[39] It is thus a thin, almost imperceptible line that separates Rand's ideological and literary trash from the ultimate feminist insight.

Such a reading of the feminine "formulas of sexuation" also enables us to draw a crucial theoretical conclusion about the limits of subjectivity: hysteria is not the limit of subjectivity, there *is* a subject beyond hysteria. What we get after "traversing the fantasy" (i.e., the pure being of drive that emerges after the subject undergoes "subjective destitution"), is not a kind of subjectless loop of the repetitive movement of drive, but, on the contrary, the subject at its purest, one is almost tempted to say: the subject "as such." Saying "Yes!" to the drive (precisely to that which can never be subjectivized), freely assuming the inevitable (the drive's radical closure), is the highest gesture of subjectivity. It is thus only after assuming a fundamental indifference toward the Other's desire, after getting rid of the hysterical game of subjectivizations, after suspending the intersubjective game of mutual (mis)recognition, that the pure subject emerges. The answer to the question: where, in the four subjective positions that we elaborated, do we encounter the Lacanian subject, the subject of the unconscious, is thus, paradoxically: in the very discourse in which the subject undergoes "subjective destitution" and identifies with the excremental remainder that forever resists subjectivization.

Notes

1 Which is why psychosis is excluded: it designates the very breakdown of the symbolic social link.

2 This same gap is also exemplified by the two names of the same person. The pope is at the same time Karol Wojtyla and John Paul II: the first name stands for the "real" person, while the second name designates this same person as the "infallible" embodiment of the institution of the church—while the poor Karol can get drunk and babble stupidities, when John Paul speaks, it is the divine spirit itself that speaks through him.

3 In Ernesto Laclau's terms, the Master's gesture signals the introduction of a new ideological hegemony; see his *Emancipation(s)* (London: Verso, 1996).

4 See Paul-Laurent Assoun, *Le pervers et la femme* (Paris: Anthropos, 1996), 30–36.

5 Furthermore, are we not dealing here with a clear parallel with Wagner's *Parsifal?* Does Kundry, this archetypal hysterical figure, also not hystericize Parsifal through her "indecent proposal," by defiantly offering herself to him? When the horrified Parsifal, like Hyppolite, violently rejects his role of sexual object, does this rejection also not function as the hysterical disavowal of castration (the hysteria being clearly discernible in his identification with Amfortas's wound)?

6 The crucial point not to be missed here is how Lacan's late identification of the subjective position of the analyst as that of *objet petit a* presents an act of radical self-criticism: earlier, in the 1950s, Lacan conceived the analyst not as the *small* other (*a*), but, on the contrary, as a kind of stand-in for the *big* Other (A, the anonymous symbolic order). At this level, the function of the analyst was to frustrate the subjects' imaginary misrecognitions and to make them accept their proper symbolic place within the circuit of symbolic exchange, the place that effectively (and unbeknownst to them) determines their symbolic identity. Later, however, the analyst stands precisely for the ultimate inconsistency and failure of the big Other (i.e., for the symbolic order's inability to guarantee the subject's symbolic identity).

7 It is homologous with the notion of desire: in Kant's philosophy, the faculty of desire is "pathological," dependent on contingent objects, so there can be no "pure faculty of desiring," no "critique of pure desire," while for Lacan, psychoanalysis precisely *is* a kind of "critique of *pure* desire." In other words, desire *does* have a nonpathological ("a priori") object-cause: the *objet petit a,* the object that overlaps with its own lack.

8 For this crucial distinction, see also Charles Shepherdson, "The *Role* of Gender and the *Imperative* of Sex," in *Supposing the Subject,* ed. Joan Copjec (London: Verso, 1994).

9 For a more detailed account of these paradoxes, see Appendix III of Slavoj Žižek, *The Plague of Fantasies* (London: Verso, 1997).

10 This paradox also enables us to account for the fact that a man who finds the fulfill-ment and goal of his life in a happy love-relationship, when confronted with a choice between love and professional cause—doing his duty toward his country, follow-ing his professional or artist's career—inevitably chooses his cause, as if the direct choice of love would somehow devalue love itself and/or make him unworthy of love: although love is that which matters *most* to him, the professional cause nonetheless matters *more*. . . .

11 Nietzsche's famous claim that Christ was the only true Christian also relies on the reversal of the usual role of the founding figure, which is that of the constitutive ex-ception: Marx was not a Marxist, since he himself *was* Marx and couldn't entertain toward himself the reflective relationship implied by the term "Marx*ist*." Christ, on the contrary, not only was a Christian, but—for that very reason, following an in-exorable necessity—has to be the only (true) Christian. How is this possible? Only if we introduce a radical gap between Christ himself and Christianity and assert that Christianity is grounded in the radical misrecognition, even active disavowal, of Christ's act. Christianity is thus a kind of defense-formation against the scandalous nature of Christ's act.

12 Another way to put it is to say that when a woman offers her presence instead of the symbolic message, she thereby posits her body as the *envelope of a secret* (i.e., her presence becomes a "mystery").

13 In contrast to such a letter that, apparently, does *not* arrive at its destination, there are (at least) two types of letters that *do* arrive at their destination. One is the "Dear John" letter, explaining to the husband or boyfriend not love but the end of love (i.e., the fact that she is leaving him). The other is the suicidal letter destined to reach its addressee when the woman is already dead, as in Zweig's *Letter from an Unknown Woman.*

14 See Darian Leader, *Why Do Women Write More Letters Than They Post?* (London: Faber and Faber, 1996).

15 Although here, again, the obverse also holds: is the famous *an die ferne Geliebte,* to the distant beloved, not the motto of all love poetry? Is therefore the male love poetry not the exemplary case of the sexualization of the gap that separates the poet from the beloved, so that, when the barrier disappears and the beloved comes too close, the consequences can be catastrophic? The thing to do would be, again, to construct two almost-symmetrically-inverted couples of opposites: men prefer their beloved to remain distant in contrast to women who want their man close to them, but, simul-taneously, men want to enjoy directly the partner's body, while women can enjoy the very gap that separates them from the partner's body.

16 I owe this point to Anne-Lise François, of Princeton University.

17 Furthermore, the princess of Clèves subverts the logic of adultery as inherent trans-gression by turning around the standard adulterous procedure of "doing it" (having sex with another man) and not telling it to the husband: she, on the contrary, tells about it (her love) to her husband, but doesn't "do it."

18 This perverse position of the instrument of Other's *jouissance* is, of course, always in danger of turning into aggressivity ("You dirty whore, how could you do this to me!") when the subject loses his instrumental distance and undergoes hystericization.

19   I rely here on an unpublished paper by Monica Pelaez, of Princeton University.

20   *The Complete Poems of Emily Dickinson,* ed. Thomas H. Johnson (Boston: Little, Brown and Company, 1960), 359.

21   See Elisabeth Badinter, *XY: On Masculine Identity* (New York: Columbia University Press, 1996).

22   At a more elementary biological (and also scientifically more convincing) level, some scientists claim that complex forms of organic life resulted from the malignancy of simple (monocellular) life forms that, at a certain point, "ran amok" and started to multiply in a pathological way—complex life is thus inherently, in its very notion, a pathological formation.

23   See James Naremore, *The Magic World of Orson Welles* (New York: Oxford University Press, 1978), 61–63.

24   Ibid., 48, 50.

25   A further point to be made about the Wellesian use of the depth of field, is that it confers a kind of positive ontological density on darkness and shades: when, in an "expressionistic" shot, we perceive in the background an overilluminated object, surrounded on both sides by the impenetrable dark shades, this darkness is no longer simply the negative of the positively existing things, but in a way "more real than real objects themselves"—it stands for the dimension of primordial density of matter, out of which definite objects (temporarily) emerge.

26   Quoted in Joseph McBride, *Orson Welles* (New York: Da Capo, 1996), 36.

27   Quoted in ibid., 157.

28   Quoted in ibid., 47. The paradigmatic example of Kane's gesture of excessive generosity that characterizes the attitude of the Master is the famous scene in which, after firing Leland, his longtime friend, for writing a detrimental critique of his wife's opera debut, Kane sits down at Leland's desk, finishes Leland's critique in the same injurious spirit, and has it printed.

29   The point not to be missed here is that Prince Hal's father (King Henry IV) is, no less than Falstaff, an impostor whose throne is contested—Falstaff's mocking of royal rituals is so striking since it points toward the imposture that already characterizes the "true" bearer of the title. The two paternal figures of Prince Hal, his father the king and Falstaff, are thus opposed as the desiccated dying man clinging to the symbolic title, and the generous ebullience that mocks all symbolic titles. However, it would be wrong to say that we should strive for the ideal father uniting the two sides: the message of Welles is precisely that this split of the paternal figure into the desiccated bearer of the symbolic title and the ebullient *jouisseur,* is insurmountable—there must be two fathers.

30   Another supreme example of this fidelity-through-betrayal is found in Dashiell Hammett's *Glass Key* (for a detailed analysis of it, see chapter 5 of Slavoj Žižek, *Enjoy Your Symptom!* [New York: Routledge, 1993]).

31   I owe this example to Robin Blackburn, who discusses it *in extenso* in the chapter 1 of his *The Making of New World Slavery* (London: Verso, 1997).

32   Rand's ideological limitation is here clearly perceptible: in spite of the new impetus the myth of the "prime movers" got from the digital industry (Steve Jobs, Bill

Gates), individual capitalists are today, in our era of multinationals, definitely not its "prime movers." In other words, what Rand "represses" is the fact that the "rule of the crowd" is the inherent outcome of the dynamic of capitalism itself.

33 Ayn Rand, *The Fountainhead* (New York: Signet, 1992), 143–44. Further citations will be given parenthetically in the text.

34 See Paul-Laurent Assoun, *La voix et le regard* (Paris: Anthropos, 1995), 2:35–36.

35 *Atlas Shrugged* contains a whole series of such hysterical inversions of desire—suffice it to quote from the blurb on the cover of the pocket edition: "Why does [John Galt] fight his hardest battle against the woman he loves? . . . why a productive genius became a worthless playboy. Why a great steel industrialist was working for his own destruction . . . why a composer gave up his career on the night of his triumph . . . why a beautiful woman who ran a transcontinental railroad fell in love with the man she had sworn to kill."

36 Parsifal resists Kundry's advances by means of his identification with Amfortas's wound: at the very moment of Kundry's kiss, he retreats from her embrace, shouts "Amfortas! The wound!" and seizes his thighs (the site of Amfortas's wound); as it was demonstrated by Elisabeth Bronfen's penetrating analysis (see her "Kundry's Laughter," *New German Critique* 69 [fall 1996]), this comically pathetic gesture of Parsifal is that of hysterical identification, (i.e., a step into the hysterical theater). The true hysteric of the opera, of course, is Kundry, and it is as if Parsifal's very rejection of her contaminates him with hysteria. The main weapon and index of Kundry's hysteria is her laughter, so it is crucial to probe into its origins: the primordial scene of laughter is the Way of the Cross where Kundry was observing the suffering Christ and laughing at him. This laughter then repeats itself again and again apropos of every master Kundry served (Klingsor, Gurnemanz, Amfortas, Parsifal): she undermines the position of each of them by means of the surplus-knowledge contained in her hysterical obscene laughter, which reveals the fact that the master is impotent, a semblance of himself. This laughter is thus profoundly ambiguous: it does not stand only for making a mockery of the other, but also for despair at herself (i.e., for her repeated failure to find a reliable support in the Master). The question that one should raise here is that of the parallel between Amfortas's and Christ's wound: What do the two have in common? In what sense is Amfortas (who was wounded when he succumbed to Kundry's temptation) occupying the same position as Christ? The only consistent answer, of course, is that *Christ himself was not pure in his suffering:* when Kundry observed him on the Way of the Cross, she detected his obscene *jouissance* (i.e., the way he was "turned on" by his suffering). What Kundry is desperately searching for in men is, on the contrary, somebody who would be able to resist the temptation of converting his pain into a perverse enjoyment.

37 The subject of the university discourse is only able to make the best choice (rational strategic decision) within the conditions of the given situation—what he is not able to do is to perform an excessive gesture that, as it were, retroactively redefines/restructures these very conditions, or, to put it in popular terms, a gesture that "changes the entire picture," so that, after it, "things are no longer the same."

38 Even in *Touch of Evil,* one cannot avoid the impression that, when the straight Var-
gas (Charlton Heston) successfully entraps the corrupted Quinlan (Orson Welles),
he somehow betrayed him.

39 It is well known that a thwarted (disavowed) homosexual libidinal economy forms
the basis of military community—it is for that very reason that the Army opposes so
adamantly the admission of gays in its ranks. Mutatis mutandis, Rand's ridiculously
exaggerated adoration of strong male figures betrays the underlying disavowed lesbian economy, that is, the fact that Dominique and Roark, or Dagny and Galt, are
effectively *lesbian couples.*

PART II | **cogito's body**

4

The Case of

Polyphemus,

or, a Monster

Alain Grosrichard | **and Its Mother**

. . . it is difficult to understand how only seeing or imagining an object could cause a disturbance as great as the one we see in the written account that Monsieur Le Duc, Master Surgeon in Paris and one of the most experienced in deliveries, gave me of a most singular monster:

On the 25th of September 1696, I was summoned between one and two o'clock in the morning to care for a woman suffering pains from a difficult delivery. Having done what the profession requires on these occasions, I happily delivered a small full-term baby girl with a well-proportioned body, except for the face, where one could see the following deformities. First of all, there was in the middle of the face, above the upper jaw, one eye the size of a calf's, in which one could distinguish two lenses through the cornea and, beyond, two pupils joined side by side. This eye was in a socket, surrounded by a fleshy rim or border, which could be said to replace the eyelid, as it had lashes set in the extreme interior of its circumference. About half a finger above it one could see, to the right and left, thin flat semi-circular eyebrows, and between them, in the place of a nose, a protuberance more than an inch long, straight and thick as one's little finger. One could feel that it was composed of a narrow cartilage covered with fleshy skin, similar to that of the nostrils. It was pierced at its extremity, and when one inserted a stylette into the cavity, one could feel the cranium at the end; otherwise, it resembled a man's penis, as it had a kind of glans covered by something resembling a foreskin. I opened the head and found that the brains were more than three quarters full of hydropic fluid, which could account for the brief life of this child. I saw her move this one double eye, which shone with great vivacity, but after emitting a few sighs, she expired.

This head was exhibited to the Association of Surgeons, and Monsieur Le Duc *fils,* also Master Surgeon and present at this birth, out of curiosity keeps a portrait of it produced by an adept painter when the head was still fresh. . . .[1]

The extraordinary constitutes the ordinary in Claude Brunet. Author of a *Traité de la superfétation* (1696), he is best known for his *Journal de la médecine,* which in 1686 succeeded the journal of the Abbé de la Roque, and in 1697 became *Le Progrès de la médecine, contenant un recueil de tout ce qui s'observe d'utile à la pratique.*

The text published above is only one example of what one might find in this type of semiperiodical publication; the strangeness of the poorly researched cases, generally known only secondhand, serves almost always as a pretext for hasty and wild digressions resulting in a series of baroque and defective theorizations. Seen in this light, Brunet's text is nothing more than a historical curiosity, too familiar to a reader of Bachelard and Canguilhem to be remembered for long.

This would not be the case for a reader versed in psychoanalytic theory, who will easily find material there for interpretation. That is, if he can detach himself from the fascination of this hybrid figure, where the Cyclops and the Unicorn combine their emblems to form an obscene avatar of the Medusa's head—because it is Medusa who is being revealed to him in the silent call-to-attention of this child-monster. Monster? Only in that it reveals in an exemplary fashion to every mother the truth of her child and the reality of her desire. "I saw her move this one double eye, which shone with great vivacity, but after emitting a few sighs, she expired." As impossible existence and as a fleeting glimpse of the real, she dies from having said the whole truth.

It is difficult to resist the temptation to make monsters speak; for a long time, they were created for that very purpose. They provoked interpretation before eliciting an explanation. As divine sign of an impending threat or punishment, the monster delivered a truth from elsewhere. As objects of study and experiments, the truth with which we illuminate them transports us elsewhere. But whether the monster delivers the truth to us or receives it from us, only the direction of flow changes. Truth always passes through the monster.

The observations of Brunet are precisely from such a period when the truth of monsters was changing direction. In 1703 Fontenelle writes, "Philosophers are convinced that Nature does not play games, and that all her creations are equally serious. There can be extraordinary creations, but not irregular ones, and it is often the most extraordinary ones which most open up access to the discovery of the general rules which they all follow."[2] An opening that is no longer the mouth of truth but a passage leading to it.

Fontenelle, permanent Secretary of the Academy of the Sciences, was not thinking of Brunet when writing these lines. He was engaging in a debate that would soon see the participation of renowned anatomists armed with all their scientific authority. These included Littre, Duverney, and Winslow and Lémery, who were the Horatius and Curiatius of the nascent science of teratology. For someone like Brunet, Fontenelle writes "l'Histoire de la dent d'or," which is still relevant for those naive and credulous readers who even today might be tempted to take his monster seriously and make it speak.

For in claiming to explain it, Brunet makes his monster speak; he refuses to adhere to a mechanical determinism and therefore sees this extraordinary effect to be an effect of meaning. He thinks he can perceive there, as Freud did in the joke, the admission of a desire.

Against the theory of these "physicians" who "are beginning to say that these bizarre tendencies were already present in the egg, and that they are merely the result of unusual rearrangements occurring in the first stages of the embryo, for which neither the imagination nor that which provoked it has any part," Brunet argues that only the effects of the mother's imagination on her fetus can help us understand a monstrous birth of this kind.[3] This is a timeless belief, fostered since antiquity by fantastic examples that were then carefully collected in the Renaissance by compilers such as Martin Weinrich (*De ortu monstrorum commentarius* [1595]) or Johannes Georg Schenk (*Monstrorum historia memorabilis* [1609]). It circulates within doctrines, espouses them, saves them, or brings them to ruin, depending on the period and the author. It plays upon correspondences and resemblances, mobilizes the doctrine of the four causes, and animates the dialectic of the Same and the Other, which haunts all questions relating to reproduction, bathing a form of love sickness (*maladie d'amour*) in a tragic half-light.

We will try elsewhere to write the history of these beliefs in the role of the maternal imagination. We will then hear a grotesque cohort of child-monsters answering the ancient question that lurks behind their parents' desire for knowledge: "Where do children come from?" Here I have chosen to study one text, which seems notable to me both because of the incontestable scientific prestige granted at the time to its author and the influence he had for a long time, and in the most diverse branches of human knowledge, and because of the central position held by the question of the maternal imagination in its system. It is a chapter from *The Search after Truth* by Nicolas Malebranche, orator and member of the Royal Academy of the Sciences from 1699 on.

Let us abandon Claude Brunet for a moment to the oblivion from which we have prematurely removed him. We will bring him out again later so that he can make Malebranche say what the Christian philosopher could not or would not say completely. We will then see what is really at stake in this question of the maternal imagination, where the historian and the psychoanalyst will meet, beyond the self-assured positivism of the one and the interpretive pathos of the other.

We will assume that the reader knows the Malebranchian doctrine of the imagination, which book 2 of *The Search after Truth* explains to be the "second cause of error," after the senses. "[W]ith regard to what occurs in the body, the senses and the imagination differ only in degree."[4] To imagine is therefore only a weak form of sensing and of representing an object as absent. But one can imagine vividly, and believe to sense what is not there. If the explanatory principle is a strict mechanism inspired by Descartes, the privileged metaphor is one of imprinting or engraving, which acknowledges that two senses—sight and touch—were predominant in classical theories of representation. Therefore one will imagine more vividly or more feebly based on how forceful the burin is ("the animal spirits"), and how resistant the plaque is (the "sensorium," whose precise place in the brain is open to discussion but not its existence). "[T]he greater and more distinct the traces of the animal spirits, which are the strokes of these images, the more strongly and distinctly the soul will imagine these objects. Now, just as the breadth, depth, and clarity of the strokes of an engraving depend upon the pressure applied to the burin, and the pliancy of the copper, so the depth and clarity of the traces in the imagination depend upon the pressure of the animal spirits, and upon the constitution of the brain fibers. And it is the variety found in these two things that constitutes nearly all the great diversity observed among minds" (*ST*, 89).

The strength of the animal spirits is a function of food, drink, and the quality of the air we breathe. Because the body is a sympathetic system of organs, the strength of the animal spirits also varies with the heat of the heart, the shrinking of the liver (which produces yellow bile, exciting maniacal impulses), or of the spleen (which secretes cold, black bile, responsible for melancholy), and, of course, with the humor of the uterus.

As for the brain fibers, which form the sensorium, their resistance or flexibility varies according to age (they are "soft, flexible and delicate" in infancy. "With age they become drier, harder, and stronger. But in old age they are completely inflexible" [*ST*, 110]) and, as we will see later, to gender.

By varying these two elements (the animal spirits and the sensorium) only within the register of the body, a whole typology of different minds can be constructed, which could be used for both a universal taxonomy of character types and a psychopathology.

Is this simply a development of Cartesianism? Yes, but based on metaphysical principles opposed to Descartes's, because one can only build "psychology" on a wholly mechanistic base by renouncing the Cartesian notion of the reciprocal action of the soul and the body: every idea (image) corresponds to an imprint, and vice versa. But this correspondence is explained in Malebranche by a parallelism established by God between thought and extension (*l'étendue*), which makes changes in one the *occasion*, but never the *cause*, of changes in the other. The idea (image) in the mind does not cause the traces left in the brain, and inversely, "it is inconceivable that the mind receive anything from the body and become more enlightened by turning toward it, as these philosophers claim who would have it that it is by *transformation* to fantasms, or brain traces, *per conversionem ad phantasmata*, that the mind perceives all things" (*ST*, 102; original emphasis).

This vertical and reciprocal connection between ideas and traces, which is necessary and yet arbitrary (whether referring to the "natural" connections established by God or to the connections brought about by education), is integrated into a theory of the sign expressed in Arnauld's *Logique de Port-Royal*. Here the sign is not considered an instrument of thought, but its very *element*. To imagine is to think, not *through* the sign, but first and foremost *in* the sign.

Another connection must be added to this one: the "horizontal" connection of traces to each other. "[T]he brain traces are so well tied to one another that none can be aroused without all those which were imprinted at the same time being aroused" (*ST*, 105). Through this "syntax" of traces, which relates back to a simultaneity of impressions, we can account for memory, habits, and instinct, which are only aspects of the imagination. But above all, Malebranche sees in the signifying substitution and sliding that this syntax permits, "the basis for all rhetorical figures," since, for example, "when we do not recall the principal name of a thing (or a person), we designate it sufficiently by using a name that signifies some property or circumstance of that thing (or person)" (*ST*, 105; translation modified).

Structured like a language, as it was understood at the time, the imagination has all the same powers and surprising effects. Going even further, metaphor and metonymy are primarily the rhetorical games of this originary language, of which the other language is merely an annex and a copy. That the second language permits the philosopher, through the application of method, to discipline the first—or rather to neutralize it with the artifice of algebraic symbolism—does not mean that it is not attached to it. Beneath the illusory transparency of words, it is in and through the language of the imagination that we communicate. As the originary language, this is what unites man, weaving together those "invisible and natural ties" established by God to supplement those of charity that have been broken by sin. "[B]ut we do not notice it. We allow ourselves to be guided without considering what guides us or how it guides us" (*ST*, 113). We do not think about it, because along with the imagination, here it is the body that leads us, and we do not know what the body can do: "we feel the motions produced in us without considering their sources" (*ST*, 113). As for knowing how it leads us, and by which ties it subjects us to each other, it is precisely this that the Malebranchian theory of imitation and compassion attempts to explain.

"[It is] necessary that children believe their parents, pupils their teachers, and inferiors those above them" (*ST*, 113). Imitation, by rendering relations of dependence necessary, makes civil society possible: "These natural ties we share with beasts consist in a certain disposition of the brain all men have to imitate those with whom they converse, to form the same judgments they make, and to share the same passions by which they are moved" (*ST*, 161). In other words, every conversation tends to take the form of a conversion, and what we consider to be a communication between souls or between equals through the neutral intermediary of language, is really a communication between *bodies*, where one body, having captivated the other, always ends up by assimilating it.

Along with the initial engraving metaphor (burin and copper plate), we must therefore add another: the body as mirror, which is *imitation*. Combining the two gives us the body as a registering and sensitive mirror, and we end up with the metaphor for *compassion*: "Thus, it is necessary to know that not only are the animal spirits borne naturally into the parts of our bodies in order to perform the same actions, and the same movements that we see others perform, but also for the purpose of suffering their injuries in some way and to share in their miseries. For experience teaches us that when we carefully attend to a man someone has rudely struck, or who has a serious wound, the spirits are forcefully borne into the parts of our bodies that correspond to those we see wounded in another" (*ST*, 114).

This "sympathy," in the strong sense, varies of course with the type of imagination, that is, with the vivacity of the animal spirits and the fragility of the fibers of the brain: "sensitive people with a vivid imagination and very soft and tender flesh" will be more affected than those who are "full of strength and vigor" (*ST*, 114). Thus, "[women] and children . . . suffer much pain from the wounds they see others receive. They mechanically have much more compassion for the miserable, and they cannot see even a beast beaten or hear it cry without some disturbance of mind" (*ST*, 115; translation modified).

"Mechanically," it is worth repeating, because this compassion is not a virtue of the soul but a mechanism of the body. No doubt compassion corresponds to that in the mind that is called "pity," which is nothing but "compassion in the mind" and is explained in the same manner as compassion in the body: "It excites us to help others because in so doing we help ourselves" (*ST*, 114). To see someone being beaten is unbearable because it is like being beaten. To kill is "[to be] wounded by the counterblow of compassion" (*ST*, 114). Every aggression is in itself its own reprisal. Ultimately, there are no longer torturers or victims, active or passive, and one should not say "*I* beat" or "*I* am beaten," but rather, a man, a woman, a child, or an animal "is being beaten." The impersonal and the reflexive, which are the mode and means of Freudian fantasy, are also those of Malebranchian compassion.[5] Producing the same effects as charity but by an inverse route, compassion thus ironically (or with a terrible literalness) honors the biblical maxim "love your neighbor as you love yourself." In this it still bears witness to God, who through it constructs as a universal law of physical nature what can only be a futile and nostalgic maxim of reason after original sin.

Imitation and compassion work, therefore, to make one Body from the fragmented body of Adam's descendants. But this unity is only the simulacrum of the City of God (the "community of spirits") which is One for all eternity. The fragile *unanimity* of the earthly city ("the society of commerce") is only based on a *consensus* of bodies that are sympathetic when under attack, and where the differences—the stigma of sin—are resolved into an identity only by way of an identification with the body of the Master.

This is why power belongs always to "strong imaginations," imaginations that can penetrate those of others (with "vivid" imaginations) and imprint their traits upon them. The Master is he who turns others into his mirrors and transforms them into the very image in which, one and many, he is reflected. "The contagious communication of strong imaginations," writes Malebranche (*ST*, 161). The entire third part of the second book of *The Search after Truth* addresses only this theme in a series of variations. One can read in them the portrait of a hierarchical society where power is seized (as Louis XIV knew) by playing imaginary identities. This is a world where the smallest crime is always *lèse-majesté* to a degree, *lèse-majesté* itself is a crime against each and every one, and where torture is public, as Michel Foucault reminds us,[6] and the Malebranchian doctrine of the imagination explains (in its own way). But one must also see there a general theory of power, conceived as the result of a hand-to-hand struggle.

Consequently, for example, rhetoric is only elevated when it touches the body, as the cases of Tertullian, Seneca, and Montaigne prove. It is only then that words "are obeyed without being understood, and we yield to their orders without knowing them" (*ST*, 173). They are like icy projectiles that thought melts "when we wish to know precisely what we believe or want to believe; when we approach, so to speak, these phantoms in order to scrutinize them, they often vanish into smoke with all their display and luster" (*ST*, 173). We believe what the orator, "visionary," prince, or father says only because we believe in them, and we believe in them only because as listener, zealot, courtier, or child, our body has already been seduced.

The body always precedes us; it has already made its allegiance when it occurs to us to recognize in the other our Master: "It sometimes happens that unknown people, who have no reputation, and for whom we were not biased by any esteem, have such strength of imagination and as a result such vivid and affective expressions that they persuade us without our knowing either why or even precisely of what we are persuaded. It is true that this seems quite extraordinary, but nonetheless there is nothing more common" (*ST*, 171). Mechanistic psychology here clarifies and establishes the Law. When the jurists elaborated the fateful notion of "abduction by consent" (*rapt de séduction*) after the Council of Trent as a complement to "abduction by force" (*rapt de violence*) in order to invalidate love marriages entered into without the consent of the father, they were not so far off the mark in their claim that they were defending liberty. And if these notions were followed in Malebranche's time and later, it was because there were new reasons to think these men had judged correctly: marriage for love, where the body has arranged everything ahead of time even more despotically than a father, is the least free of all.[7]

The force of imagination reaches its peak, however, when it flows through institutional channels; then, "there is nothing so bizarre or extravagant of which it cannot persuade people" (*ST*, 170). "If Alexander tosses his head, his courtiers toss theirs. If Dionysius the Tyrant applies himself to geometry upon the arrival of Plato in Syracuse, geometry then becomes fashionable, and the palace of this king, says Plutarch, is immediately filled with dust by so many people tracing figures. . . . It seems . . . that they are enchanted, and that a Circe transforms them into different men" (*ST*, 169). And one finds the paradigm for all types of power in this account of Diodorus of Sicily, who reports that "in Ethiopia the courtiers crippled and deformed themselves, amputated limbs, and even killed themselves to make themselves like their princes. It was . . . shameful to appear with two eyes and to walk erect in the train of a blind and crippled king" (*ST,* 170).

One finds in Malebranche a deep unease when faced with this despotic phenomenon, an unease that La Boétie had articulated earlier in a torrent of unanswerable questions.[8] This was the preoccupation, tinged with fascination, of the entire eighteenth century. In this manner, one may conclude (and this goes for Montesquieu as much as Rousseau) that what makes the social bond possible is the same as what destroys it: there is no power that does not also encompass its abuse. And before Rousseau, Malebranche implies that there is no "enlightened" despotism and that in every domain of society the master of the house (*maître du logis*) is always also the madman of the house—the imagination (*folle du logis*).[9] Because "those who have a strong and vigorous imagination" are, as such, "completely unreasonable" and "there are very few more general causes of man's errors than this dangerous communication of the imagination" (*ST,* 161).

How can one defend oneself then? There are, of course, some absurd techniques offered. For example, when faced with a tortured body, one should turn away the flow of the animal spirits going toward the part of our body that we see wounded in the other "by deliberately stimulating with some force, a part of the body other than that seen to be injured" (*ST,* 114). But we remain nonetheless subject to our bodies, determined as we are by the order of the imprints in the brain, which are in fact disorder and absence of reason.

The only way, apart from the extraordinary saving powers of grace, to escape this dangerous contagion and the traps of the discourse of the body, which lead us without our knowing, is to think without the body, to reach "the clear and evident ideas . . . of understanding or the pure mind" (*ST,* 195), this being the "mind's faculty of knowing external objects without forming corporeal images of them in the brain" (*ST,* 198). This is the path to salvation, which leads to the full light of the "vision through God." But the path is difficult since it supposes that men can tear themselves, in order to become the children of God, from what the order of things wishes them to be: the sons of their mothers, in whose womb—whether that of a saint or a prostitute—they are irrevocably marked with the damning seal of the imagination.

"About seven or eight years ago, I saw at the Incurables a young man who was born mad, and whose body was broken in the same places in which those of criminals are broken. He had remained nearly twenty years in this state. Many persons saw him, and the late queen mother, upon visiting the hospital, was curious to see and even to touch the arms and legs of this young man where they were broken" (*ST*, 115). The facts are explained in this manner: "the cause of this disastrous accident was that his mother, having known that a criminal was to be broken, went to see the execution. All the blows given to this miserable creature forcefully struck the imagination of this mother and, by a sort of counterblow, the tender and delicate brain of her child," where it produced destruction great enough that he lost his mind forever. (*ST*, 115). Furthermore, "[a]t the sight of this execution, so capable of frightening a woman, the violent flow of the mother's animal spirits passed very forcefully from her brain to all the parts of her body corresponding to those of the criminal, and the same thing happened in the child" (*ST*, 115). But in the places where the mother felt perhaps only a shudder, the body of the child, infinitely more delicate, was broken.

Like the case of the Ethiopians who mutilated themselves to resemble their one-eyed or lame king, this famous case of the boy who was born mad and broken illustrates Malebranche's analyses of imitation and compassion. This is not surprising, in that "[v]ery common examples of this communication of the imagination are found in children with regard to their fathers (and still more in daughters with regard to their mothers)," since the relation of dependence here is a fact of nature (*ST*, 167). "A young boy walks, talks, and makes the same gestures as his father. A little girl dresses like her mother, walks like her, and speaks as she does; if the mother lisps, so does the daughter; if the mother has some unusual motion of the head, the daughter adopts it. In short, children imitate their parents in everything, in their defects and their affectations, as well as in their errors and vices" (*ST*, 168).

But the parent-child relation is more than just an example, since all the others develop from it. This explains the stake of the question of education for all sociopolitical relations. Malebranche treats the subject at length, and we know the great interest this subject held for the eighteenth century, which did not separate it from the question of despotism. This constituting relation, however, is itself constituted from before birth in the maternal womb: "Infants in their mothers' womb, whose bodies are not yet fully formed and who are, by themselves, in the most extreme state of weakness and need that can be conceived, must also be united with their mother in the closest imaginable way. And although their soul be separated from their mother's, their body is not at all detached from hers, and we should therefore conclude that they have the same sensations and passions, i.e., that exactly the same thoughts are excited in their souls upon the occasion of the motions produced in her body" (*ST,* 112).

This is precisely what a close examination of the case cited by Brunet implies that we should believe, as will be confirmed by several others later on. Anticipating the writings of Fontenelle, for whom studying monsters would "most open up access to the discovery of the general rules" that all of nature's works follow, Malebranche sees in his explanation of monstrous births "the principles of an infinity of things ordinarily thought to be very difficult and very complex" (*ST,* 115). The examples become proof for the suppositions that they illustrate. Hypotheses at the outset, imitation and compassion become theoretical principles founded on experimentation, as does the direct communication of the mother with her fetus. To the reproach that he is merely "guessing," Malebranche responds emphatically: "I have given a sufficient demonstration of this communication through the use I make of it to explain the generation of monsters. . . . Thus, I am not making any guesses about this because I do not venture to give any precise indication of the nature of this communication. I even believe that the means by which this occurs will always elude the skills of the cleverest anatomists. I might say that it happens through the roots that the foetus grows into the womb of the mother and through the nerves with which this part of the mother seems to be replete. And in doing so, I would be guessing no more than a man who, never having seen the machines of the Samaritan pump, would assert that there are wheels and pumps for raising the water." [10] Hypotheses, experimentation, return to the hypotheses that then become theoretical principles, consequences, and generalizations; one sees here a discourse that insists on its conformity with the requirements of the new experimental science of living things. [11] The significant alterations made to chapter 7 of the first part of book 2, between the first (1674) and second (1675) editions of *The Search after Truth,* attest to the desire to turn what was at first only an illustration into a proof of the power of the imagination.

But if Malebranche has such a strong desire to prove his concept of the maternal imagination, it is because his entire system depends on it. As the radical origin of all social bonds, it ultimately accounts for the nature of power and its perversions, and as such, the communication of the mother to her fetus occupies a decisive position in the political problematic. It is also a crucial piece of the theory of generation, and, finally, it makes possible a "rational" solution to the question of the transmission of original sin. The political, the biological, and the theological are thus all based and intertwined in it. And the orator, the member of the French Academy, and the subject of the King of France will all keep a unified front in order to maintain it.

It would require a long historical detour to fully understand the role of the maternal imagination in Malebranche's theory of generation. Suffice it to say that this theory, which reigns supreme in the first third of the eighteenth century, systematically brings together and combines three theses that had hitherto been separate:

(1) *Ovism* ("omne vivum ex ovo"): Every living being comes from an egg, enclosed in the ovaries (or the testicles, according to a widespread analogy from the period) of all females, including mammals.

(2) *Preformation:* Living things are already completely formed within these eggs. Mechanical laws by themselves can explain their development, but they cannot account for their formation or their structure, as Harvey's and Descartes's theories of epigenesis had argued.

(3) *The encasement of seeds:* Eggs are encased one in the other, ad infinitum, from the first day of Creation. The first female of each species carried in her all her descendants (male and female).

As fanciful as it may seem, this theory pretends to be based on anatomical observations (the discovery, among other things, of eggs—which were in fact only ovarian vesicles—in the ovaries of mammals by Régnier de Graaf), microscopic observations (by Swammerdam, Kerkring, and Malebranche himself), and on the physico-mathematical principle of the infinite divisibility of "extension," which is to say, in a Cartesian world, of matter itself.[12]

Malebranche undoubtedly reduces the problem of generation to one of reproduction, which he then resolves ultimately by eliminating it, since, according to the general rules of mechanism, the reproduction of living things is nothing more than development of preformed organisms. But in this manner he does salvage Cartesian mechanism, which Descartes himself had realized hinged on the question of generation and yet never resolved, despite repeated efforts.[13]

The preexistence and the encasement ad infinitum of eggs explain the fact that a specific living being always reproduces another of the same type. But how then do we account for individual differences? As multiple copies of a unique essence, people should be indistinguishable except for their position in time and space. How can we explain then that the identity of the species is only experienced in the form of resemblance—which may be taken as far as identification—and the individuality of the species in the form of difference—which may be taken as far as monstrosity?

Malebranche answers: "by means of the effects of the maternal imagination." This is what allows us to understand the concepts of resemblance (parents-children) and difference among people at the same time, since it is the maternal imagination that makes the originally identical figure within the egg different by assimilating it. And one must not think that this correspondence between mother and fetus "is a useless thing, or an ordained evil in nature" (*ST,* 117). "I do not deny that God could have disposed all things necessary for the propagation of the species throughout the infinite ages in a manner so precise and regular that mothers would never abort, but would always give birth to children of the same size and color or, in a word, so similar they would be taken for one another, without this communication of which we have just spoken" (*ST,* 118). But the world would have been less perfect, because perfection consists in producing the largest number of effects from the smallest means. Furthermore, the fact that God "had a plan to produce an admirable work by the simplest means, and to link all His creatures with one another" made this communication necessary (*ST,* 118). This principle of differentiation, which makes the world richer and more varied, is also a principle of union. It makes the child resemble its mother and at the same time permits it a first attempt at adapting to its social world. Having seen, felt, feared everything that its mother has seen, felt, and feared, the newborn will instinctually know what it must do or avoid in order to survive. Birth is a catastrophe, whose effects chapter 8 of *The*

Search after Truth describes in the darkest terms. But how much worse would it be if the mother's imagination had not "already accustomed their children somewhat to the impressions of objects," thus keeping men "from being mad from birth" (*ST*, 126).

This does not negate the fact that it is in fact this imagination that sometimes makes them so. The maternal imagination is only orthopedic at the risk of being teratogenic. Not that God intended to create monsters; he did not desire their existence, but rather foresaw it. And though the "simplicity of means" renders them foreseeable, it does not make them inevitable. That is the result of the dissoluteness of the imagination of mothers, the fruit of original sin.

In a theory of reproduction conceived as the repetition of a type, the action of the maternal imagination is the only entity that strictly speaking *engenders*, or produces something new. What is engendered, though, is not a new being, but an aspect of *semblance*—the basis for all resemblance and difference—in a being as old as the world and created by the hands of God. One engenders only in and through the imagination. The real repeats itself.

As a being of semblance, the monster is however not a semblance of being. As a being, what it communicates to us is the admirable simplicity of the means of creation. To the savant, it is an argument for theodicy. But as a semblance, it accuses and problematizes the mother, unveiling her nature as a woman and as a sinner.

The mother is a woman, which means first of all that she has a "vivid" (i.e., weak) imagination. Imagining vividly is a characteristic of women: "Everything abstract is incomprehensible to them. . . . They consider only the surface of things, and their imagination has insufficient strength and insight to pierce it to the heart, comparing all the parts, without being distracted. A trifle is enough to distract them, the slightest cry frightens them, the least motion fascinates them. Finally, the style and not the reality of things suffices to occupy their minds to capacity because insignificant things produce great motions in the delicate fibers of their brains" (*ST*, 130).

With her "vivid imagination," woman is essentially imitative and compassionate. Like the child, she is a being of semblance. She defines herself only in relation to an other who makes an impression on her: the complete man. Heir to the entire Western philosophical tradition,

Malebranche implies that Woman does not "ex-sist" as such. Infinitely and unpredictably malleable, a woman is never identical to herself. Her mode of being is multiplicity. Like Plato's sophist, whose alterity is his only identity, *there is no concept for woman.*

But also, with her vivid imagination (like that of the child), a woman does not think, desire, or love except as determined by the marks imprinted on her brain. This is why she cannot reach Truth, or the ideas of pure reason, which are independent of bodily traces. If she turns toward God, she will only know him through images, or rather she will only worship metaphors: *she has no access to the concept.* In brief, like the child, she eludes concepts in the same way that concepts elude her.

"Suffice it to say of women and children that . . . they are not involved in seeking truth and teaching others" (*ST*, 131). It is here, of course, that Malebranche is mistaken. The pregnant woman has at once a weak imagination in relation to what surrounds her, and a strong one in relation to her fetus, so that the child, if it makes itself resemble the mother, will make itself resemble her resemblance. It imitates its mother in what she herself imitates, and empathizes with that with which she empathizes. The case of the child born mad and broken serves as an illustration.

Here is another, also "witnessed," which will take us even further:

> It has not been more than a year since a woman, having attended too carefully to the portrait of Saint Pius on the feast of his canonization, gave birth to a child who looked exactly like the representation of the saint. He had the face of an old man, as far as is possible for a beardless child; his arms were crossed upon his chest, with his eyes turned towards the heavens; and he had very little forehead, because the image of the saint being raised towards the vault of the church, gazing toward heaven, had almost no forehead. He had a kind of inverted miter on his shoulders, with many round marks in the places where miters are covered with gems. In short, this child strongly resembles the tableau after which its mother had formed it by the power of her imagination. This is something that all Paris has been able to see as well as me, because the body was preserved for a considerable time in alcohol. (*ST*, 116)

In this case, it is the mere view of a painting that moves the spirits of the mother, and brings about an outline of imitation. (We can set aside the aesthetic theory that supports this explanation, and that states that the effect of representation, which is itself an imitation, is to make the spectator imitate it.) What the child imitates is what the eye perceives and that which is impressed on the brain of the mother, in other words, a flat representation that creates the effect of relief, distance, and depth through the artifice of perspective. A "natural judgment," combined with experience, is what allows us as adults not to be fooled by paintings. We associate visual images with the ideas of tangibility with which they are naturally associated. But the child is fooled; not only does it see what its mother sees, and not what she knows she is seeing, but its body is transformed into what she sees. The representation of the saint is foreshortened by the perspective, and so we understand why the child has "very little forehead." In terms of geometrical optics, one would say that rather than metamorphose, the child "*anamorphoses.*"

Furthermore, bearing in mind that the classical theory of representation proceeds by means of a theory of signs, and the theory of perception by means of figures of rhetoric, we can follow Leibniz when he writes: "When a painting deceives us there is a double error in our judgments; for in the first place we substitute the cause for the effect, and think we are seeing immediately that which is the cause of the image, rather like a dog who barks at a mirror. . . . In the second place, we are mistaken in substituting one cause for another, and thinking that what only comes from a flat painting is derived from a body; so that in this case there is in our judgments at the same time both a metonymy and a metaphor; for the very figures of rhetoric become sophisms when they impose upon us." [14]

As innocent victim of this sophistry of the imagination (and is sophistry anything else but that?), the child, by making himself "identical to the image which he saw," has been taken in by literality, or by the pure signifier that is the visible image. Anamorphosed, we can say that he has identified through his entire body with an imaginary signifier.

There remains one last step: from the first case to the second, we go from a real scene to a represented one. The first means to excite horror, and the second devotion, but the effect produced on the child remains the same: seeing what its mother sees, it identifies with what she sees. But "[t]here are many other examples of the power of a mother's imagination in the literature, and there is nothing so bizarre that it has not been aborted at some point. For not only do they give birth to deformed infants but also fruits they have wanted to eat, such as apples, pears, grapes, and other similar things" (*ST*, 117).

These are all effects of pure imagination, because the cause is not in the objects seen but in the simple marks imprinted in the brain of the mother. In other words, they are effects of objects of desire. If these traces are brought forth by an active circulation of the animal spirits of the mother (due to a modification in the equilibrium of the brain's interior), they will be imprinted in the brain of the child. Going even further, "the flow of spirits excited by the image of the desired fruit, expanding rapidly in a tiny body, is capable of changing its shape because of its softness. These unfortunate infants thus become like the things they desire too ardently" (*ST*, 117).

Desiring as its mother desires, the child desires what she desires, and by identifying itself with the signifier that is the cause and object of the desire of the mother, the child comes to offer itself to itself as the cause and object of its own desire. But if the gift of love taken to the extreme can meet and even be confused with absolute self-love, it can do so only in the absurd absolute that is death.

A living thing, impossible because it has become the same as what it sees in the gaze of the Other, or as what it desires in the desire of the Other—so appears the monster, at least as explained by the effect of the maternal imagination. But this is also true of the madman, if we loosely define madness as "identification without meditation." The principle of parallelism forces Malebranche to think of the possibility of physical monstrosity and of madness as belonging together, as he does in paragraph 4 of chapter 7. Even if the monster is a madman in both soul and body, one must not however assume that madness is to monstrosity what the mind is to the body, but rather what the brain is to the entire body. The madman loses his mind because he carries in his head the mark of the maternal imagination and desire, without having the ability to withstand them. The monster dies from having become, with its entire body, not the base and the subject of the mark, but the mark itself.

So we have here, mutatis mutandis, a tragic version of Descartes's vertiginous metaphor in the "Third Meditation," where he attempts to illustrate the way in which man—as an immortal soul, granted a will and reason—is made "in the image of God." The *idea* of an infinite God "placed . . . in me" when I was created, is "like the mark of the crafts-man stamped on his work, not that the mark need be anything distinct from the work itself. But the mere fact that God created me is a very strong basis for believing that I am somehow made in his image and likeness, and that I perceive that likeness, which includes the idea of God, by the same faculty which enable me to perceive myself" and by which also "I understand that I am a thing which is incomplete and de-pendent on another and which aspires without limit to even greater and better things."[15]

But what is a mark that is not distinct from the subject itself? "Are you yourself both the mark which is stamped and the subject on which it is stamped?" objects Gassendi as a good Epicurean. "What is the form of this mark, and how is the stamping carried out?"[16]

To which Descartes responds by slipping from one metaphor into another; we resemble God as a painting resembles the painter. "Sup-pose there is a painting in which I observe so much skill that I judge that it could only have been painted by Apelles, and I say that the in-imitable technique is like a kind of mark which Apelles stamped on all his pictures to distinguish them from others. The question you raise is like asking, in this case, 'What is the form of this mark, and how is the stamping carried out?' "[17]

But a painting also resembles its model. Does saying that we are "in the image of God," not mean that God is "like a man"?[18] That would be to misunderstand, responds Descartes, that "it is not in the nature of an image to be identical in all respects with the things of which it is an image, but merely to imitate it in some respects" or in some traits.[19] It is as if, in order to deny that Apelles had made portraits resembling Alexander, one were to say "that this would mean that Alexander was like a picture, and yet pictures are made of wood and paint, and not of flesh and bones like Alexander."[20]

Therefore we resemble God in two different ways at once, just as a painting resembles both the painter and its model. It must be added that, in the case of the human soul, the painting would be a kind of self-portrait that, having the faculty of self-reflection, could recognize the perfections of the painter and the model blended together, at the same time that it recognized itself as a portrait.

One could spend much time analyzing this pictorial metaphor, in which are combined several of the important themes of classical ideas of representation. Let us simply retain this, which leads us back to Malebranche: the two types of resemblance which the metaphor introduces vary in inverse relation to each other. Suppose that the painting imitates the model too closely: the resemblance to the painter will diminish. If, instead, this latter resemblance dominates, then the quality of the image-copy will diminish. In short, by taking either aspect (model, painter) to the extreme, either the image or the style ("cachet") will be privileged, without one ever being able to completely negate the other, since in that case there would be no real image or style as such. One would go from the (almost) anonymous realism of an identical copy, to the fantastical expressionism of a work of (almost) pure fiction, two extremes that the canon of classical painting rejects as aesthetically nonviable. A successful painting is one in which the two resemblances are balanced.

And this balance between two resemblances is required, according to Malebranche, for a child to be born healthy of body and spirit, because a child is always both an image and a style, imprinted on the egg that has been the white canvas since Creation. The child who is born broken and mad, or the Saint Pius child, are cases of image prevailing over style. The pear- or apple-child, or more generally the miscarried child with the most bizarre deformities, is style prevailing over image. For Descartes, for whom God, who possesses all perfections, is simultaneously painter and model, the painting (the soul) is necessarily perfect, or as much as possible given its finitude. According to Malebranche, for whom the mother plays the role for the body of a painter who has not mastered her art (a kind of evil genius), the extraordinary thing is not that monsters are born but rather that there are so few of them. It is true, he says, that they are disposed of, like bad paintings, as soon as they are produced. It is also true that if observed closely, many children carry marks (desires) on their bodies, or otherwise display, by some strangeness of the mind (like James I of England, who could not stand the sight of a drawn sword), the irregularities of the imagination of their mothers. The question remains, however: if the power of the imagination (*folle du logis*) is so strong, how is it that it does not cause more destruction?

To pose this question is to interrogate Malebranche on a subject about which he remains curiously silent. Among the objections made to his theory of reproduction, this one returns again and again: if one can explain the resemblance between mother and child by the maternal imagination, how can one explain the fact that a child *also* resembles its father? But if Malebranche does not touch upon this, it is because the answer is taken for granted, and because what is problematic is that the child should resemble its mother. The eyes of the mother most frequently encounter the body of her husband, whose strong imagination cannot fail to impress the vivid imagination of his wife. This assumes that the husband is a man worthy of the name, that he has a strong imagination, or at least that his wife's is weaker than his, in brief, that she remains a woman. However, as light imprints often repeated produce the same effect as a single strong imprint, regular cohabitation suffices to correct the effects of a weak paternal imagination or of a strong maternal imagination—conditions that the early eighteenth century sees as becoming increasingly widespread. This period begins to preoccupy itself with a degeneration for which the confusion of the sexes is seen as both cause and effect.

This last remark calls for two additional comments: first, that a child resembles its two parents through the effects of the maternal imagination, which permits a double imitation or identification; but this identification is not the same in both cases. The child identifies with its mother, in that it feels, sees, and desires *as* she does; she marks the child with her style. The identification with the father, on the contrary, is an identification with *that which* the mother feels, sees, and desires. The child, in its mother's womb, identifies with the representation of its father in its mother's imagination.

This identification with the representation of the father is necessary. Through it, the unregulated imagination of the mother can to a certain extent be disciplined, which saves the child from the monstrous avatars to which it would be condemned by the unchecked caprices of maternal desire. This identification must not be taken to the extreme however, again at the risk of monstrosity. The child should become not a copy, but an image of its father, or in Descartes's definition, a representation that takes from its model only a few characteristic *traits*. So the child runs the risk of monstrosity or madness both if the father does not play his proper role in the original structuring language of the maternal imagination, and if his role is excessive.

Second, these demands refer back to an ethics of conjugal and domestic life, which assigns determined roles to husband and wife. This ethics is not yet a hygiene, as it will become toward the end of the eighteenth century, when the intimate life of the married couple will become caught in a tight network of medical, moralist, political, and economic discourses, which build upon the morality of the confessor without eliminating it. This is because in Malebranche's time a child is not yet what it shall become to a successful bourgeoisie, which fears less the corruption of the heart of its offsprings than their physical deformations, and for whom "orthopedics"—which shall become the rage in 1741 due to the work of the physician Nicolas Andryis—meant to produce not exemplary Christians but, rather, useful citizens and a serviceable work force. For Malebranche's contemporaries, a newborn, even a completely healthy one, is considered "abject" and "hated by God" because it is born in sin. And his contemporaries base the principles of their conjugal morality on authorities who are theological rather than medical, and Saint Augustine in particular, the great theoretician of original sin, whose book *De nuptiis et concupiscentia* was translated in 1680 by Jean Hamon as *Du mariage et de la concupiscence, pour les personnes mariées.*

This does not prevent the fact that when Malebranche writes that "as there are few women without some weakness, or who have not been disturbed by some passion during pregnancy, there must be very few children whose minds are not distorted in some way, and who are not dominated by some passion" (*ST*, 119), he may be thinking of the shortcoming that must be overcome to reach the City of God, but one can also understand this to apply to the earthly city. The effort of the technicians of salvation to retake control over the life of the married couple prepares the way for the later technicians of health, even if the norms that they impose are founded on different systems. This is why, in my view, we must not hesitate to give the improbable sounding doctrine of the maternal imagination all the weight that it carried during this period. It is in and through what was called the imagination—a corporeal faculty—that "power," whose rise since the seventeenth century Michel Foucault describes and analyzes and which penetrates and invests the body through disciplines, begins to be exercised. As we have seen, if the imagination is all-powerful, it is because it is the power of bodies upon bodies. That these powers are all rooted in that of the mother over her child, and from that of the husband over his wife, points out clearly the stakes of a discipline of the imagination and its privileged object: woman—because the ever-present dangers of the imagination (*folle du logis*) exist only because a woman is always more or less a madwoman (*folle au logis*). It is up to her husband to keep her under control by keeping her occupied with the sedative tasks of domestic life, and by turning her away from what could impress her imagination, like novels or the theater, and thus liberate her hysterical desire.

One could perhaps claim that Malebranche's rantings are those of a solitary philosopher, but this is not true. He proved what everyone *believed*. It suffices to read, for example, the many prayers of pregnant women, whether traditional, Jansenist, or reformed, to measure the intensity of the anxiety associated with pregnancy. It is not so much that they feared the pains of childbirth and its deadly effects, but rather that they did not know the nature of the being that they would bring to life. It is as if a woman alienated from her own desiring body as well as from the spectacle of the world were capable of anything: "My God, my Father, who by your power and providence have formed the child that I am carrying inside me, save me during my pregnancy from injuries and dangerous predicaments, and also from strange and extravagant thoughts which leave their deformed impressions on children . . . and if I am preserved while the child expires in the womb, give me grace that I may worship your judgments, full of equity, and that I may know that the child has completed its course early in order not to see this terrible century and to feel its soul sheltered presently in celestial glory."[21] A child who dies before birth, abandoned to God in its first form, and which simply testifies to the woman's incapacity to become a mother, is still preferable to a monster, like Brunet's, whose birth reveals that its mother is a woman by revealing all of her desire.

Whether Brunet read Malebranche or not, there is no doubt that the case that he describes and the explanation that he proposes are very close to what we have just read: "One must suppose that the pregnant woman was shocked to imagine herself vividly with such a protuberance attached to her forehead while trying to bring together her two eyes beneath it, either in a dream, or while conversing with her husband, or perhaps while looking closely at a representation of the feast of Priapus."[22] Brunet's monster is thus comparable to the second and last cases cited by Malebranche.

There is, however, something that is exemplary about this monster. It is a monster within a monster, since in it are juxtaposed the excess of style and the excess of image. That this little girl had identified herself with the gaze and the desire of a fascinated mother is demonstrated by this "one double eye" that is itself fascinating: style here turns into signature. As to the organ attached to her forehead, which is the effect of an excessive identification with the object of this gaze and desire, it is surely more than a mere image. It is as if the emblems of women and of man were found side by side on this serene visage. Of women: the essence to which finally these beings with vivid imaginations can be reduced—the gaze. Of man: what he has and she does not, and which, as the signifier of the difference between the sexes, is the most likely object to fascinate the gaze of woman and to mark her imagination—the phallus.

But it is not as an illustration, albeit exemplary, of Malebranche's theory that Brunet's monster holds our attention, because it does more than illustrate. It illuminates Malebranche, one could even say that it interprets him luminously, on the one point toward which lead all of the considerations of the future Member of the Academy: original sin. One could expect that theology would come into play in the writings of a man whose ambition was to, "as much as possible, put reason at the service of religion":[23] "But what I want to have especially well noticed is that there is every possible evidence that men retain in their brains even today traces and impressions of their first parents. For just as animals produce other animals that resemble them, with similar traces in their brains that are the reason why animals of the same species have the same sympathies and antipathies, and perform the same actions in the same circumstances, so our first parents after their sin received such great vestiges and such deep traces in the brain from the impressions of sensible objects that these could well have communicated them to their children. Accordingly, this great attachment we have since birth to all sensible things, and this great gulf between us and God in this state, could somehow be explained by what we have just said" (ST, 120).

All of his later texts confirm what is here only a probable hypothesis. Being born from a woman's womb, it is not possible for a child to be born without concupiscence—if concupiscence is defined as the "natural effort made by the brain traces to attach the mind to sensible things"— or to be born without original sin—if original sin is "the reign of concupiscence" and its victory (*ST*, 120). Concupiscence is indeed neither a depraved desire nor the desire for sinful objects; it is the determination of the mind by the order of the traces, whatever they may be. And this determination is the rule for all children, whoever the mother may be. This is easy to accept if the mother is careless of her own salvation and abandons herself to the concupiscence toward which her imagination naturally leads her. But it is also true of a mother who is righteous and pious. Because one of these two things must occur: either she will succeed, extraordinarily since she is a woman, in thinking of God through pure reason, and she will love an idea that as such can leave no mark on the brain of the fetus, and thus can have no saving effect on it. Or, like all women, she will think of God and love him only through an image, a metaphorical signifier, and it is only this image that shall be impressed on the brain of the fetus. "A mother, for example, who is excited to the love of God by the movement of spirits that accompanies the impression of the image of a venerable old man, because this mother has attached the idea of God to this impression of age . . . , this mother, I say, can only produce the trace of an old man in her child's brain, and a favorable attitude toward old men, which is not at all the love of God by which she was touched" (*ST*, 123).

Ultimately, it is the righteous woman who will lead her child most deeply into concupiscence, because her love of God is accompanied by the strongest passion, and it is this passion that the child will inherit: "the child she engenders, never having loved God with a voluntary love and its heart not having been turned toward God, it is clear that it is disordered and deranged, and that there is nothing in it not deserving the anger of God" (*ST*, 123).

It is then solely through the mother, in that she is a woman, that original sin is transmitted. And Malebranche insists: it is transmitted *in reality*, like a hereditary disease, and one must not say that newborns, not being responsible, are only sinners by the "imputation" of the sins of their parents. "The inclinations of children are *actually* corrupt [and] they are *actually* in a state of disorder" through their mothers.[24]

Every child is born guilty, which is to say that there is no innocent mother. The loveliest newborn, hated by God, is already an accusation of its mother. But through her, it accuses all women, and the first ever woman. In the *Elucidations* attached to *The Search after Truth*, Malebranche addresses this objection: "If Original Sin is transmitted because of the communication found between the brain of the mother and that of her child, it is the mother who is the cause of this sin and the father has nothing to do with it. Yet Saint Paul teaches us that it is through man that sin has entered into the world. He does not speak only about woman."[25] To which he responds, first with a contrasting text from Ecclesiasticus ("sin comes from woman and . . . it is through her that we are all subject to death"), and then by a sociolinguistic argument: "In speech, we never attribute to woman something in which she plays no role and which belongs to man only. But we often attribute to man something that belongs to woman, because the husband is her lord and master."[26] Also, because *man* is a generic term and because women do not form a separate species and are always simultaneously singular and plural, man will always come off well. One must therefore interpret Saint Paul, and since "what belongs to woman can be attributed to man, . . . if we were obliged through faith to excuse either man or woman, it would be more reasonable to excuse man."[27]

But this is not the true solution. The solution can be found in the original scene of Genesis, where the essence of both concupiscence and desire can be understood simultaneously, as can the reasons for their transmission through woman. We will not analyze the different versions that Malebranche proposes for the fall of our original parents.[28] Let us bear in mind only this: in paradise, their happiness and their innocence were characterized by the faculty of total mastery of their bodies. Not that they did not have the same senses, or did not feel, like us, pleasure and pain. But they could suspend at will the course of the animal spirits, which are the occasion of pleasure and pain in the mind, and could keep them from filling their brain with traces. In this manner their reason, within the limits of its finitude, took full pleasure in God. Eve is at the origin of sin when she gives in to the temptation to eat the forbidden fruit offered to her by the Evil one who says to her: "You shall be as Gods." The first step toward the fall is thus the pride of the woman who, substituting a fatal love for the pure love of God that fills her mind, becomes enamored of herself and of the idea of her own perfection. The punishment should have been, according to the decree, the immediate rebellion of her body, and her incapacity to control the movement of the animal spirits. However, "because her body belonged to her husband,

and because her husband was still in a state of innocence, she received no punishment through this body. This punishment was deferred until he himself had eaten of the fruit she gave him. It was then that they *both* felt the rebellion of their bodies." [29]

In this manner the "rebellion of the body" (which is to say, the rise to power of the imagination, and the reign of concupiscence) is both the punishment for *and* the sign of a rebellion against God that originates in Eve (and is then transmitted to Adam). One can understand then why a woman is fundamentally a creature of the imagination, and why "this wretched fecundity of begetting sinful children" falls to her. [30] We said before that every child is an accusation. The monster is even more so. And no doubt it is not by chance that the examples of monsters Malebranche offers in the third case are of fruit-children. Every monster in Malebranche tends to take on the form of an apple: a form in which the psychoanalyst is delighted to find a phantasm related to orality, a good example of cannibalistic identification, or an illustration of certain Kleinian notions about the bad mother. But we, however, should hear the monster say most clearly to its mother what every child says without showing it: that it is, literally, the fruit of sin.

If the fruit-child attests in this manner to the original rebellion of the body, we shall see that Brunet's cyclopic and phallophoric little girl is an even more scrupulous interpreter of the Bible. "It was then that they *both* felt the rebellion of their bodies," Malebranche goes on to add, "and saw that they were naked, and it was then that shame forced them to cover themselves with fig leaves." [31] The rebellion of the body is accompanied then by what the Bible calls an "opening of the eyes," inseparable from the shame of the naked body. Of course, Adam and Eve saw their nakedness before the fall, and one could explain this in Malebranchian terms by saying that this vision of their nakedness left no traces on their brains, because they were masters of their bodies. It remains to be explained, however, why it is that by an exchange of glances at their bodies they felt in shame the first effect of their sin.

Malebranche says nothing on this point. This is made more remarkable by the fact that his interpretation of the scene from Genesis is apparently inspired by the commentaries of Saint Augustine, who is much clearer on the subject. The beginning of "evil" is already present for Saint Augustine in the pride wakened in Eve's soul by the serpent's words. "[T]o leave God, and to have being in oneself, that is, to follow one's own pleasure";[32] these are the first acts of concupiscence (which cannot be reduced to the concupiscence of the flesh) that will recur throughout history as the *libido dominandi* or *gloriandi* of despots, conquerors, and the proud. "The initial wrong therefore was that whereby, when man is pleased with himself, as if he were in himself a light, he is diverted from that light through which, if he would but chose it, he himself also becomes a light. This wrong, I repeat, came first in secret and prepared the way for the other wrong that was committed openly."[33]

Once the error has been committed, and the revolt against God has been carried out, what punishment could be inflicted on the rebel but the rebellion itself? "For man's wretchedness consists only in his own disobedience to himself, wherefore, since he would not do what he then could, he now has a will to do what he cannot."[34] In this way, against his will, his flesh will have to suffer, age, and die. This disobedience of the flesh is the sign through which, *after the fact,* and having "opened his eyes," man feels the suffering of his disobedience to God. This is the true significance, according to Saint Augustine, of " 'the opening of his eyes' which the serpent had promised him in his temptation—the knowledge, in fact, of something which he had been better ignorant of."[35]

In opening their eyes, Adam and Eve come to know something that it would have been better to ignore. What exactly? The disobedience of the body, as in Malebranche? Not at all, according to Saint Augustine, because "the eyes, and lips, and tongue, and hands, and feet, and the bending of back, and neck, and sides, are all placed within our power to be applied to such operations as are suitable for them."[36] There are even men who can move their ears or sweat at will, or "produce at will without any stench such rhythmical sounds from their fundaments that they appear to be making music."[37] But there is one case in which the body does not obey us: "when it must come to man's great function of the procreation of children, the members which were expressly created for this purpose will not obey the direction of the will, but lust has to be waited for to set these members in motion, as if it had legal right over them, and sometimes it refuses to act when the mind wills, while often it acts against its will."[38]

What "opens the eyes" of the first man and woman is the uncontrollable presence of the organ of procreation. Does it even deserve the name *organ,* given that it no longer corresponds to the definition of *instrument?* We see it, notice it, it attracts the gaze, only in that it is the intolerable reminder of that first sin by which Adam and Eve, turning away from God, presumed to set themselves up as their own masters. Whether erect or limp, it always represents more than itself. As a place-holder for the entire body, it is the signifier of the new Master: the de-siring body, and the master-signifier of its new power.

This is why, when we speak of "libido," which in principle desig-nates all desire, "nothing comes to mind usually but the lust that excites the shameful parts of the body." [39] And this libido "convulses all of a man when the emotion in his mind combines and mingles with the car-nal desire to produce a pleasure unsurpassed among those of the body. The effect of this is that at the very moment of its climax there is an almost total eclipse of acumen and, as it were, sentinel alertness." [40] The pleasure associated with the libido therefore marks the greatest possible distance from this luminous Other, in whom we live and see.

Man and woman are therefore subject to the phallus, this organ be-come signifier. For even if it is connected to the man's groin, it is none-theless the signifier of their common subjection, and the libido that animates it affects the woman as much as the man. The proof is in the universal shame that, despite the ridiculous provocations of the Cynics, both sexes attach to seeing the parts of the body that serve for procre-ation. [41] Humans are subject to many other passions than sexual libido, such as anger for example. But anger is not accompanied by shame. Why not? Because, in these other passions, "the members of the body are not put into operation by the emotions themselves but by the will, after it has consented to them, for it has complete control. . . . But in the case of the sexual organs, lust has somehow brought them so completely under its rule that they are incapable of activity if this one emotion is lacking and has not sprung up spontaneously or in answer to a stimulus. Here is the cause of shame, here is what blushingly avoids the eye of onlookers; and a man would sooner put up with a crowd of spectators when he is wrongly venting his anger upon another than with the gaze of a single individual even when he is rightly having intercourse with his wife." [42]

The gaze, the phallus: what Brunet's monster carries on its face, are perhaps the emblems of femininity and virility. But, more profoundly, it is a summary and reminder of the entire original scene when, the organ becoming a signifier at the same time that the look became a gaze, something that should never have been known was revealed. A repetition of an effect after the fact, it brings about the Law in the very punishment for its transgression, and inspires dreams of what might have been if Eve had not transgressed: the contentment of an obedient life without the constraints of order. If this organ obeyed the will, like all the others, it "would have sown its seed upon the field of generation, as the hand does now upon the earth."[43] "[T]he male seed could then be introduced into the wife's uterus without damage to her maidenhead, even as now the menstrual flow can issue from a maiden's uterus without any such damage."[44]

By making it appear in *The Search after Truth*, we have turned Brunet's monster into a kind of hallucination of Malebranche. It never stops signifying, and that is why it dies so quickly. As biological historians, we could have chosen to consider the being of the monster, but its meaning would have disappeared. We have chosen, along with Brunet, to interpret the meaning, or rather to "reduc[e] the non-meaning of the signifiers, so that we may rediscover the determinants of the subject's entire behaviour."[45] Because it is ultimately the gaze and the phallus that the death of the child-monster makes into enigmatic and all-powerful signifiers, since, from the family to the State, from the love of the couple to the love of the despot, they rule the world.

Leaving the mother's belly to die and to accuse its mother, a being of semblance, Brunet's monster is the Cyclops leaving his lair with the stake in his eye to accuse Nobody. And as it has no name, not having been baptized, we who want to be forgiven for having made it speak too much choose to call it Polyphemus, a good name for the unconscious.

Translated by Marina Harss and Sina Najafi.

Notes

1   Claude Brunet, *Le Progrès de la médecine, contenant un recueil de tout ce qui s'observe de plus singulier par rapport à sa théorie et à sa pratique . . . pour l'année 1697* (Paris, 1698), 49–51.

2   Fontenelle, *Histoire de l'Académie des Sciences, pour l'année 1703,* 37; quoted in Claire Salomon-Bayet, "l'Académie des Sciences et l'expérience du vivant" (unpublished dissertation, Université Paris VII, 1968).

3   Brunet, *Le Progrès,* 45.

4 Nicolas Malebranche, *The Search after Truth*, trans. Thomas M. Lennon and Paul J. Olscamp (Columbus: Ohio State University Press, 1980), 88. Hereafter, citations to this work will be abbreviated *ST* and given in the text.

5 The French grammatical form being discussed here is the impersonal "on bat un enfant," which is the French title of Freud's essay "A Child Is Being Beaten." The German and English use the passive voice, while French uses the impersonal. *Trans.*

6 Michel Foucault, *Discipline and Punish*, trans. Alan Sheridan (New York: Vintage, 1979), 3–31.

7 On the notion of "abduction by consent," see for example G. Lepointe, *Histoire des faits sociaux* (Paris: PUF, 1967).

8 Estienne de La Boëtie, *Slaves by Choice*, trans. and ed. Malcolm Smith (Egham, England: Runnymede Press, 1988).

9 "Folle du logis" is the name given by Malebranche to the imagination. *Trans.*

10 Nicolas Malebranche, *Elucidations of the Search after Truth*, trans. Thomas M. Lennon (Columbus: Ohio State University Press, 1980), 601–2.

11 Cf. Salomon-Bayet, "l'Académie des Sciences."

12 On these points, see J. Roger, *les Sciences de la vie dans la pensée française du XVIIIème siècle* (Paris: A. Colin, 1971).

13 See René Descartes, *Oeuvres complètes*, ed. Charles Adams and Paul Tannery, vol. 11 (Paris: Le Cerf, 1897).

14 G. W. Leibniz, "New Essays on the Human Understanding," in *Leibniz: Philosophical Writings*, trans. Mary Morris (New York: Dutton, 1968), 176.

15 Descartes, "Meditations on First Philosophy," in *The Philosophical Writings of Descartes*, trans. J. Cottingham et al. (Cambridge: Cambridge University Press, 1984), 2:35.

16 Descartes, "Objections and Replies," in ibid., 2:256.

17 Ibid.

18 Ibid.

19 Ibid., 2:256–57.

20 Ibid., 2:256.

21 Pasteur Merlin, "Le Bouquet d'Eden, ou recueil des plus belles prières et méditations . . ." (1673), quoted in H. Brémond, *Histoire du sentiment religieux en France* (Paris: Gallimard, 1959), 9:305–6.

22 Brunet, *Le Progrès*, 53.

23 Malebranche, "Réponse au Livre I des Réflexions philosophiques et théologiques de M. Arnaud contre le Traité de la Nature et de la Grâce," in *Oeuvres complètes*, ed. Robinet (Paris: Librairie J. Vrin), 9:760.

24 Malebranche, *Elucidations of the Search after Truth*, 597.

25 Ibid., 599.

26 Ibid., 600.

27 Ibid.

28 On this point, see Martial Guéroult, *Malebranche* (Paris: Aubier, 1959), vol. 3, chap. 10.

29 Malebranche, *Elucidations of the Search after Truth*, 601; emphasis added.

30   Ibid., 600.

31   Ibid., 601.

32   Saint Augustine, *City of God,* trans. Philip Levine (Cambridge, Mass.: Harvard University Press, 1966), 4:339.

33   Ibid., 4:341.

34   Ibid., 4:349.

35   Saint Augustine, "On Marriage and Concupiscence," in *Saint Augustine's Anti-Pelagian Works* (Grand Rapids, Mich.: Eerdmans, 1971), 266.

36   Ibid.

37   Saint Augustine, *City of God,* 4:391.

38   Saint Augustine, "On Marriage and Concupiscence," 266.

39   Saint Augustine, *City of God,* 4:353.

40   Ibid.

41   Ibid., 4:369–71.

42   Ibid., 4:367.

43   Ibid., 4:383–85.

44   Ibid., 4:397–99.

45   Jacques Lacan, *The Four Fundamental Concepts of Psycho-Analysis,* trans. Alan Sheridan (London: Penguin, 1991), 212.

5

Malebranche's Occasionalism, or, Philosophy in the Garden of Eden

Miran Božovič

According to Malebranche, the mind is situated and, as it were, constantly torn between God and body. It is united to both God and body. Each of the mind's two unions is governed by its specific laws, the former by laws of the union of mind with God, or intelligible substance of universal Reason, and the latter by the laws of the union of mind and body, or psycho-physical laws. The more the union of mind with body is increased and strengthened, the more its union with God is diminished and weakened, and vice versa. Whereas the mind's union with God can be strengthened through knowledge of truth, the modifications occasioned in the mind by the body it animates, weaken this union.[1]

According to Malebranche, God, with his will, not only creates bodies, but also continues to "conserve" them in their existence from the moment that they pass from nothing into being.[2] Every body is in its place solely by the will of God: "only the one who gives being to bodies can put them in the places they occupy."[3] A body cannot be moved from its place unless God moves it. Hence a power capable of moving even the smallest of bodies from the places in which they are conserved by God, would have to not only equal, but surpass the power of God. This means that even the greatest of powers cannot set a body into motion "if God does not intervene."[4] Thus, the moving force of a body is nothing other than "the efficacy of the volition of God who conserves it successively in different places."[5] Wherever bodies happen to be, they are there at all times solely by the will of God. Strictly speaking, "it is only the Creator of bodies who can be their mover."[6]

Let us now consider the case of one's own body and the movement of one of its members. According to Malebranche, by ourselves, we are incapable of changing places, moving our own arm, or even uttering a one-syllable word; in short, we are incapable of making the slightest change in the universe by ourselves. Unless God comes to our aid, all we are capable of doing is making "efforts in vain," or forming "desires that are without power."[7]

How then does Malebranche think it possible to carry out a bodily movement, the movement of one's own arm for example? In purely physiological terms, an arm can be moved "only by means of animal spirits flowing through the nerves to the muscles, contracting the muscles, and drawing to them the bones to which they are attached."[8] However, even if we were familiar with the anatomy of our bodies to the extent that we knew the very nerve ducts through which to direct the animal spirits in order to contract the biceps, we would still be incapable of moving our arm by ourselves. This is simply because, as these animal spirits are themselves nothing other than bodies, that is to say, the smallest particles of the blood and humors, they can only be moved by God.[9] Thus, it is God who moves our bodily members by "successively conserving" the animal spirits on every point of their path from brain to nerves, and from nerves to muscles.

Whatever we imagine our union with our own body to be, if God were not willing to attune his "always efficacious" volitions to our "always powerless" desires, we would remain "motionless and dead."[10] The power that we have over our bodies is not our own, but rather, the power of God himself. And God has communicated his power to us, by establishing the laws of the union of soul and body—it is by virtue of these laws that our arm moves at the instant we will it to move. Thus, through certain modalities of our mind, we are able to determine the efficacy of God's will, the sole moving force of all bodies, including the smallest particles of our blood and humors. Or, in other words, certain modalities of the mind were established by God as the occasional causes of certain modalities of the body, that is to say, as causes of the "effects which He produces Himself."[11] Since we owe all the power we have over our own bodies to God, or, in other words, since it is God who wills that our arm move the instant we will it to move, if we were, for example, to kill an enemy with our own hands, in the eyes of God not only would we be guilty of murder, but also of "l'abus criminel" (the criminal abuse) of the power he communicated to us through the psycho-physical laws.[12]

Strictly speaking, these psycho-physical laws do not give us direct power over the body, but rather, over God, who himself has power over our bodies. What is within our power, is the ability to activate the power God has over our bodies. Since the power that moves the body is no less external to the body than it is to the mind, by determining the will of God, we have only an indirect control over our own bodies. Although it seems that our bodies respond to our every will, that we are able to control the body with our very thoughts, it is in fact not the body we are influencing, but God. The body, then, for all its perfection, is no less a machine.

What the soul is immediately united to is not the body, but God; the soul is united only indirectly to the body it animates, that is through its union with God: Malebranche observes, "only through the union it has with God is the soul hurt when the body is struck."[13]

Without God not only are we unable to make the slightest move-ment with our bodies, not only are we unable to sense anything unless God modifies our minds, but without God, we are also unable to know anything. According to Malebranche, minds can "know nothing unless God enlightens them."[14] Thus, not only are we powerless in the ma-terial world, we are powerless in the intelligible world as well. Just as it is in regard to the movement of our own bodies that we are completely dependent upon God's will, so with regard to our mind's knowledge we are entirely dependent upon God's understanding, or more precisely, upon ideas within it. The fact that the mind is capable of thought only by virtue of the union it has with God, places us "in a position of com-plete dependence on God—the most complete there can be."[15]

According to Malebranche, when we wish to think about a certain thing, God reveals the idea of that thing to our minds. However, God does not produce ideas directly in our mind, that is, he does not modify our mind; God merely reveals to us his own ideas, that is, the ideas he himself has of the things we wish to think about. Although "presentes à l'esprit" (present to the mind),[16] the ideas are not present in it: the mind, as it were, sees them outside of itself, namely in God, or in the intelligible substance of universal Reason. Accordingly, our ideas can be said to have a certain reality independent of our thought, in that, they exist even when we are not thinking of them.[17] Since God reveals his own ideas to our mind, every idea that is present to the mind has the status of divine revelation. Furthermore, every attention of our mind, that is, every effort with which we summon up ideas, is "une priere naturelle" (a sort of natural prayer),[18] since through it we are addressing ourselves directly to God. And God answers the mind's prayer by revealing the appropriate idea to it. Thus, when we think, we are literally thinking through God's ideas. It is in this sense that Malebranche's God is *la Raison universelle des esprits*, the universal Reason of minds,[19] since all created minds think through the ideas of this Reason.

In order to solve a problem in geometry or examine some metaphysical principle, all we have to do is focus our attention, and the light of reason will spread itself within us in proportion to our attention. As this light comes from God, it is in fact God himself who is "l'auteur de nos connoissances" (the author of our knowledge).[20] Whatever philosophers may think of their own knowledge, Malebranche writes, "it is God Himself who enlightens philosophers in the knowledge that ungrateful men call natural though they receive it only from heaven."[21] Or, as Christ says to the subject of *Meditations chrétiennes et métaphysiques:* "sans moi tu ne penserois a rien, tu ne verrois rien, tu ne concevrois rien" (without me you would think of nothing, see nothing, and conceive of nothing). "Toutes tes idées sont dans ma substance, & toutes tes connoissances m'appartiennent" (all your ideas are contained within my substance, and all your knowledge belongs to me).[22]

Let us now briefly consider the relation between ideas and sensations. Sensations are closer to the soul than ideas are. Ideas are external to the soul, and they "do not modify or affect it."[23] Although the ideas are in God, they are not modifications of God's mind, as God is "incapable of modifications"[24]—ideas constitute "the efficacious substance of Divinity"[25] itself. Sensations, on the other hand, are "within the soul itself—they modify and affect it."[26] Sensations are thus modifications of the mind, or more precisely, as modalities are often termed by Malebranche, "they are but the soul itself existing in this or that way."[27] Whereas ideas cannot even be said to belong to us—strictly speaking, they are God's own, and we can be said to have an idea only when God reveals to us one of his ideas—in contrast, sensations belong exclusively to us: God who causes the sensation of pain in us, knows pain, namely in the sense that he knows what that modification of the soul is in which pain consists, but he does not feel it (whereas we feel pain, but do not know pain).[28]

Since, on the one hand, although present to the mind, ideas are ontologically distinct from it, and since, on the other hand, sensations are nothing other than "the soul itself existing in this or that way," the mind can be distracted from its contemplation of the most sublime truths (of God, etc.) by the slightest sensation—for example, by the bite of an insect or the buzzing of a fly: "si un insecte nous picque, nous perdons de vue les vérités les plus solides" (if an insect bites us, we lose sight of the most solid truths); "si une mouche bourdonne à nos oreilles, les ténèbres se répandent dans notre esprit" (if a fly is buzzing around our ears darkness spreads in our minds).[29] Thus any sensation, however faint, is capable of distracting the mind and diverting all of its attention away from God and toward the body. The soul being finite and limited, sensations can quickly exhaust its capacity for thought, so that it cannot sense pain or pleasure and simultaneously think freely about God.

As minds, we were created "to know and love God,"[30] and in order to carry out this task we do not need the body. Since, strictly speaking, "we are not our body,"[31] we could exist without it. However, we do not know that "we are not our body," because God deliberately keeps us ignorant of our true nature. There is, then, in universal Reason an idea—the idea of our mind—that God is not willing to reveal to us despite all of our mind's attention. The reason for God's withholding the idea of our mind from ourselves is for us to preserve the body we animate: if the idea of our mind were accessible to us, in other words, if we thus clearly saw what we really were, we would no longer look after the body that God has ordered us to preserve.[32] It is, then, because of God's blinding us to our true nature that we mistakenly take ourselves to be our bodies and look after their preservation. God expects us to maintain our union to the body we animate, to the thing that in fact weakens the union that we have with him.

In order that the mind's concern for the preservation of the body to which it is united does not distract it from fortifying its union to universal Reason, God, in the presence of bodies, produces in the mind various sensations, by which he informs us of the relations these bodies have with the one that we animate. For example, when we taste an apple, God produces a certain sensation of sweetness or pleasure in our mind, through which he informs us that this body is suitable for the preservation of our own body, and is therefore appropriate for us to join ourselves to it. By informing us through "les preuves courtes du sentiment" (short proofs of sentiment)[33] of the utility of the bodies surrounding us for the preservation of our own body, God economizes on our mind's attention: if we had to find out by ourselves the exact relations the bodies surrounding us have with the one we animate, it would occupy our mind to the extent that it would be distracted entirely from thinking about God, the mind's true good.[34]

Our experience of bodies is governed by an "artifice"[35]—in order for the mind to willingly join itself to certain bodies (and separate itself from others), according to the pressing needs of the body it animates, God makes the mind "sense as in bodies the qualities which the bodies do not have."[36] Although, for example, an apple is in itself completely tasteless (there is no sweetness in the apple, and even if there were, the apple could not communicate it to us since it is causally inefficacious and cannot act on the mind) by virtue of God's artifice, the mind finds it "filled with taste."[37] If the mind saw the bodies "such as they are, without sensing in them what in fact is not in them,"[38] it would find the preservation of the body it animates unbearable. God, then, represents bodies to the mind not as they are in themselves, but disguises them with "borrowed qualities."[39] Seeing the bodies differently than they truly are should enable us to see God as he truly is. However, it is precisely that which God, in the presence of bodies, produces in our mind in order not to distract us from himself, that distracts us from him and attaches us to bodies— not only do we join ourselves to certain bodies or separate ourselves from others, we also love or hate them precisely for what is not in them.

The artifice of "short proofs of sentiment" is not only the source of our greatest pleasures, but also the source of our greatest evils. For example, when the body is hurt, the sensation of pain that God produces in our minds, not only warns us that we have to do something for the well-being of the body, it entirely fills the mind, that is to say, it diverts, against our will, all of the mind's attention toward the body, thereby preventing the mind from thinking of its true good, that is, of God. And therein lies "the terrible contradiction":[40] whereas, on the one hand, the light of reason makes us see that as minds we are superior to our bodies, that we were made to know and love God, on the other hand, the modifications that God produces in our minds persuade us to the contrary, namely, that the mind is fatally dependent upon the body it animates, even to the extent that, because of the body, it loses sight of its own true good, God.

Moreover, why is God, who produces pleasure in our minds when we strive after the goods of the body, after false goods, unwilling to produce even the slightest sensation of pleasure in our minds when we strive after him, our only true good? Why is it that when the mind thinks of God and approaches him through its love, God sometimes fills it with "dryness"?[41] Or, in other words, why is our striving after the goods of the mind—that is, the knowledge of God—at best affectively neutral? After all, we were made to know and love God.

In order to arouse our interest in bodily goods, in sensible objects or bodies that are necessary for the preservation of our own body, God has to present these goods to the mind differently than they really are, that is, endowed with qualities they do not have. In contrast, God believes that he himself, in order to arouse our love for him, does not need any such "borrowed qualities."[42] Whereas God believes that we will love him as soon as we come to see him as he really is, the use of bodies such as they really are would be "très-pénible" (very painful), "très-incommode" (very inconvenient),[43] and even "insupportable" (unbearable for us).[44]

While the love brought about by the sensation of pleasure for the cause that produces, or seems to produce, this pleasure in us, is instinctive and blind, the love that arises solely as a result of the light of reason is free and enlightened. While pleasure "instinctively" attaches us to its (apparent) cause, the affectively neutral light leaves the will entirely to itself, so that it is entirely up to us whether or not we respond to the light with love.[45] And God expects us to love him through reason, that is through free and enlightened love.

Furthermore, it is not only the case that our striving after the goods of the body, the false goods, is "easy and pleasant," while our striving after the goods of the mind, after God, is not, our striving after the latter is often even "hard and painful."[46] Thus, not only does God reward us for our sinful actions through the pleasure he produces in us when we turn our backs on him and strive after false goods, through the pain he produces in us when we strive after him, our only true good, he also punishes us for our virtuous actions. By making the ways of virtue "hard and painful," and those of vice "easy and pleasant," that is, by producing in us horror or distaste with regard to the goods of the mind, and pleasure with regard to the goods of the body, God acts as if he wanted to distract us from himself and have us attach ourselves to sensible objects or bodies.

The ways of virtue being "hard and painful," the contemplation of the goods of the mind quickly tires us, and it is only with the greatest of difficulties that we are able to keep our attention focused on them for long. In contrast, the ways of vice being "easy and pleasant," we are quick to abandon ourselves to the goods of the body, to idleness or to whatever brings us sensible pleasure. Thus, beneath the utterly ordinary, everyday occurrence of growing tired of theory and being overcome with laziness, an occasionalist philosopher is capable of recognizing the hidden hand of God at work—a God who, by producing in the philosopher horror or distaste with regard to the goods of the mind, distracts the philosopher from fortifying his union with universal Reason, that is, distracts him from God himself. When faced with his aversion for theory, the occasionalist philosopher cannot even say to himself: as the aversion I feel for theory reflects not my own laziness, but rather, the horror or distaste God produces in me with regard to the goods of the mind in order to punish me for approaching him, or, in other words, since it is in fact God who wants me to put down my pen and abandon myself to the goods of the body, I can act autonomously by not succumbing to his will and by continuing to work diligently. Not only does God reject the occasionalist philosopher with utter disregard when he strives after him, for the occasionalist philosopher, the contradiction in God's conduct must be all the more "terrible"—in his eyes, it is God himself who produces and sustains the impulse that makes him strive after God.[47] It is no small wonder, then, that Malebranche's theoretical opus is so vast.

In the eyes of the occasionalist philosopher, God, the only object worthy of love, then, turns out to be perverse; yet, any occasionalist philosopher worthy of the name, must love God as his only true good.

According to Malebranche, the difficulties we experience in uniting ourselves to universal Reason, that is, the fact that we find every attention of the mind relating to true goods "pénible & désagréable" (hard and unpleasant),[48] stems from "la rebellion du corps" (the rebellion of the body).[49] "We are no longer such as God made us,"[50] writes Malebranche; the relation between mind and body, which God had established as a "union," has changed through our own fault to one of "dependence" of mind upon body. A mind that becomes dependent upon the body, to the extent that it loses sight of its sovereign good, God, is no longer worthy of thinking of God, or of loving and worshipping him. Consequently, God has withdrawn himself from the mind "as much as He could without losing and annihilating it."[51]

The body, then, rebels against us. It rebels against us because Adam revolted against God. Adam having disobeyed God, his body ceased to obey him. It is thus through the rebellion of the body that God punished the original sin. Since, according to Malebranche, sin is hereditary,[52] from the first man's Fall onward, we all inhabit a rebellious body.

And it is precisely because we are no longer masters of our own bodies, that we can no longer be masters of our attention. True, we are still able to think of whatever we will—the laws of the union of our mind with the intelligible substance of universal Reason have not changed since the first man's sin: God is still willing to answer every "natural prayer" of our mind, our desires are still the occasional causes of the presence of the ideas to our mind—but we are no longer masters of our own desires; our desires are fatally affected by our mind's dependence upon our bodies. Since the mind is no longer simply united with the body, but rather, dependent upon it, sensations bring a certain disorder and confusion into our ideas, and "ainsi nous ne pensons pas toujours à ce que nous voulons" (thus we do not always think of what we will).[53]

God did not subject the mind to the body; he merely united the two through laws of the union of mind to body. This union consists in the "reciprocity" of modalities of the two substances, between which there is no relation of causality: "[God] willed, and He wills unceasingly that modalities of mind and body be reciprocal. This constitutes the union and the natural dependence of the two parts of which we are composed. It consists exclusively in the mutual reciprocity of our modalities based on the unshakeable foundation of divine decrees, decrees which, by their efficacy, communicate to me the power that I have over my body and through it over others, decrees which, by their immutability unite me to my body and through it to my friends, to my belongings, to everything surrounding me." [54] The reciprocity of the modalities of mind and body is thus the result of God's decrees. What we take to be power over our own body, is in fact nothing other than "the efficacy of divine decrees"; while what we take to be the union of mind and body, is nothing other than the "immutability" of these decrees. The laws of the union of mind and body, along with the laws of the communication of motion, were established by God at the creation of the world. They were no different then than they are now; however, at that time God was still willing to suspend them in Adam's favor, so long as Adam did not sin.

While our senses "blur our ideas" and "tire our attention," [55] in short, while our senses "tyrannize" [56] us, Adam's senses still "respectfully" informed and warned him. Adam was advised by his senses of what was necessary for his body "without being distracted from God." [57] And it is precisely because he was still absolute master of his own body, that Adam was master of his attention, of his mind and its ideas. Whether sensible objects would act upon his mind and distract its attention, was completely dependent upon his will. Sensible objects act on our minds only when the motion of the animal spirits, occurring in the body as a result of its contact with sensible objects, is communicated to "the principal part" of the brain, to the part to which the soul is immediately joined. The affections of this part of the brain are the only modalities of the body that are always followed by corresponding modalities of the mind. In other words, it is the affections of this part of the brain that determine the efficacy of the laws of the union of mind and body. Since, prior to the sin, the motion of the animal spirits was "perfectly submissive" [58] to his will, Adam was capable of arresting this motion immediately after it reached and affected the principal part of his brain, that is, immediately upon feeling a certain sensation (e.g., a pain). As the motion of the animal spirits no longer affected the principal part of his brain, Adam simply did not feel the pain. Thus, he was able to silence his senses at will. He was capable of detaching, as it were, the principal part of his brain from the rest of his body. [59] Thus, by detaching the principal part of his brain (i.e., the seat of the soul) from the rest of his body, Adam was able literally to separate his soul from his body. Since, then, the principal part of his brain was "perfectly submissive to him," [60] the attention of Adam's mind was never distracted against his will.

Thus, by virtue of the power he had over his body, Adam was able to "eat without pleasure, look without seeing, sleep without dreaming." [61] Life in paradise, it seems, must have been rather dreary and unappealing. But such a reaction on our part to Malebranche's description of life in paradise betrays precisely our own corruption, that is, our own subjection to "the law of concupiscence": our own bodies have enslaved us to the extent that we find it absolutely inconceivable that we should rely on pleasure exclusively in discerning whether a certain body is suitable for the preservation of our own body and that we should, upon joining ourselves to that body, renounce the pleasure completely.

Where does the exceptional power that Adam had over his body come from? It has already been said that the laws of the communication of motion and the laws of the union of mind and body were established by God at the creation of the world, and that before the sin they were no different than they are now. Thus, it was also the case that every affection of the principal part of Adam's brain was invariably followed by a corresponding sensation in his soul. The distinction being, that Adam was capable of arresting the motion of the animal spirits before, or immediately after, it reached and affected this part of his brain. And he arrested the motion of the animal spirits whenever he wanted to devote himself to the contemplation of ideas. Adam's power over his own body, the power to control even the motion of the smallest particles of his blood and humors, was due to the fact that, in certain cases, God was suspending the laws of the communication of motion and making exception to the laws of the union of soul and body in Adam's favor.[62] And God was doing this in order that Adam's body not distract him from thinking of what he willed. Thus, as an exception to the laws of nature, Adam's power over his body was nothing other than "an anomaly," [63] as Ferdinand Alquié observes.

But, having once sinned, Adam was "no longer worthy of there being exceptions to the laws of nature on his account." [64] As a result, he lost the power he had had over his body, and his mind, once simply united to his body, became dependent upon it. Consequently, since all of the motions of "the rebellious [animal] spirits" [65] were now communicated to the principal part of his brain, Adam's mind was subject to as many modifications.

It seems as if Malebranche's God, who took such pride in "la simplicité de ses voyes" (the simplicity of his ways),[66] could hardly wait for the first man to succumb to temptation and fall, as it released him from suspending, and making exceptions to, the laws of nature on Adam's account, that is, from debasing himself by acting through particular wills. For this reason, during the Fall of man, God preferred to observe indifferently the world crumbling into ruins rather than intervening through a particular will; since the first man's sin, we thus inhabit "des ruines" (ruins), or "débris d'un monde plus parfait" (a debris of a more perfect world).[67] And, according to Malebranche, it is precisely by God's remaining "immobile" during the Fall, that is, through the utter disregard he shows for his most excellent creature on the occasion of its sin, that God declares his infinity and asserts his divine character.[68]

It was, then, through his sin, rebelling and turning against God, that Adam released God from debasing himself in acting through particular wills, and thereby enabled God to begin behaving as one worthy of the name, that is, acting through general wills or laws. Indeed, the very act of punishment, that is to say, the act by which God stripped Adam of the power he had over his body is, in itself, the epitome of the simplicity of divine ways: in order to punish Adam, not only did God not need to introduce any new particular will and incur an additional imperfection in his conduct, he could even abandon the one particular will that he had been acting through, thereby ridding himself of the last imperfection in his conduct. God stripped Adam of his power over the body by beginning strictly to obey his own laws. Hence, it is only through the first man's sin that God truly becomes God.

Before the Fall, Malebranche writes, Adam's "happiness consisted mainly in that he did not suffer pain."[69] The reason why Adam "did not suffer pain" was that he was able to arrest the motion of the animal spirits in his body and prevent the occurrence of those affections in the principal part of his brain that would inevitably have been followed by sensations of pain in his soul. What constituted paradise qua paradise was, then, nothing other than the power that Adam had over his own body, that is, his psycho-physical privilege. Thus, paradise itself was based on an exception to, or suspension of, the laws of nature. Not only, then, does God become God through the first man's sin: the moment God punishes Adam by stripping him of his psycho-physical privilege, the last anomaly disappears from the world, and thus the world truly becomes the world.

Before the Fall, Adam knew that "only God was capable of acting on him."[70] Knowing "more distinctly than the greatest philosopher ever"[71] that God was the only true cause, the first man should thus be considered as an occasionalist philosopher par excellence. Not only, then, did philosophy originate in paradise, but it in fact originated as Malebranchian occasionalism. However, whereas Adam knew through the light of reason that God was acting upon him, "he did not sense it."[72] What he sensed was, on the contrary, "que les corps agissoient sur lui" (that bodies were acting upon him); and although he sensed that bodies were acting upon him, "il ne le connût pas" (he did not know it).[73]

Thus, even the first occasionalist philosopher, Adam, would most likely have agreed with modern critics of occasionalism: that not only is there no sensible proof for occasionalism's central tenet, that God is the only causal agent, but that this tenet is also directly contrary to all sensible experience. Although, upon tasting a fruit with pleasure, Adam, as an occasionalist, knew that it was the invisible God who was causing this pleasure in him, his senses were persuading him to the contrary, namely that it was the fruit that he saw, held, and ate, that was causing this pleasure in him. Thus, the first and most firmly convinced occasionalist philosopher was without sensible knowledge of God's continual acting upon him, and his own philosophy must have already been, in his eyes, directly contrary to the testimony of his senses.

Since, as an occasionalist philosopher, Adam undoubtedly knew that he could know nothing unless God enlightened him, and sense nothing unless God modified his mind, the fact that what he knew was never what he sensed, and vice versa, must have, in his eyes, reflected a certain contradiction in God's conduct: First, since what Adam knew was that God was acting upon him, and since what he sensed was that bodies were acting upon him, it must have been God himself who wanted Adam's sensible experience to be contrary to his knowledge of God's causal efficacy, that is, to that which God himself was making Adam see through the light of reason. Second, since Adam never sensed that which he knew, it was of course God himself who withheld from Adam sensible proof of what he was making Adam see through the light of reason; or, in other words, it was God himself who was hiding his omnipotent hand from Adam, God himself who made his causal efficacy imperceptible in Adam's eyes. And third, since Adam never knew that which he sensed, it follows that he could not have expected to see, through the light of reason, that bodies were acting upon him. In short, just as, on the one hand, Adam had no sensible proof of the causal efficacy of God, that is, of occasionalism, so on the other hand, neither did he have any rational knowledge of its direct opposite, that is, of the causal efficacy of bodies.

Why was it, then, that despite "a very clear knowledge of God's continual acting upon him,"[74] Adam did not sense that God was acting upon him? And why was it that he sensed that it was, in fact, bodies that were acting upon him? It was because "the sensible knowledge of God's continual acting upon him" would have "invinciblement" (invincibly),[75] attached him to God. Or, in other words, had Adam sensed that God was acting upon him, it would have made him love through instinct, that good which he was to love only through reason. Insofar, then, as occasionalism is itself nothing other than a free and rational love of God, Adam's lack of sensible knowledge of God's continual acting upon him, far from being a weakness of occasionalism, is rather its constitutive feature.

Where, on the one hand, God expects us to love him through a free and rational love, on the other hand, by causing all our sensations, it is precisely the blind and instinctive love for himself that he constantly arouses in us. The difficulties that the God of occasionalism faced, then, were not in making Adam love him, but rather, in keeping Adam from loving him blindly and instinctively. This was not an easy matter for God, since he had to remain imperceptible to Adam, despite the fact that God himself was the cause of all of Adam's sensations; his hand had to remain invisible, despite its being present behind all of Adam's ideas, sensations, and bodily movements.

And it was for this reason that God lent, as it were, his own causal efficacy to otherwise causally inefficacious bodies. In disguising from Adam's gaze, God's own causal efficacy as that of bodies, that is, in making Adam sense that bodies were acting upon him, God did succeed in keeping Adam from blindly and instinctively loving him; however, at the same time, God thereby exposed Adam to the attraction of bodies. And it was in order for Adam to be able to resist the blind and instinctive love of bodies, aroused in him by sensible objects—or rather, God acting through sensible objects—that God gave Adam his psycho-physical privilege. It was only in continually detaching the principal part of his brain from the rest of the body and silencing his senses, that Adam was able to see, despite the apparent acting of bodies upon him, that God was the only true cause, and love God through reason. It was, then, precisely in order to be able to persist in his occasionalist belief, despite the unmistakable testimony of his senses to the contrary, that Adam was given his psycho-physical privilege. Thus, it was nothing less than Adam's belief in God's causal efficacy, that is, his enlightened love of God, his occasionalism, that was ultimately contingent upon the power he had over his body.

Wherein, then, lies the first man's sin? What was it that Adam did? Or, more precisely, what was it that he did *not* do? What was he guilty of? What Adam did not do was to make use of the power he had over his body: upon joining himself to a certain body, that is, to "the forbidden fruit," Adam did not suppress the sensation of pleasure that God was producing in his mind, but rather, abandoned himself to it. And it was precisely by not renouncing the pleasure immediately after it fulfilled its advisory function, that Adam crossed the line between innocence and sin. In failing to silence his senses, that is, in failing to detach the principal part of his brain from the rest of the body, Adam allowed his mind's capacity to be exhausted by the sensation of pleasure, to the extent that the darkness of modifications entirely obscured the light of reason. Having thus been distracted, Adam never regained his mind's attention. What the sensation of pleasure, which Adam was unwilling to renounce, erased from his mind, was the mind's "clear perception, which informed him that God was his good, the sole cause of his pleasures and joy, and that he was to love only Him." [76] It was, therefore, nothing less than the very truth of occasionalism that was erased from Adam's mind. And therein lies Adam's sin.

Adam, no longer seeing through the light of reason that only God was capable of acting upon him, still, uninterruptedly sensed that the body he had joined himself to, "the forbidden fruit," was acting upon him; thereupon he came to recognize that the cause of his pleasure was the body, in the presence of which, God was producing pleasure in his mind. In short, he came to believe in the causal efficacy of bodies; his enlightened love of God yielded to the love that the sensation of pleasure necessarily brings about for the object that seems to produce it, that is, to the blind and instinctive love of bodies.

Having failed to make use of the power he had over his body, Adam thereupon lost it. In stripping him of his psycho-physical privilege, God, then, appears to have punished Adam for radically shifting his philosophical position, by readjusting his physiology to conform to his newly discovered philosophy. Having voluntarily relinquished his occasionalist belief for a belief in the causal efficacy of bodies, Adam was thereafter condemned to non-occasionalism. Having voluntarily renounced his love of God, he was thereupon doomed to love bodies.

As long as Adam persisted in his occasionalist belief, God, making exceptions to, and suspending, the laws that he himself had established, clearly did not act as would be fitting for the God of occasionalism, one who prides himself on the simplicity and generality of his ways; however, after the Fall, when God began to behave as an occasionalist God, one worthy of the name, that is, inviolably following His general laws, occasionalism itself became an utterly untenable philosophy. Contingent upon an exception to, and suspension of, the laws of nature, occasionalism is thus possible only in paradise—it is a philosophical reflection on an anomalous world.

Whereas prelapsarian physiology made Adam's belief in the causal efficacy of God possible, that is, his love of God, postlapsarian physiology, in contrast, necessarily engenders and sustains belief in the causal efficacy of bodies, that is, the love of bodies. What is more, it was only as a result of the postlapsarian physiology that some of the central problems of early modern philosophy arose. It was precisely because of the exceptional power Adam had over his body that, for instance, the existence of the external world and the distinction between appearance and reality presented no difficulties for him at all. The course of the animal spirits having been "perfectly submissive to his volitions," Adam could tell whether his brain was affected by an external or internal cause— thus, says Malebranche, "he was not like the mad or the feverish, nor like us while asleep, that is, liable to mistake phantoms for realities."[77] It was, then, God's stripping Adam of the power he had had over his body, that gave rise to these questions in philosophy. Or, in other words, through these unanswerable questions in philosophy, we are all punished for the first man's sin, that is, for his having relinquished his occasionalist belief.

Having lost power over our bodies, that is, the power to detach the principal part of the brain from the rest of the body, we inevitably love bodies. After the first man's loss of the power over his body, the love of bodies, as the direct opposite of occasionalism, that is, the belief that bodies are our good and that they can act upon us, is inscribed, as it were, into the very bodies we animate. The mind contracts this love immediately upon being united to the body it will thereafter animate, that is, already inside the mother's womb. Thus, it is even before birth, that a child loves bodies.

According to Malebranche, it is by virtue of the communication between the brain of the mother and that of a fetus by way of the animal spirits, that the child's soul is "nécessairement tournée vers les corps" (necessarily turned toward bodies),[78] and consequently turned away from God. Unavoidably, the mother has traces in her brain, representing sensible objects: it suffices simply that she see a body or nourish herself on it, for if she is to survive, she must eat; yet she cannot eat without at the same time receiving at least some brain traces. Every brain trace is followed by a certain motion of the animal spirits, inclining the mother's soul to love the object, present to her mind at the time of the impression. Since only bodies can act upon the brain, the ensuing love can only be a love of bodies. Malebranche observes that there is no woman without at least some brain traces and subsequent motions of the animal spirits, inclining her toward sensible things.[79]

As a result of the communication between its brain and that of its mother, during the period of gestation, the child has "les mêmes traces & et les mêmes émotions d'esprits que sa mere" (the same traces and the same motions of [animal] spirits as its mother);[80] therefore, although created "to know and love God,"[81] it is already inside its mother's body that the child "connoit & aime les corps" (knows and loves bodies).[82] Having, thus, already as fetuses been turned away from God and toward bodies, we are all invariably born believing in the causal efficacy of bodies, that is, born as non-occasionalists.

Love of bodies, that is, the belief in their causal efficacy, is thus propagated by the very bodies we animate. However, whereas the love of bodies, as the direct opposite of occasionalism, can be said to result directly from postlapsarian physiology—the mind contracts this love immediately upon being united to the body it will thereafter animate—the love of God, that is to say, the belief in God's causal efficacy, or, in a word, occasionalism, cannot be communicated, by way of the animal spirits, from one mind to another. This is simply because God is not sensible, and consequently, there is no trace in the brain representing, by the institution of nature, God, or any other purely intelligible thing. Thus, for example, a mother, loving God "with a voluntary love,"[83] may well imagine him in the form of "a venerable old man";[84] however, in this way, she can only communicate to the unborn child her own brain trace and the idea joined to it by the institution of nature, that is, the idea of an old man; in contrast, she can never communicate to her unborn child the idea that she herself has learned to associate with the trace of an old man, that is, the idea of God. Therefore, not even the most pious mother can communicate the love of God to the infant in her womb, whereas, through the brain traces giving rise to ideas of sensible things and arousing passions, she necessarily communicates the love of bodies to her child. Thus, while the mother may well be thinking of God, the child will think of an old man; while the mother loves God, the child only loves bodies; though she herself might be saintly, she cannot fail to give birth to a sinner.[85]

Occasionalism, then, cannot be passed on by way of the animal spirits, to a child from its mother before it is born. Or, more precisely, occasionalism can only be inherited in the form of its direct opposite, that is, as a love of bodies. Loving God "with a voluntary love" and therefore an occasionalist philosopher herself, the mother cannot help but engender non-occasionalist offspring. Thus, in a sense, occasionalism itself, as a love of God, can be said to contribute to the growth of a love of bodies.

Since, as a result of Adam's loss of the power over his body, we cannot help but sense surrounding bodies acting upon us, and since we blindly and instinctively love bodies, clearly the light of reason alone cannot suffice to convert us to the belief that God is the only true cause, to the pure and rational love of God, that is, to occasionalism. As the sensations giving rise to the love of bodies in us cannot be overcome by *grâce de lumière* (grace of enlightenment), God opposes them by *grâce de sentiment* (grace of feeling), that is, by occasionally producing in our minds certain sensations "contrary to those of concupiscence."[86] For example, God opposes the sensations resulting from the first man's loss of the power over his body, that is, the pleasures relating to sensible goods or bodies and the pains relating to true goods, by producing in our minds "pleasure relating to true goods" and "horrors or distastes relating to sensible goods."[87] "Grace of feeling," thus, consists of the sensations that God produces in our minds in order to counteract "the influence of the first man"[88] and to resist his "continual action"[89] upon us.

As a result of the loss of the power over our bodies, our virtuous actions appear to be punished through the pain God produces in us when we strive after true goods, and our sinful actions rewarded through the pleasure he produces in us when we strive after false goods; whereas, in counteracting the first man's influence on us, that is, in producing in us pleasures relating to true goods, and horrors or distastes relating to false goods, God clearly makes the ways of virtue "easy and pleasant," and those of vice "hard and painful." It is only in the realm of the "grace of feeling," then, that God, in his acting, ceases to be perverse.

The pleasures relating to true goods give rise to a blind and instinctive love of God, that is, they make us love through instinct that good which should only be loved through reason.[90] In other words, in order to remedy the disorder of the first man, that is, "la concupiscence criminelle" (the criminal concupiscence), God produces a new disorder in us, that is, "une sainte concupiscence" (a holy concupiscence).[91] Thus, lest the blind and instinctive love of bodies be substituted by an equally blind and instinctive love of God, the "grace of feeling" should act only to the extent that the pleasures relating to false goods be counterbalanced, but not outweighed, by pleasures relating to true goods. It is only at the point when our mind's equilibrium has been restored through the equal weights of contrary pleasures, that we are in a position "to follow our light in the movement of our love";[92] it is only at the point when the mind is drawn by pleasure neither to God nor to bodies, that we are able to determine the movement of our love toward what we see through the light of reason to be our true good. Having lost the power over our bodies, the "grace of feeling" is necessary for the "grace of enlightenment" to take effect in us. Through the "grace of feeling," God aims at restoring the precarious equilibrium of the mind between God and bodies—the equilibrium that Adam maintained by exercising his psycho-physical privilege.

However, since the Fall, not only do we believe in the causal efficacy of bodies, but also in the causal efficacy of our own will. For example, as our bodily members move the instant we will them to move, we judge that it is our will that is the true cause of their movement. Furthermore, the internal sensation of the effort of the will we make to move a bodily member makes us sense ourselves to be the cause of its movement. Just as, since the loss of the power over our bodies we cannot help but sense the surrounding bodies acting upon us, so in the same way we cannot help but sense our will causing the movement of our bodily members. Although it is our own impotence that God makes manifest to us through the sensation of the effort of the will, nonetheless, we come to recognize it as a sign of our own power.[93]

That which veils God's almighty hand at work and simultaneously strengthens our belief in the causal efficacy of our own will, is precisely the fact that a movement of one of our bodily members follows, with unfailing regularity, our will to move it. A movement of one of our bodily members, the presumed effect of our will, never fails to occur when we will it, nor does it occur against our will. Thus, the greater the uniformity in God's acting, the stronger our belief in the causal efficacy of our own will; the more unfailingly the effects follow the occasional causes, the more they veil their true cause, God. The more God is present as a cause, the harder he is to perceive.

Accordingly, the less power we have over our bodies, the more we seem to be the cause of their movements. Although we have less power over our bodies than Adam had over his—in fact, the field of occasional causes is narrower for us than it was for Adam—it is precisely because of the loss of the power to detach the principal part of the brain from the rest of the body, that we sense ourselves to be the cause of the movement of our bodies.

How, then, is it possible for God to counter our belief that it is our own will that causes the movement of our bodies, that is to say, the belief that, no less than belief in the causal efficacy of the surrounding bodies, reflects the first man's "influence" or "continual action" upon us? A way in which God could counteract this particular influence of the first man on us, analogous to that of God's acting through the "grace of feeling," would be for him to directly oppose the sensations of our will's causing the movement of our bodily members. The obvious way to do this would be for him to occasionally divest us of the occasional causality over the movement of any of the bodily members that we believe we move ourselves. By divesting us of the occasional causality over one of our bodily members, that is, by moving it against our will or by refusing to move it when we will it to move, God confronts us with a frustrating situation in which the presumed effects of our will do not occur, or occur contrary to our will.

Among our bodily members, there is one whose movement occasionally resists our will, that is to say, our presumed causal efficacy, in precisely the above-mentioned way: namely, the male sexual organ— its erection sometimes occurs directly contrary to our will, and sometimes does not occur despite all our will. By occasionally moving this bodily member against our will, or by refusing to move it when we will it to move, God reveals the causal inefficacy of our own will. What God makes us sense through the missing or unintentional erection is that our will is not its cause.

Insofar as grace consists of sensations that God produces in us in order to counteract those sensations that are contrary to that which he is making us see through the light of reason, namely that he is the only true cause, the missing or unintentional erection can be considered as a species of grace. Just as it is through the pleasures relating to true goods that God opposes the pleasures relating to false goods, so it is through the missing or unintentional erection that he opposes the sensations of our will's causing the movement of our bodily members. Just as, after the pleasures relating to false goods have been counterbalanced by pleasures relating to true goods, we are in a position to follow the light of reason and come to see that God is the only cause of all our pleasures, so, in the same way, after the sensations of our will's causing the movement of our bodily members have been neutralized through the missing or unintentional erection, we are in a position to follow the light of reason and come to see that God is the true cause of all our bodily movements.

The fact that the missing or unintentional erection of the male sexual organ reveals a certain loss of the power over one's body is perhaps what led St. Augustine to the conclusion that, through the disobedience of this bodily member, we are punished for the first man's disobedience to God.[94] Although the missing or unintentional erection of the male sexual organ clearly reveals the narrowing of the field of the occasional causes available to us, that is, a further loss of the power over our body, nevertheless, it is precisely the occasional loss of the power over this bodily member that embodies the exact postlapsarian counterpart of Adam's onetime exceptional power over his body: the immediate result of the missing or unintentional erection can be said to be epistemically equivalent to the result of Adam's exercising his psycho-physical privilege—in both cases, an opportunity opens up for us to freely follow the light of reason, that is, to realize that God is our good, the sole cause of our pleasures and bodily movements, since he is the only one capable of acting upon us, and that we are to love only him. While Adam had this opportunity, whenever he silenced his senses and their testimony contrary to the light of reason, we in turn have this opportunity when God, through certain sensations he produces in us, neutralizes the sensations that are contrary to the light of reason, that is, the sensations that, as a result of Adam's not silencing his senses at the time of the sin, and of his not following the light of reason, we cannot help but sense. *Having lost the power over our bodies,* that is, the power to detach the principal part of the brain from the rest of the body and silence our senses, *a further loss of power over our bodies* is necessary for the "grace of enlightenment" to take effect in us. Thus, rather than a "just punishment,"[95] the missing or unintentional erection is nothing other than a manifestation of God's counteracting the first man's influence on us; of his seeking to bring about our conversion to occasionalism. No less than the "grace of feeling," then, the missing or unintentional erection is an opportunity, occasionally granted by God, for us to freely recognize him as the only true cause; a possibility for us to love him through enlightened love; a possibility for us to abandon the philosophy of the serpent and to embrace occasionalism anew.

According to Malebranche, since Adam's sin, we inhabit "ruins," or "a debris of a more perfect world."[96] As it was already on account of the *first* man's sin that it crumbled into ruins, this world is not unlike the Egyptian pyramids, which Alain considered to be "monuments construits déjà écroulés" (monuments constructed already collapsed).[97] The objection that our world as "la demeure des pécheurs" (the abode of sinners), is "un ouvrage négligé" (a neglected work) would be met by Malebranche with the contention that it was not the present, but rather the future world, that was the proper object of creation;[98] the present world being merely a transitional stage in the construction of the *Temple Éternel* (eternal temple), composed of those souls saved through grace. Like the laws of nature, the laws of grace are general and blind. Just as it is because of the simplicity and generality of the laws of nature that the rain does not fall only on "seeded ground where it is necessary," but also in "the sea where it is useless," so it is because of the simplicity and generality of the laws of distribution of grace, that "the rain of grace" or "heavenly rain" falls indiscriminately on "prepared souls" and on "hardened hearts."[99] Since, then, grace is diffused utterly regardless of the burdens of the concupiscence to be counterbalanced, the amount of grace given is, most often, either insufficient to bring about our conversion and therefore goes to waste, or, it is excessive and only succeeds in replacing the blind and instinctive love of bodies with an equally blind and instinctive love of God. Although undoubtedly a very rare resource, it is because of the simplicity and generality of the laws of the distribution of grace, that God, in fact, sometimes seems to be wasting grace.[100] Thus, the God of occasionalism holds to the simplicity and generality of the laws governing our salvation even at the cost of the damnation of most of us. Since, in counteracting the first man's influence through grace, God tends to overshoot or undershoot the mark, the "ruins" that we, sinners and rebels, inhabit, are most likely to be no less persistent and long-lasting than the pyramids, persistent and long-lasting precisely as a result of their being built already as ruins.

Notes

Unless otherwise noted, all translations are author's own.

1   See *The Search after Truth*, Preface, trans. Thomas M. Lennon and Paul J. Olscamp (Columbus: Ohio State University Press, 1980), xix–xxix.

2   See *Dialogues on Metaphysics*, trans. Willis Doney, in Nicolas Malebranche, *Philosophical Selections*, ed. Steven Nadler (Indianapolis: Hackett, 1992), 228–30.

3   Ibid., 231.

4   Ibid.

5 Ibid.

6 Ibid., 234.

7 Ibid., 233.

8 Ibid., 233–34.

9 Ibid., 234; see also Malebranche, *The Search after Truth*, 671.

10 Malebranche, *Dialogues on Metaphysics*, 234.

11 Ibid., 231.

12 See *Entretien d'un philosophe chrétien et d'un philosophe chinois*, in *Oeuvres complètes de Malebranche*, ed. André Robinet (Paris: J. Vrin, 1986), 15:29; hereafter abbreviated as *OC*, and referred to by volume and page number.

13 Malebranche, *The Search after Truth*, 366.

14 Ibid., 449.

15 Ibid., 231.

16 Ibid., 213.

17 See Malebranche, *Dialogues on Metaphysics*, 154.

18 Malebranche, *Méditations chrétiennes et métaphysiques*, in *OC* 10:144.

19 Malebranche, *Treatise on Nature and Grace*, trans. Patrick Riley (Oxford: Clarendon Press, 1992), 114; see also *The Search after Truth*, 613–15.

20 Malebranche, *Entretien d'un philosophe chrétien et d'un philosophe chinois*, in *OC* 15:23.

21 Malebranche, *The Search after Truth*, 231.

22 Malebranche, *Méditations chrétiennes et métaphysiques*, in *OC* 10:125.

23 Malebranche, *The Search after Truth*, 213.

24 Malebranche, *Elucidations of the Search after Truth*, 625.

25 Malebranche, *Conversations chrétiennes*, in *OC* 4:79; see also *The Search after Truth*, 233.

26 Malebranche, *The Search after Truth*, 213.

27 Ibid., 218.

28 See Malebranche, *Dialogues on Metaphysics*, 170.

29 Malebranche, *Conversations chrétiennes*, in *OC* 4:159.

30 Malebranche, *Dialogues on Metaphysics*, 237.

31 Malebranche, *The Search after Truth*, 359; see also *Méditations chrétiennes et métaphysiques*, in *OC* 10:190; and *Entretiens sur la mort*, in *OC* 12–13:412.

32 See Malebranche, *Méditations chrétiennes et métaphysiques*, in *OC* 10:104–5.

33 Ibid., 113.

34 See Malebranche, *Dialogues on Metaphysics*, 190–92.

35 Malebranche, *Conversations chrétiennes*, in *OC* 4:39; *Entretiens sur la mort*, in *OC* 12–13:412–13.

36 Malebranche, *Dialogues on Metaphysics*, 195.

37 Ibid., 192.

38 Malebranche, *The Search after Truth*, 580.

39 Malebranche, *Dialogues on Metaphysics*, 195.

40 Ibid., 193.

41 Malebranche, *Treatise on Nature and Grace*, 189.

42 Malebranche, *Dialogues on Metaphysics*, 195.

43 Malebranche, *Conversations chrétiennes*, in OC 4:37.

44 Malebranche, *Méditations chrétiennes et métaphysiques*, in OC 10:154.

45 Malebranche, *Treatise on Nature and Grace*, 181.

46 Malebranche, *Conversations chrétiennes*, in OC 4:88; see also *The Search after Truth*, 365.

47 See Malebranche, *The Search after Truth*, 449.

48 Malebranche, *Méditations chrétiennes et métaphysiques*, in OC 10:140.

49 Malebranche, *Dialogues on Metaphysics*, 176.

50 Ibid., 193; see also *Entretiens sur la mort*, in OC 12–13:393.

51 Malebranche, *The Search after Truth*, 339.

52 See Malebranche, *Conversations chrétiennes*, in OC 4:98–105.

53 Malebranche, *Entretiens sur la métaphysique et sur la religion*, in OC 12–13:289.

54 Malebranche, *Dialogues on Metaphysics*, 234.

55 Ibid., 193.

56 The expression "cette puissance qu'ils [*sc.* les sens] ont de *tyranniser* des pécheurs" (OC 1:75) is somewhat imprecisely rendered by Lennon and Olscamp as "their power of *victimizing* sinners"; see *The Search after Truth*, 22.

57 Ibid.

58 Malebranche, *Dialogues on Metaphysics*, 217.

59 See Malebranche, *Conversations chrétiennes*, in OC 4:40.

60 Malebranche, *Dialogues on Metaphysics*, 218.

61 Ibid., 194.

62 See Malebranche, *Méditations chrétiennes et métaphysiques*, in OC 10:113; see also *Dialogues on Metaphysics*, 193.

63 Ferdinand Alquié, *Le cartésianisme de Malebranche* (Paris: J. Vrin, 1974), 470.

64 Malebranche, *Dialogues on Metaphysics*, 194; see also *Entretiens sur la mort*, in OC 12–13:386; and *Conversations chrétiennes*, in OC 4:102.

65 Malebranche, *Dialogues on Metaphysics*, 218.

66 Malebranche, *Entretien d'un philosophe chrétien et d'un philosophe chinois*, in OC 15:29.

67 Malebranche, *Méditations chrétiennes et métaphysiques*, in OC 10:73.

68 See Malebranche, *Traité de la nature et de la grâce*, in OC 5:18; see also *Réflexions sur la premotion physique*, in OC 16:118; and *Entretiens sur la mort*, in OC 12–13:387.

69 Malebranche, *Elucidations of the Search after Truth*, 564.

70 Ibid., 565.

71 Ibid.

72 Ibid.

73 Malebranche, *Conversations chrétiennes*, in OC 4:95.

74 Ibid., 97.

75 Ibid.

76 Malebranche, *Elucidations of the Search after Truth*, 581.

77 Malebranche, *Dialogues on Metaphysics*, 217.

78 Malebranche, *Conversations chrétiennes*, in OC 4:98.

79 See ibid., 98–99.

80 Ibid., 99.

81 Malebranche, *Dialogues on Metaphysics*, 237.

82 Malebranche, *Conversations chrétiennes*, in OC 4:99.

83 Malebranche, *The Search after Truth*, 123.

84 Malebranche, *Conversations chrétiennes*, in OC 4:99.

85 See ibid., 99–100; see also *The Search after Truth*, 123.

86 Malebranche, *Treatise on Nature and Grace*, 151.

87 Ibid.

88 Ibid.

89 Ibid., 192.

90 Ibid., 154; see also *Méditations chrétiennes et métaphysiques*, in OC 10:153.

91 Malebranche, *Méditations chrétiennes et métaphysiques*, in OC 10:155.

92 Malebranche, *Treatise on Nature and Grace*, 190.

93 See Malebranche, *Elucidations of the Search after Truth*, 670; see also *Méditations chrétiennes et métaphysiques*, in OC 10:12.

94 St. Augustine, *De Nuptiis et Concupiscentia* (*Patrologia Latina* series, vol. 44, book 2, chap. 53, 467–68); see also *The City of God*, book 14, chap. 24, in St. Augustine, *Political Writings*, trans. Michael W. Tkacz and Douglas Kries (Indianapolis: Hackett, 1994), 107–8; and Michel de Montaigne, 'On the power of the imagination,' in *Essays*, trans. J. M. Cohen (Harmondsworth, England: Penguin, 1958), 42–43.

95 St. Augustine, *De Nuptiis et Concupiscentia*, PL 44.468.

96 Malebranche, *Méditations chrétiennes et métaphysiques*, in OC 10:73.

97 Quoted in Roger Caillois, *Meduse et Compaignie* (Paris: Editions Gallimard, 1960), 45.

98 Malebranche, *Méditations chrétiennes et métaphysiques*, in OC 10:73.

99 Malebranche, *Treatise on Nature and Grace*, 129.

100 See Jon Elster, *Leibniz et la formation de l'esprit capitaliste* (Paris: Editions Aubier Montaigne, 1975), 192.

6

The Silence of
the Feminine

Renata Salecl | **Jouissance**

When we hear the sound of a siren, we immediately think, "Danger!" or maybe even, "Death!" During wartime, the codified signal of sirens warns of enemy attacks; and during peacetime, sirens alert people to fires or medical emergencies. In some countries, sirens are also used on national holidays to invoke solemn events from the past. In the former Yugoslavia, sirens went off every year at 3 P.M. on the day commemorating Tito's death; and in Israel, sirens announce the moment of silence on Memorial Day, when people remember the soldiers who fell during the war for independence. When the sirens sound, life is interrupted: people stop, the traffic stops, and for a minute everyone stands motionless. The sound of sirens invokes the stillness of time: it freezes the moment and petrifies the hearers.

In this petrifying effect, today's public sirens very much resemble their predecessors—the ancient Sirens of classical mythology, half-human being, half-bird, who lived on an island to which they enticed sailors with their seductive singing.[1] Those sailors who succumbed to the Sirens' song immediately died. As a result, the island was covered with piles of white bones, the remains of the perished sailors. Hence, the very setting in which the Sirens dwelled was filled with death. Whenever a ship approached the Sirens' island, the wind died away, the sea became still, and the waves flattened into a calm sheet of glass: the sailors entered the land where life is fixed forever. The Sirens themselves were neither dead nor alive: they were creatures in between—the living dead. Or, as Jean-

Pierre Vernant writes, they were, on the one hand, pure desire, and, on the other hand, pure death: they were "death in its most brutally monstrous aspect: no funeral, no tomb, only the corpse's decomposition in the open air."[2]

As many theorists of Greek mythology have observed, the Sirens present danger to particular men's lives, while also presenting a challenge to the social order as such, especially the family structure. In the *Odyssey* we thus read: "Whoever draws too close, off guard, and catches the Sirens' voices in the air—no sailing home for him, no wife rising to meet him, no happy children beaming up at their father's face."[3] This danger of the Sirens to the family life and, more generally, to the social order is supposedly linked to their status as creatures that are closer to nature than to culture.[4] In the context of psychoanalytic theory, the trouble that their bestiality presents for culture as well as for individual men has to be placed into the context of the subject's confrontation with that special form of "cultured" animality that is known as drive. But before we put the Sirens through the hoop of psychoanalytic theory, let us first recount some points from Odysseus's encounter with them.

Paradoxically we learn more about the deadliness of the Sirens from Circe's warnings to Odysseus than from Odysseus's own account of his adventure with them. Odysseus sees no heap of bones around Sirens' island. He only says that the Sirens were encouraging him to stop his ship and listen to their honey-sweet voices, which bring pleasure and wisdom to man. The Sirens were thus boasting to Odysseus: "We know all the pains Achaeans and Trojans once endured on the spreading plain of Troy when the gods willed it so—all that comes to pass on the fertile earth, we know it all!"[5]

These words incite Odysseus's desire to stop and surrender himself to the Sirens' lure: he is willing to endure a collusion with the singers that excludes everything else.[6] But the paradox of the *Odyssey* is that we never learn what the Sirens actually sing about. Did the Sirens ever sing, and if they did sing, why is this song not recounted by Homer? Pietro Pucci gives two explanations for this. First, "the *Odyssey* presents the Sirens as the embodiment of the paralyzing effects of the Iliadic poetics because their song binds its listeners obsessively to the fascination of death."[7] Death is therefore something that lies at the center of the *Odyssey,* the song of survival, but it is also something that must be left unspoken. The second explanation concerns the fact that "the *Odyssey*'s own sublime poetry cannot be inferior to that of the Sirens. No text can incorporate the titillating promise of a song as sublime as the Siren's without implying that this sublimity resides in the incorporating text itself." [8] Thus, the *Odyssey* itself has to be understood as the embodiment of the Sirens' song. The Sirens' song is thus "the negative, absent song that enables its replacement—the *Odyssey*—to become what it is." [9] In sum, the Sirens' song is left unsung either because death as such is something that has to be left unspoken, or because the *Odyssey* itself comes to incorporate or represent the Sirens' song. In both cases, the Sirens' song stands as an empty, unutterable point in the *Odyssey,* which, with the allusion to deadly pleasure, brings a sublime quality to the poem.

Tzvetan Todorov gives another answer to the question, Why do we know nothing about the Sirens' song? His thesis is that the Sirens said to Odysseus just one thing: We are singing. In other words, the Sirens' song is just a self-referential claim that there is a song. And death is always linked to this song. It is not only that the listeners die upon hearing the Sirens' song: if the Sirens fail to seduce their prey, they themselves commit suicide. (Some post-Homeric interpretations of the *Odyssey* maintain that the Sirens threw themselves from the rock into the sea, when Odysseus escaped their lure.) Thus, the only way for the Sirens to escape death is to seduce and then kill those who hear them. On another level this also explains why we do not know the secret of the Sirens' song: "The song of the Sirens is, at the same time, that poetry which must disappear for there to be life, and that reality which must die for literature to be born. The song of the Sirens must cease for a song about the Sirens to appear. . . . By depriving the Sirens of life, Odysseus has given them, through the intermediary of Homer, immortality." [10] In other words, the Sirens' song is the point in the narrative that has to remain unspoken for the narrative to gain consistency. It is an empty point of self-referentiality that a story has to omit in order to attain the status of a story. From the Lacanian perspective, this empty point is another name for the real, the unsymbolizable kernel around which the symbolic forms itself. This kernel is not simply something prior to symbolization; it is also what remains: the leftover, or better, the failure of symbolization. The Sirens' song is the real that has to be left out for the story of the *Odyssey* to achieve form. However, there is no song of the Sirens before the story of the *Odyssey*. The Sirens' song is thus, on the one hand, that which incites the *Odyssey* as narration, while, on the other hand, it is also that which results from this narration: its left-over, which cannot be recounted.

What kind of knowledge of the past do the Sirens have? In regard to this knowledge, there is a significant difference between the Sirens and the Muses, who are also supposed to have voices that are delicately clear, immortal, tirelessly sweet and unbroken. The Muses are the daughters of Zeus and the Titaness Mnemosyne (Memory); as the fruits of their parents' nine nights of lovemaking, the Muses became the singers that preside over thought and artistic creativity.[11] The Muses bring memory to their listeners, along with the divine help that produces inspiration: "according to Hesiod, a singer (in other words a servant of the Muses) has only to celebrate the deeds of men of former days or to sing of the gods, and any man beset by troubles will forget them instantly."[12] The memory of the past that the Muses bring is thus essentially linked to forgetfulness.

With the Sirens, the knowledge of the past has a different meaning: "The Sirens know the secrets of the past, but it is a past that has no future life in the 'remembering' of successive generations."[13] How is one to understand here the difference between knowledge and memory? For Lacan, memory primarily has to do with non-remembering of trauma, the real around which the subject centers his or her very being. When we tell our stories, it is at the point where we touch the real that our words fail, but fail so as to always come back to the trauma without being able to articulate it: "The subject in himself, the recalling of his biography, all this goes only to a certain limit, which is known as the real. . . . An adequate thought, *qua* thought, at the level at which we are, always avoids—if only to find itself again later in everything—the same thing. Here the real is that which always comes back to the same place—to the place where the subject in so far as he thinks, where the *res cogitans*, does not meet it."[14] The subject forms memory in order to get consistency, to fashion a story that would enable the subject to es-cape the traumatic real.

In regard to the difference between the Muses and the Sirens, we can say that only the Muses provide memory, since they enable their listeners to forget the traumas of their life, while the Sirens put the listeners in touch with what Lacan calls the *knowledge in the real,* that knowledge that the listeners do not want to know anything about. Inspired by the memory that the Muses provide, their listeners are able to create works of art, while those who hear the knowledge offered by the Sirens' song immediately die. In a different theoretical context, Adorno and Horkheimer make the same point when they claim that the Sirens' singing cannot be perceived as art precisely because of the way it deals with the past: the Sirens' "allurement is that of losing oneself in the past. . . . The compulsion to rescue what is gone as what is living instead of using it as the material of progress was appeased only in art, to which history itself appertains as a presentation of past life. So long as past declines to pass as cognition and is thus separated from practice, social practice tolerates it as it tolerates pleasure. But the Sirens' song has not yet been rendered powerless by reduction to the condition of art."[15] The past in the Siren's song has not been symbolized yet, it has not become a memory; such unsymbolized past is traumatic for the listener, since it evokes something primordial, something that is between nature and culture that the subject does not want to remember. And for Odysseus, it becomes essential to symbolize his encounter with the Sirens and to form a narrative about them. Here Odysseus significantly differs from his colleagues, who had their ears closed with wax in order not to succumb to the voices of the Sirens. Odysseus wants to hear their singing. Circe, who instructed Odysseus how to escape the Sirens' enchantment, also gave him a mandate to remember this event and recount it to his colleagues and to Penelope. Odysseus thus becomes obliged to form a memory of his encounter with the Sirens, that is, to cover up the trauma that the Sirens present.

The impasse of drive

The Lacanian term for this "knowledge in the real" that resists symbolization is *drive,* the self-sufficient closed circuit of the deadly compulsion-to-repeat: the paradox is that that which cannot ever be memorized, symbolized by way of its inclusion into the narrative frame, is not some fleeting moment of the past, forever lost, but the very insistence of drive as that which *cannot ever be forgotten* in the first place, since it repeats itself incessantly.

Drive first needs to be understood as a leftover that pertains to the fact that something is left out when the subject becomes the subject of the signifier and is incorporated into the symbolic structure. When the subject becomes a speaking being, he or she will no longer be able to have sex in an animal's instinctive way. However, in the place of this loss, we encounter a force that essentially marks the subject by imposing a constant pressure on him or her. This force is what Lacan named variously: libido, drive, or lamella. Through this naming, Lacan does a rereading of Freud that offers another perspective on and to Freudian theory.

For Freud, libido primarily concerns the subject's ability to find sexual satisfaction in different ways. Aside from having sex, the subject can find this satisfaction through such activities as eating, shitting, looking, speaking, writing, and so on. Libido is always linked to a libidinal object, which is not simply a material object, but what Lacan names object *a*.

It is crucial for the subject that only partial drives exist, and no genital drive as such. The subject is determined on the one hand by these partial drives, and on the other hand by the field of the Other, the social symbolic structure. For Freud, love, for example, is not to be found on the side of the drives, but on the side of the Other. And it is in this field of the Other that anything which could resemble some kind of genital drive finds its form.

Drive and desire each have a different relation to the symbolic law. Desire is essentially linked to the law, since it always seeks out something that is prohibited or unavailable. The logic of desire would be: "It is prohibited to do this, but for that very reason, I will do it." Drive, in contrast, does not care about prohibition: it is not concerned about overcoming the law. Drive's logic is: "I do not want to do this, but I am nonetheless doing it." Thus, we have an opposing logic in drive, where the subject does not want to do something, but nonetheless enjoys doing just that. Drive paradoxically always finds satisfaction, while desire has to remain unsatisfied, endlessly going from one object to another, positing new limits and prohibitions. Drive is thus a constant pressure, a circulation around the object *a,* which produces *jouissance*—a painful satisfaction.[16]

Drive is in the final instance always the death drive, a destructive force, which endlessly undermines the points of support that the subject has found in the symbolic universe. In regard to drive, desire plays a paradoxical role of protection, since desire, by being subordinated to the law, pacifies the lawless drive and the horrible *jouissance* that is linked to it. The subject of desire is the subject of identification: this is the subject who constantly searches for points of support in the symbolic universe, the ego-ideals with which he or she can identify and thus achieve an identity. Such a point of identification can be a teacher, lover, analyst, etcetera. But on the level of drive, there is no identification anymore, there is only *jouissance*. Paradoxically, the subject is always happy at the level of drive: although because of drive, the subject actually suffers terribly and tries to escape its enormous pressure, in this suffering *jouissance* is at work, which means precisely this painful satisfaction that is the highest happiness on which the subject can count.[17]

The problem of the subject is that he or she is nothing except through the love and desire of others. The subject by him- or herself has no value. Recognizing this fact causes the subject's devastating depressive moods. So, it turns out that the subject is not the phallus that would complement the Other. The Other can function very well without the subject. And to overcome this traumatic truth, the subject endlessly tries to leave a mark on the Other, on the social symbolic structure, on history, and so on. However, the subject can find a special form of happiness when he or she is not at all concerned with the Other, that is, through *jouissance* that pertains to drive.

One can discern this *jouissance* in the partial drives related to voice and gaze. It is in the tonality of the voice, for example, where we encounter *jouissance,* that is to say, this is the place where the surplus enjoyment comes into being, which is something that cannot be inscribed in the series of signifiers. This excessive *jouissance* that pertains to voice is what makes the voice both fascinating and deadly. If we take as an example the diva's singing in the opera, it is clear that the very enjoyment of opera resides in her reaching the peak of the voice. At this moment, her voice assumes the status of the object detached from the body. The singer has to approach "self-annihilation as a subject in order to offer himself or herself as pure voice. The success of this process is the condition for the dissolution of the incongruity between singer and role, a dissolution that . . . is at the foundation of the lyric arts."[18] But if this process does not succeed, the public reacts sometimes with violence.

The singer who fails to produce this effect of the object detached from the subject reopens the incongruity between object and subject and thus becomes "a failing subject": "the singer is cast back by the public into the position of object, but now a fallen object, a piece of refuse, to be greeted in kind with rotten egg or ripe tomato—or . . . with the vocal stand-in for refuse: booing and catcalls." [19] The public reacts so violently because it is denied its moment of ecstasy; its fantasy of finally possessing the inaccessible object has fallen through. And the same goes for the Sirens: if they do not succeed in seduction, they are punished. Many stories about the Sirens stress their failure to seduce with their voices. The unsuccessful singing contests with the Muses supposedly caused the Sirens to lose their wings. Later they tried to outcharm Orpheus's lyre, but failed again and as a result supposedly committed suicide.

From the Other's Desire to the Other's *Jouissance*

For psychoanalysis, the problem of the encounter between Odysseus and the Sirens thus concerns the logic of desire and drive: How does the subject react to the drive in the other? How does the subject respond to hearing the seductive voice of the other? Could it be that the desire that the subject (Odysseus, in our case) develops in response to the luring other (the Sirens) is actually a protection from the destructive nature of the drive? In this precise sense, one is tempted to claim that the Lacanian object small *a*, the object-cause of desire, is none other than drive itself: that which arouses the subject's desire for the Other is the very specific mode of the Other's *jouissance* embodied in the object *a*. In the case of hatred (which is always a counterpart of love), as with racism or nationalism, the subject is primarily bothered by the way he or she enjoys: when racists object to how the others enjoy their food or music, the ungraspable *jouissance* of the other materialized in these practices of everyday life sets in motion the subject's desire and incites all kinds of fantasies. In the case of love, this *jouissance* of the Other (which can easily turn into repulsion) gets inscribed in the gaze of the other, his or her voice, smell, smile, laughter . . . all the features that exert on the loving subject an irresistible attraction.

In Homer there is a certain ignorance at work in the Sirens' lure: they would like to get Odysseus into their trap, but they are not at all struck by him (i.e., he is not the object of their desire). Why is desire of the

Other such a problem for the subject? For Lacan, this dilemma concerns the subject's very being; this dilemma is first formulated as the question of what was the subject's place in the desire of his or her parents. The subject tries to answer this question by way of forming a fundamental fantasy: a story of his or her origins that will provide the grounds for his or her very being.

The desire of the Other incites horror on the side of the subject (i.e., it produces anxiety). This anxiety arises because the Other's desire remains an enigma to the subject—which also means that the subject can never really know what kind of an object he or she is for the Other. Lacan exemplifies this anxiety by asking us to imagine that one day we encounter a giant female praying mantis; as it happens we are wearing a mask, but we do not know what kind of a mask it is: we do not know if it is a male or female mask. If it is a male mask, we can, of course, expect to be devoured by the female praying mantis. Lacan's example of the female praying mantis returns us to the subject's encounter with deadly feminine creatures, such as the Medusa or the Sirens. In this encounter, the subject's urgent question is: What kind of mask am I wearing? In other words, what kind of an object am I for her? Am I a man or a woman? This would be the question for the male hysteric. He has doubts about his sex and his being, therefore, he expects to get an answer from the Other, just as a female hysteric does. And, in order to obtain this answer, he places himself as the ultimate object of the Other's desire, but the object whose allure is linked to the fact that he always vanishes and can never be possessed.

Since most men are not hysterics but are obsessionals, the question is: what is the obsessional strategy in regard to the monstrous female? In contrast to the hysteric, who sustains her desire as unsatisfied, the obsessional maintains his desire as impossible. While for the hysteric every object of desire is unsatisfactory, for the obsessional this object appears too satisfactory, that is why the encounter with this object has to be prevented by all means. The hysteric, by always eluding the Other, slipping away as object, maintains the lack in the Other. She wants to be the ultimate object of the desire of the Other; but she nonetheless prevents this from happening, and by doing so, thus keeps her desire unsatisfied. But the obsessional maintains his desire as impossible and does so in order to negate the Other's desire.[20]

The obsessional wants to be in charge of the situation, he plans his activities in detail. An encounter with the woman who is the object of his desire will be thought out well in advance; everything will be programmed and organized, all to prevent something unexpected from happening. The unexpected here concerns desire and *jouissance*. The obsessional tries to master his desire and desire of the Other by never giving up thinking or talking. His strategy is to plug up his lack with signifiers and thus to avoid the object of his desire. Lacan also points out that the obsessional does not want to vanish or to fade as a subject, which happens when the subject is eclipsed by the object of his desire and *jouissance*. The obsessional tries to demonstrate that he is the master of his own desire and that no object is capable of making him vanish.[21] Even during sexual intercourse, he will go on planning, thinking, and talking, always in efforts to control his *jouissance* and *jouissance* of the Other.

This obsessional strategy can be best exemplified by the case of a man who was waiting for two nights for a telephone call from the woman who was the object of his love. In the middle of the night he got the idea that the phone might not be working, thus he repeatedly picked up the receiver and listened to check the dial tone. The man knew, of course, that picking up the receiver would hinder the woman's efforts to call him, so as soon as he was convinced that the phone was working, he quickly put the receiver down. But after a short while, he would repeat the test procedure. He continued this ritual throughout the night to the point of utter exhaustion. And after two nights, he fell into a serious crisis, which brought him to analysis.[22]

Odysseus's position is obsessional: he resorts to a series of strategies in order to keep at bay the *jouissance* of the Other and his own desire for the Other. Odysseus thus performs a whole ritual to prevent a genuine encounter with the Sirens. It can even be said that he finds his very *jouissance* precisely in this ritual of thinking and planning about how to escape the Sirens' lure.

While the hysteric endlessly questions the desire of the Other, the obsessional, in contrast, does not want to know anything about this desire. For the obsessional it is crucial that he put himself in the place of the Other, from which point he can then act so that he avoids any risk: thus he wants to escape from situations that might involve confrontation, or might in any way disturb his equilibrium. While the hysteric deals with the dilemma, "Am I a man or a woman?" the obsessional agonizes over the question, "Am I dead or alive?" He hopes that with the death of the Other who continually imposes obligations on him, he will finally be free. Thus the obsessional also questions whether the Other is still alive or dead. Thus the encounter with the Other who is the living-dead becomes the most horrible thing for the obsessional. But paradoxically, the obsessional is himself a special kind of a living-dead, since the rituals and prohibitions that he imposes on himself make him a robotlike creature, apparently drained of desire.

Odysseus also acts in an obsessional way in his passion to narrate his encounter with the Sirens. It is well known that obsessionals find great joy not only in planning the encounter with the object of their desire and at the same time preventing this from happening, but also in narrating this failure, in creating a story about it. Odysseus also has been mandated to recount his meeting with the Sirens, and his *jouissance* is at work not only in planning how to avoid an actual encounter with the Sirens, but also in telling others about this missed encounter.

In sum: for both the hysteric and the obsessional, it is crucial to understand their dilemmas with desire as defenses against *jouissance*. The hysteric, for example, wants to be the ever elusive object of the Other's desire, but she does not want to be the object of the Other's *jouissance*. She does not simply want to be a partial object through which the Other enjoys, but something else—the never attainable object of desire. The hysteric masquerades herself as a phallic woman, all with the intention to cover the lack in the Other, to make the Other complete. Since this attempt always fails, she needs to repeat her seductive strategy again and again. Through seduction, the hysteric tries to provoke the desire of the Other for her, which will, of course, never be satisfied. Although the hysteric may enjoy this game of seduction and unsatisfaction, she cannot deal with the situation when the Other takes her as his object of *jouissance* and not simply as the inaccessible object of desire. The hysteric is therefore attracted to the desire of the Other, but horrified by his *jouissance*.

Let us exemplify this aversion to the Other's *jouissance* with the help of the short story by O. Henry, "The Memento." This story is about a young Broadway dancer Lynnete who decides to change her life: she gives up dancing, moves to a small village, and happily falls in love with the local priest, whom she does not want to know about her dishonorable past. Rumor has it that the priest was unhappily in love sometime before and that he keeps a secret memento from his beloved locked in a box. One day, Lynnete finds and opens this box. What she discovers presents an absolute horror for her: in the box is one of the very garters that she, as a Broadway dancer, used to throw into the audience at the end of each performance. After this discovery, Lynnete flees from the village and, disillusioned, returns to the Broadway theater.

The story makes it clear that the priest did not know that he fell in love with the same woman twice. When Lynnete questioned him one time about his past love, the priest simply explained that some time ago he was infatuated with a woman whom he did not really know. He admired this woman only from a distance, but now all this has been forgotten, since he is finally happily in love with a woman who is real. Although the priest tries to distinguish fantasy from reality, he actually fell in love with the same object. Both the first and the second time, he loved the woman because of something that was more in her then herself. Since it was always the object *a* in the woman that attracted the priest, for his love to emerge it did not really matter whether the beloved was a "fantasy" or "reality"—a distant dancer in a Broadway show or an innocent country girl.

But the crucial problem of the story is: Why was Lynnete repulsed when she discovered the memento? Why wasn't she happy that she herself was his great past love? One of the explanations for her horror could be her fear that the priest might stop loving her if he found out about her deception. However, there is another explanation for Lynnete's repulsion: Lynnete's horror is to encounter the very elusive object of love itself—the object *a*. The garter stands here for the object *a*. However, this object is for the priest not only the always elusive object of his desire, but also the object through which he enjoyed. And this created a problem for Lynnete: she wanted to be the object that is desired by the priest, but not the object through which he had found his particular form of *jouissance*.

This story can help us to understand the universal dilemma of the neurotics, which has to do with the subject's desire to be desired by another subject, while he or she does not want to be the object through which another enjoys.[23] Returning to the story of Odysseus and the Sirens: it can be said that Odysseus actually desires the Sirens (and maybe even wants to be desired by them); however, what causes problems for him is the peculiar way the Sirens enjoy.

Feminine *Jouissance*

Odysseus's encounter with the Sirens has to be understood as a failure. However we read this encounter, as the seduction of Odysseus by the Sirens or vice versa, whatever attraction existed between them never brought the two parties together. That Odysseus escaped the Sirens is commonly understood as his triumph; however, it can also be understood as his failure to confront and pursue his desire. This failed encounter between Odysseus and the Sirens can also be taken as the prototype of the impossibility of the sexual relationship between men and women.

A man falls in love with a woman because he perceives in her something that she actually does not have, the object *a*, object cause of desire. He will therefore fall in love with a woman because of some particularity—with her smile, some gesture, her hair, or the tone of her voice, whatever will fill the place of the object *a* for him. And around this object a man will form the fantasy scenario that will enable him to stay in love. The problem for a woman is that she knows very well that a man will fall in love with her because of some particularity that distinguishes her from other women and, as a result, she will desperately try to enhance what she thinks is special about herself. However, a woman can never predict just what particularity will make a man fall in love with her. Thus one woman might nurture her beautiful lips, thinking that men are attracted by her sensual smile, meanwhile a man does fall in love with her, but mainly because of her fairly unattractive voice. It is needless to point out how the whole cosmetic and fashion industry relies on women's search for the object in themselves that makes them the object of love. And since women can never guess what is more in them than themselves, the fashion industry encourages them to always look for another product that would make them unique.[24]

In Lacan's formulas of sexual difference, a man is totally determined by the phallic function; however, there is one man, the Freudian primordial father, who is the exception. As the possessor of all the women, he is also the one who prohibits other men's access to women. This father of the primal horde is the only one that has direct access to sexual *jouis-sance* and for whom there is no prohibition of incest. The sexuality of other men is essentially linked to prohibition; they have undergone symbolic castration, after which they are not able to enjoy the body of the woman as a whole.

It is wrong to understand castration as something that prevents the subject's rapport with the opposite sex. After the subject has undergone castration, he or she will not be able to engage in simple animal copulation, that is, heterosexual intercourse will cease to be an instinctual activity linked to the preservation of the species. However, with humans, castration should not be understood as the basis for denying the possibility of the sexual relation, but as the founding condition for the possibility of any sexual relation at all. It can even be said that it is only because subjects are castrated that human relations as such can exist. Castration enables the subject to take others as other and not as the same, since it is only after undergoing symbolic castration that the subject becomes preoccupied with questions such as: "What does the Other want?" and "What am I for the Other?"[25]

Why is symbolic castration on the side of men crucial to their love-liaisons with women? The fact that a man is totally submitted to the phallic function means that he is marked by a lack. After being barred by language, a man will endlessly deal with two questions: First, what is my symbolic identity (i.e., who am I in the symbolic network)?[26] And second, Which is the object that can complement me? The subject deals with this second question in his love life when he searches for the object on the side of the woman, which would enable him to form the fantasy of an always provisional wholeness. When encountering his love-object, a man will want to know in what kind of symbolic role does the woman see him. In contrast to the woman's dilemma of wondering what kind of object she is for the other, a man's concern is whether the woman recognizes his symbolic role. Here a man's obsessions with social status, wealth, public importance all play an important part. For example, a millionaire in a film by Claude Chabrol complains that he is tired of women insisting that they love him for what he is; he would like to meet a woman who would finally love him for his millions. This man's complaint has to be understood as a confirmation that the man wants to be loved for what is in him more than himself—his symbolic status.

Although a man has access only to phallic *jouissance,* he nonetheless has aspirations to the Other *jouissance* (i.e., to the *jouissance* that is beyond the limits of the phallus). This aspiration is paradoxically caused by the superego's command to enjoy, which arouses the man's thirst for the infinity of the Other, while at the same time prohibiting access to it.

The paradox of the superego is that, on the one hand, it is linked to the law of castration (because of which man's *jouissance* can only be phallic); but, on the other hand, the superego is also a command that goes beyond any law. In sum: the superego is analogous to castration in its prohibitive function, while at the same time it is not submitted to the phallic order.[27] As a result, the superego is a demonic agency that commands the subject to go beyond the phallic order and to experience a non-phallic *jouissance,* but this agency also prohibits the subject access to this *jouissance.* That is why the superego is like the laughing voice of the primordial father, who appears to be saying to the son: Now that you have killed me, go and finally enjoy women, but you will see that you are actually unable to do so; thus, it is better that you not even try.

When Lacan speaks about feminine *jouissance* he primarily emphasizes the impossibility of defining what it is. Since women are also determined by the phallic function, feminine *jouissance* is not something that women get instead of phallic *jouissance,* but on top of it. Feminine *jouissance* is thus a supplement to phallic *jouissance:* while the man has access to only one form of *jouissance,* the woman has possible access to another, additional *jouissance.* Lacan points out that feminine *jouissance* is for women only a potentiality, since women do not expect it. And about this *jouissance* the woman knows nothing more than the simple fact that she enjoys it. She does not talk about it, since it is something that cannot be spoken of in language.

A man tries to find out what feminine *jouissance* is: he may even hope to experience it himself, but he always fails in these attempts. For Lacan, such failure is analogous to Achilles's failure to be alongside the turtle: she is either ahead of him or already overtaken.[28] In the psychoanalytic clinic, this failure is incarnated in the two most common male sexual problems: too quick or too late ejaculation.

In this context, how can we read the story of Odysseus's encounter with the Sirens and his silence about the Sirens' song? In the *Odyssey,* we have, on the one hand, a promise of a limitless *jouissance* in the form of the Sirens' song, and, on the other hand, a prohibition against the man's ever hearing this song. This promise of the Sirens' song can be understood as something that is linked to Odysseus's superego: whatever voice Odysseus hears might be nothing but the voice of his superego, which commands him to experience feminine *jouissance*. But this voice also warns Odysseus of the deadliness of such *jouissance* and thus prohibits his access to it.

However, this explanation does not address the question of whether the Sirens actually did sing. Even if Odysseus heard nothing but his superego's voice, the Sirens might still have been singing. But the question remains: did the Sirens want to be heard by Odysseus (i.e., did they need him as an audience?). Since the Sirens' song embodies the ultimate myth of feminine *jouissance,* the question is also, do women need men in order to experience this *jouissance?* The Lacan of the sixties hinted at a positive answer to this question, when he said that a man acts as the relay whereby the woman becomes the Other to herself, as she is the Other for the man.[29] But in later years, Lacan complicates the matter, when in the seminar *Encore,* he claims that the woman does not necessarily need a man to experience feminine *jouissance,* since she is in a specific way self-sufficient in her *jouissance.* A woman might experience feminine *jouissance* simply by herself, or in a mystical experience, by relating to God.

How can we understand this self-sufficiency of women? Let us take the case of a femme fatale, usually perceived as a woman who desperately tries to impress men, who masquerades herself in order to be admired by men. But a femme fatale also has a certain ignorance about men, and it is this very ignorance that actually makes her so attractive. Freud pointed out that with the femme fatale, as well as with young children and wild cats, this ignorance is related to the fact that they have not given up on some part of their libido: since other people have lost this libido, they become so attracted to the ones that still retain some of it. The paradox of a femme fatale, therefore, is that she wants to be admired for her beauty, but she is perceived as beautiful precisely because she is also ignorant about the reaction of others toward her. A femme fatale enjoys her own self-sufficiency, which is why we cannot simply say that she needs men as relays to her *jouissance.* Of course, she wants to catch and hold the gaze of men, but her attraction is linked to the fact that she quickly turns around and shows very little interest in admirers.

The Silence of the Sirens, or, Kafka with Homer

We can take the Sirens as such femmes fatales, who enjoy their singing and because of this *jouissance* are admired by the sailors: although the Sirens encourage the sailors to stop and listen to them, they possess a certain self-sufficiency because of which they will never express more than a passing interest in the ships that pass by. . . . Such a reading remains within the confines of the standard sexualized opposition between masculine desire and feminine drive: men are actively engaged in penetrating the enigma of the Other's desire, while the fundamental feminine attitude is the one of drive's closed self-sufficiency—in short, men are subjects, while women are objects. What if, however, we imagine an alternative version of Odysseus's adventure with the Sirens, in which the agents reverse their respective roles, that is, in which Odysseus, a being of self-sufficient drive, confronts the Sirens, feminine subjects of desire? It was Franz Kafka who, in his short essay on the "Silence of the Sirens," accomplished this reversal. His starting point is that the measures that Odysseus and his sailors took to protect themselves from the Sirens' song were simply childish, since it was well known that nothing can protect men from the Sirens' allure. Although it is said that no one survives an encounter with the Sirens, Kafka speculates that "it is conceivable that someone might possibly have escaped from their singing; but from their silence never."[30]

Now, what happened when Odysseus approached the Sirens? Kafka's answer is that during this encounter, "the potent songstresses actually did not sing, whether because they thought that this enemy could be vanquished only by their silence, or because the look of bliss on the face of [Odysseus], who was thinking of nothing but his wax and his chains, made them forget their singing. But [Odysseus], if one may so express it, did not hear their silence; he thought they were singing and that he alone did not hear them."[31] In short, Odysseus was so absorbed in himself that he did not notice that the Sirens did not sing. Kafka's guess is that for a fleeting moment Odysseus saw them and from the movements of their throats, their lips half-parted and their eyes filled with tears, he concluded that they were actually singing: "Soon however, all this faded from his sight as he fixed his gaze on the distance, the Sirens literally vanished before his resolution, and at the very moment when they were nearest to him he knew of them no longer."[32] Kafka goes on to speculate that "they—lovelier than ever—stretched their necks and turned, let their cold hair flutter free in the wind, and forgetting everything clung with their claws to the rocks. They no longer had any desire to allure; all they wanted was to hold as long as they could the radiance that fell from [Odysseus's] great eyes."[33] Kafka thus reinterprets the encounter between the Sirens and Odysseus by claiming that the Sirens themselves became fascinated by Odysseus and not vice versa. Many misperceptions were at work in the encounter; the first concerns Odysseus not noticing that the Sirens were actually silent. This misperception helped him to become overconfident in his strength, which also made him ignorant about the Sirens, and his ignorance sparked the Sirens to become enchanted by Odysseus's gaze. Here, we have the second misperception at work: the Sirens did not notice that the gaze of Odysseus was not directed toward them at all. The failed encounter between the Sirens and Odysseus can be thus summarized like this: the fact that Odysseus did not notice that the Sirens were silent, but had thought that he had mastered their voice, had made Odysseus's gaze so alluring in its self-confidence that the Sirens fell desperately in love with him.

Kafka's rereading of the *Odyssey* can easily be understood as a myth that endeavors to restore men to their dominant position: a man does not perish when encountering a seductive, monstrous female, if he reverses the situation and incites the female to fall in love with him. If some stories say that the Sirens committed suicide when they failed to enchant Odysseus, Kafka offers an even more devastating account of the Sirens' power: it was because they fell in love with Odysseus that they were unable to even sing. We meet a similar situation in Kafka's "Before the Law," where the peasant learns at the end of the story that the doors of the law were there all the time only for him. He is thus not a nobody in front of the law: the whole legal spectacle was made just for him. The same goes for Kafka's Odysseus: he is not just one of the many sailors who come by the Sirens' island; he is the one that the Sirens were interested in, and he is the only one.

Kafka's reinterpretation of Odysseus's story enacts Lacan's notion of the magic moment of the reversal of the loved one into the loving subject. Lacan analyzes the deadlocks of the reciprocity of love in his seminar on transference, when he introduces the myth of the two hands: one hand (the hand of the desiring subject) extends itself and tries to attract the beautiful object on the tree (the loved object immersed in the self-sufficiency of drive), while suddenly another hand emerges from the site of the object on the tree and touches the first one (i.e., the object of love returns love, turns into a loving subject).³⁴ That a second hand emerges in the place of the object is for Lacan a miracle, not a sign of reciprocity or symmetry. The touching of the two hands does not mark a moment of unification or the formation of a pair. So why does such unification fail to take place? The answer is very simple in its compelling necessity and beautifully enacted in Kafka's version: because, at that very moment, the first subject no longer notices the hand stretched back, since he himself now turns into a self-sufficient being of drive. Kafka's Sirens lose their self-sufficiency when they subjectivize themselves by falling in love with Odysseus, and, as a result of this subjectivation, the Sirens become mute.

The crucial question here is: do the Sirens give up on their *jouissance* when they subjectivize themselves? If in Kafka, this subjectivization results in muteness, for other post-Homerian interpreters, the subjectivation of the Sirens is linked to their recognition that they failed to seduce Odysseus; as a result, they commit suicide. It would be wrong to take the muteness of the Sirens or their suicide as a proof that, as a result of their subjectivization, the Sirens gave up on their *jouissance*. Although the Sirens may have subjectivized themselves, they still persisted in their deadly *jouissance*. The fact that the Sirens either became mute or died, proves that they did not compromise their *jouissance*. Was it not Freud himself who associated drives with a fundamental *silence*, claiming that they pursue their work *silently*, outside the resonating space of the public word? Had the Sirens compromised their *jouissance*, they would have become "ordinary" women who would have tried to pursue Odysseus. But in that case, they would never have gained the status of such mythical figures.

The reversal of roles between the Sirens and Odysseus in Kafka is thus not quite symmetrical, since there is a crucial difference between the way the Sirens are subjectivized, and the way Odysseus is subjectivized in his fascination with the enigma of the Sirens' song (in the standard version of the story): Odysseus did give up on his *jouissance* (which is why he was able to talk, to memorize his experience, to enter the domain of intersubjective community), while the Sirens' silence bears witness to the fact that, precisely, *they refused to do this*. What the Sirens' silence offers is an exemplary case of *subjectivization without accepting symbolic castration* (the Lacanian name for this gesture of giving up on one's *jouissance*). Perhaps, this paradox of a subjectivity that nonetheless rejects the phallic economy of the symbolic castration renders the central feature of the feminine subject. And our point is not that Kafka merely gives a modernist twist to the standard version of the encounter between Odysseus and the Sirens. In a much more radical way, Kafka's reversal provides the *truth* of the standard version: the reversal described by Kafka *always already was operative* in the standard version of the myth as its disavowed background. Odysseus, fascinated with the pre-subjectivized lethal song of the Sirens, intent on probing its secret—is this not the myth of the male desire, sustained by the reality of the male subject enamored in his own fantasmatic formation and, for that reason, ignorant of the invisible, but persistent, feminine subjectivity?

Notes

1   Various stories explain why the Sirens became half-bird and half-woman. Ovid relates that the Sirens were once ordinary girls, companions of Persephone. When she was abducted by Pluto, they asked the gods for wings to help them in their search for their companion. Other authors attribute this transformation to the anger of Demeter, since the Sirens failed to prevent the abduction of her daughter. It was also said that Aphrodite deprived them of their beauty because they scorned the pleasures of love. After their transformation from humans to half-birds they tried to rival the Muses, who then removed all their feathers. (See Pierre Grimal, *Dictionary Of Classical Mythology* [Harmondsworth, England: Penguin, 1991], 403.)

2   Jean-Pierre Vernant, *Mortals and Immortals: Collected Essays,* ed. Froma I. Zeitlin (Princeton: Princeton University Press, 1991), 104.

3   Homer, *The Odyssey,* trans. Robert Fagles (New York: Viking Penguin, 1996), 272.

4   Some theorists claim that the idea of the Sirens came from the bee-cult that existed in the pre-Hellenic Mediterranean and which associated bees with various goddesses, as well as with the spirits of the dead. See Gabriel Germain, "The Sirens and the Temptation of Knowledge," in *Homer: A Collection of Critical Essays,* ed. George Steiner and Robert Fagles (Englewood Cliffs, N.J.: Prentice-Hall, 1963).

5   Homer, *Odyssey,* 277.

6   This forceful representation of enchantment is for Pietro Pucci unique in world literature, comparable only to Plato's portrayal of Alchibiades's cursed subjugation to Socrates's beguiling discourse. See Pietro Pucci, *Odysseus Polutropos: Intertextual Readings in the Odyssey and the Iliad* (Ithaca: Cornell University Press, 1987), 210.

7   Pucci here claims that "the text of the Siren's invitation and promise . . . is 'written' in strictly Iliadic diction" (ibid., 7).

8 Ibid., 212.

9 Ibid.

10 Tzvetan Todorov, *The Poetics of Prose,* trans. Richard Howard (Oxford: Basil Blackwell, 1977), 58, 59. Maurice Blanchot also analyzes Odysseus's encounter with the Sirens as the problem of narration. However, Blanchot's thesis is that Odysseus actually heard the Sirens, but "with the disturbing deafness of he who is deaf because he hears." Odysseus "took no risks but admired the Sirens with the cowardly, unemotional, calculated satisfaction characteristic of the decadent Greek he was who should never have figured among the heroes of the Iliad." See Maurice Blanchot, "The Siren's Song," in *Selected Essays by Maurice Blanchot,* ed. Gabriel Josopovici, trans. Sacha Rabinovich (Brighton: Harvester Press, 1982), 60.

11 The Muses are "supreme in their fields, and those who dare challenge them meet with defeat and punishment." See Mark P. O. Monford and Robert J. Lenadrdon, *Classical Mythology* (London: Longman, 1991), 88.

12 Robert Graves, *The Greek Myths* (Harmondsworth, England: Penguin, 1990), 2:281, 282. "Hesiod claimed that they accompany kings and inspire them with the persuasive words necessary to settle quarrels and re-establish peace, and give kings the gentleness which makes them dear to their subjects" (ibid.).

13 Charles Segal, *Singers, Heroes and Gods in the Odyssey* (Ithaca: Cornell University Press, 1994), 103. There are also claims that forgetfulness is on the side of the men who listen to the Sirens' song. George B. Walsh thus says that "the Sirens' song is deadly in its charm, apparently because it brings men so much pleasure they forget to live." See his *The Varieties of Enchantment: Early Greek Views of the Nature and Function of Poetry* (Chapel Hill: University of North Carolina Press, 1984), 15.

14 Jacques Lacan, *The Four Fundamental Concepts of Psycho-Analysis,* trans. Alan Sheridan (Harmondsworth, England: Penguin, 1979), 49.

15 Max Horkheimer and Theodor W. Adorno, *Dialectics of Enlightenment,* trans. John Cumming (New York: Seabury Press, 1986), 32, 33.

16 As Jacques-Alain Miller points out in the later seminars of Lacan, the object *a,* the object around which the drive circulates, needs to be understood as a special kind of satisfaction: "The object that corresponds to the drive is *satisfaction as object.*" See Jacques-Alain Miller, "On Perversion," in *Reading Seminars I and II: Return to Freud,* ed. Bruce Fink, Richard Feldstein, and Maire Jaanus (Albany: SUNY Press, 1995), 313.

17 Jacques-Alain Miller, "Donc" (unpublished seminar from 1993–94), 18 May 1994.

18 Michel Poizat, *The Angel's Cry* (Ithaca: Cornell University Press, 1992), 35.

19 Ibid.

20 Jacques Lacan, *Écrits: A Selection,* trans. Alan Sheridan (New York: Norton, 1977), 321.

21 Ibid., 270.

22 See Juan-Carlos Indart, "Etude d'un symptome obsessionnel," *Ornicar?* 28 (1984).

23 Here, the perverts, of course, differ from the neurotics, since they want to be the object of *jouissance* of the Other. However, in this case, the pervert actually imposes on the Other a specific form of *jouissance.*

24 It is significant how the women's journals, which are usually very much influenced

by cosmetic and fashion corporations, advise women whose husbands cheat on them to buy new clothes, especially lingerie, to make themselves again the object of love. We can agree with the German designer Joop that designer shops today function as places for therapy. The failure of the fashion industry to find the object that would satisfy the desire of the consumers helps this industry to flourish, but it also helps psychoanalysts to stay in business, since traumas usually cannot be resolved simply by purchasing a new dress.

25   The fact that human sexuality undergoes symbolic castration means that so-called natural sexuality or even animality has been repressed when the subject became the being of language. Repression also means that with the subject something becomes sexualized that hasn't been before, i.e., the function of repression is to make out of the real a sexual reality. (See Jacques Lacan, *Le séminaire, livre XX: Encore* [Paris: Editions du Seuil, 1975].)

Repression thus contributes to the fact that with the subject the partial objects like gaze and voice, breast, etc., become sexualized and function as objects of drive. Since the subject has no genital drive, these other objects (gaze, voice, etc.) play more crucial role in the subject's sexuality than his or her sexual organs.

26   In men who stutter one finds that they very much have a problem with their symbolic role: these men do not simply have difficulty in speaking but difficulty in assuming a position in a symbolic network, i.e., occupying the place from which to speak. Although we usually perceive women as being voiceless in our patriarchal culture, one rarely finds women who stutter, which confirms that women do not experience their dilemmas over their symbolic role in the same way as men. See Darian Leader, *Why do women write more letters than they post?* (London: Faber and Faber, 1996), 127, 128.

27   Geneviève Morel, "L'hypothèse de Compacité et les logiques de la succession dans le chapitre I d'Encore," *La Cause freudienne: Revue de psychanalyse* 25 (1993): 102.

28   See Jacques Lacan, *Le séminaire, livre XX: Encore,* 13. See also, Serge Andre, *Oue veut une femme?* (Paris: Seuil, 1995).

29   Jacques Lacan, "Guiding Remarks for a Congress on Feminine Sexuality," in *Jacques Lacan and the Ecole Freudienne: Feminine Sexuality,* ed. Juliet Mitchell and Jacqueline Rose (London: MacMillan, 1982), 93.

30   Franz Kafka, "The Silence of the Sirens," in *Homer: A Collection of Critical Essays,* ed. George Steiner and Robert Fagles (Englewood Cliffs, N.J.: Prentice-Hall, 1963), 98.

31   Ibid.

32   Ibid.

33   Ibid., 99.

34   Jacques Lacan, *Le séminaire, livre VIII: Le transfert* (Paris: Seuil, 1991), 67.

PART III | cogito
and its
critics

7

Marc de Kessel

"Man shall not live by bread alone." Few in our rich and fickle tradition have ever rejected this evangelical proposition outright, and neither has Georges Bataille,[1] who adopted it, but *in his own way*. Although man may live by more than bread alone, for Bataille there is nothing besides bread to live by. In his view, man coincides with the bread he eats, with the work he makes a living from, and with the economy that sustains him. But then, says Bataille, this bready, working, and economic man can also live by *nothing;* he can ignore the fact that he cannot live by anything else and simply enjoy this light-spirited attitude, even if he is going to pay for it with his life, or at least with everything he possesses, when he, sovereign as he is and fully aware of what he is doing, rejects it, burns it, gratuitously, without any reason, as if Nothing could hurt him, not even the nothingness he keeps. And he cannot be hurt even when he loses this nothingness.

Such an attitude of human beings toward life and its nothingness, is what Bataille calls "sovereignty." This sovereign reflex is not something man does when he finds no other way out; it is an indication of what man comes down to, every man, whatever he does, thinks, and asserts. This sovereignty is something like man's universal "essence," making him what he is. According to Bataille, man expresses his "essence" when he ostentatiously destroys all the bread he lives on and wastes it in a frivolous and unbridled orgy.

And yet, sovereignty is not a romantic or unworldly concept for Bataille, something that would belong to a previous, archaic era. In his thought, sovereignty takes on the air of a constructive solution, meeting the most urgent geopolitical problems that modern man has been confronted with. Hence, it is not without reason that in the early fifties he uses the title *La Souveraineté* for a text that, in a pivotal passage, dwells upon the problem of Stalinist terror, the scope of which became apparent only after the dictator's death. Without any doubt, Bataille is convinced that in this concept of sovereignty he is handing man a concept that is essential in order to keep this disaster from striking out all over the world. Furthermore, he is very clear about the necessity and the urgency of handling the problem. Modern world policy has only two options to choose from: either "thinking Stalin," or being submerged by a Stalin and his terror. For Bataille, "thinking Stalin" is thinking sovereignty. It is *always* sovereignty that is involved—even in the case of someone like Stalin who tried to eradicate it to a greater degree than anyone else. For this reason (so Bataille said in the early fifties as the threat of the Cold War was spreading all over the planet), it is of the utmost importance to face sovereignty in this way too, precisely because sovereignty is so much more dangerous when unseen and unrecognized.

Modern Sovereignty

Sovereignty and revolution

La Souveraineté, the unpublished work written in 1953–55, demonstrates that the concept of sovereignty gives modern man unexpected insight into twentieth-century sociopolitical problems, especially into the hidden mainsprings underlying the communist revolutions that have played such a decisive role in this century. According to classical Marxist theory, these revolutions were supposed to erupt first in societies with a settled bourgeois (and hence) capitalist order, as in these societies means of production and surplus-value were monopolized by a tiny but immensely rich minority, which left only one way out for the impoverished masses: the destruction of the capitalist class and the seizure of all means of production. The actual course of history confronted Marxist theory with a question: How was it possible that revolutions broke out in precisely those societies that still were a long way from reaching the stage of extreme conflict between the classes, societies in which the accumulation of wealth and means of production had hardly started? Why did only backward, feudal countries, in which a *bourgeois* revolution was due, see successful *Communist* revolutions? Because, according to Bataille, *feudal* societies were characterized by something that drove people to revolution, much more distinctly and to a greater extent than was the case in bourgeois societies. After all, this "something" is nothing other than sovereignty, and feudal culture did explicitly stress the rulers' prodigality and ostentation, which their subservient subjects would humbly and respectfully look up to. During the revolution, these people would throw away all respect and humbleness, and, by all means possible, would attempt to capture the sovereign luxuries of the formerly revered, but now hated upper class.

The medieval, feudal lord could indeed be considered a "sovereign" in the Bataillean sense. He is by definition a person who does not work: he squanders and gambles away the earnings of others. He does not care about the future, and his life does not depend on plans, whether they are designed by others or by himself. He lives only by the yield of every "moment." He lives on pure freedom and on the luxury of regarding everything he comes across in a light-spirited manner, enjoying it as if it were his own. To put it more dramatically: he does not allow his life to be led by conservative life principles, but rather by "death principles," by everything that makes life a game or puts it at risk. He lives by the moments in which his very existence is at stake. Therefore, what he needs are "pure moments," an insouciant time, no worries whatsoever, no worries even about his own mortality. Light-spirited as he may be, he lives the life of a "perfect" man: he does not live to a certain end, but lives as if all his aspirations had already been realized, all his wishes granted, his needs fulfilled, as if there were nothing to fear. He lives as if every moment were the last in his life and there were nothing to worry about. Although his existence may express a radical finitude, he lives it as "fullness," as fulfillment of *being* as such.

For Bataille, the sovereignty of a person is the sovereignty of being itself. "Being" has no aims outside itself, and is not bothered by its own transience as it includes both life and death. "Being" *is* its own transience, and, as such, it *is* its own negation. The existence of death beside life, of disintegration beside integration, does not make "being" less perfect. Being is also aimless in that it needs no aim or cause to justify its existence: it is what it is in every single moment. The fullness of being lies not in the fulfillment of its (supposed) evolution, but in every "moment" in which it *is*, as such. By living, sovereign man asserts the sharing of this perfect "moment," which being always *is*.

From this perspective, revolution can only succeed when revolutionaries mirror themselves—whether consciously or unconsciously—in this radical sovereignty, when they enjoy their revolutionary "moment" without any further consideration of the future. The basic drive of a true revolutionary does not reside in his ideals, but rather in his merciless wish to be free, to die rather than to give up that freedom. By looking at an audacious sovereign who plays frivolously with his life and with the lives of others, man realizes who he essentially is and throws himself into the battle *game*, which, strictly speaking, has no other purpose than the battle as such, and, which will finally—man being finite—mean his death.

According to Bataille, revolution, of course, will claim to stand for a certain ideal and fight against undeniable wrongs, but the deadly risks of revolution would not have been taken if revolutionaries had not been attracted by the sovereignty of this violent "moment," secretly or unconsciously. The ideals one fights for are never more than a *secondary* revolutionary mainspring; their role is to veil, behind rational and ideological reasons, the principal purpose man seeks, and which lies in this "moment" of lethal negativity. One overthrows feudal and royal authority, not because one objects to feudalism or royalty, but because one desires to be just as wild, unjust, and irresponsible, as any feudal, sovereign lord; because one wants to dispose of one's own life just as frivolously as of the lives of others. It is only *in and during* this violent moment that the revolutionary realizes the purpose of his action, and not in the new society he thinks his revolution is aiming at. But for fear of the lethal negativity of this very sovereign moment, one will always already have filled up the emptiness of the "moment" within which "everything is possible." One thinks one is fighting for ideals, and not for the sovereign "fun" of the deadly fight itself. One will have this sovereign (and therefore lethal) *game* of revolution converted into *labor*, fighting for a different, better world.

To Bataille it is clear: the poor laborers who served as the catalyst for the Communist revolution did not want all people to be *equal*, they wanted to be *as rich* and *as prodigal* as the wealthy sovereigns above them. It was not the difference between their own hunger and the wealth of others that pushed them into revolution and violence, but wealth and luxury *as such*, the prodigality and the "glamour" of the rich. The revolutionary zest of the working classes was not aroused by the capitalists who hid their wealth, but rather by gaudy aristocrats who, although probably not even wealthy, did their best to ostentatiously exhibit the (often false) splendor of their feudal ancestry. Revolution did not break out in highly capitalist countries like Germany, France, or England, but in countries that had not really done away with feudalism as yet: Russia and China (8:320-21; 3:278-79). Successful Communist revolutions were not carried through by a politically conscious working-class, but by largely "unconscious," illiterate peasant masses with an almost completely feudal mentality.

The sovereign "sovereignlessness" of communism

Communism may take its sociopolitical position by revolutionary force, but once settled as a society, it is far from existing in a state of permanent revolution. On the contrary, it attempts to ban the same violence from its own political order, which it had previously used to ascend to power. But here too, the ultimate mainspring behind this solid political and economic system is sovereignty. Here again, Communism will repeat—but in a better, more decisive way—what all previous revolutions have done: the sovereign, negative force used to attain power, will now be employed to fight this same headstrong sovereignty, in order to utilize within a new and stern economy the things sovereignty so easily spills and wastes.

According to Bataille, Communism should be understood within the historic process in which man continually finds better ways to control and neutralize his fickle and prodigal sovereignty. Sovereignty has become increasingly aware of its own infinite power, and has therefore tried to reduce the destructive forces, or convert them into constructive ones. Essentially, man will forever remain the free sovereign he has always been, but it is the fear of this unfathomable freedom, of this infinite lethal emptiness as it is manifested in his wasting prodigality, that causes him to check his sovereign freedom and curb it, to invest the passion he has spent for his *game* in more useful things like *labor* and economy. Man has always become increasingly addicted to labor; more and more, he has sacrificed his sovereign freedom, be it, paradoxically, only to obtain a world full of sorrow and distress, caused by the very (and ultimately vain) intention to save and not to spoil his world. Communism fits perfectly into this evolutionary development; it even constitutes its ultimate moment.

The hatred that Communism bears toward capitalism is not related to fundamental ideological antagonisms, but should be understood as part of the competition between the two systems concerning the final conquest of sovereignty. More than simply being critical of capitalism, Communism is the perfection of the mentality that had served the former, especially since Calvinism (7:128; 1:134). This ideology sternly condemned the economic extravagance and waste of the medieval sovereign, and in its criticism of religion it focused on exactly the aspects that Bataille considered so essential to religion: excesses, squander, and prestige. In freeing the economy of any kind of waste, it brought about a mentality in which capitalism was to flourish. Capitalism, in turn, indeed enslaved everything and everyone to its economic law, but at least individual capitalists would still enjoy a limited measure of freedom and, hence, of sovereignty. Strong as the Calvinist mentality was, it still allowed for the choice between accumulating wealth and not doing so.

Communism will close this last loophole of economic waste and finally bring the capitalist economy and its mentality into power on a universal scale. Sovereignty will be entirely invested in a collective *sovereignly renouncing sovereignty*. No man will be able to permit himself (private) luxury or any other economic excess, and as the economy will be led by a collective of equals, no man will be able to maintain the pretense of sovereignty. It is only through Communism that the accumulation of wealth will be brought to perfection: the circular movement by which all revenues (all surplus-value) flow back into "creation of means of production" will no longer be skimmed by luxurious excesses, but will finally be absolute. The abolishment of sovereignty, which bourgeois revolutions had never fully achieved, will finally be realized by the apparent countermovement of the Communist revolution. No traces of wasteful sovereignty will remain when the people *themselves* will command over the revenues of their labor and economy. Ultimately, *nobody* will be able to exempt himself from being part of the people, *nobody* will be able to keep up the appearance of reigning sovereignly over others or to be a kind of sovereign "on his own."

But paradoxically, this implies that with the final blow to sovereignty, *everybody* will become sovereign, as the collective absolute death of sovereignty plants it anew within each member of society—this is Bataille's conclusion when he reads the then newly published study of Stalin and a recent text by Stalin himself.

Bataille quotes a casual remark by Stalin, in which sovereignty, albeit suppressed by Stalin, almost symptomatically seems to reappear. The Soviet leader argues against a certain Yarochenko, who claimed that the aim of the Communist economy was production (a notion through which he proves to be true to the previous aggressive industrialization policy of Stalin himself), by stating explicitly that the goal of all efforts he demands from the Soviet workers is not the high working pace as it is, but something akin to "leisure." When the "socialist" stage makes room for a genuine "Communist" economy, a worker will have to work a mere six, and perhaps later even five, hours a day, and then be free for the rest. Free for what? Free for further schooling, studying, or anything else, eventually freeing him from the "job" he ended up with.

Of course, according to Stalin, leisure is to be seen entirely in the function of labor; in this way, the worker seems hindered from obtaining sovereign liberty once again. But precisely because this leisure gives the worker the chance to become a *perfect* one (according to the logic of the economic system), he reaches the point at which he can master *all* work, so that no work and no labor will ever again master him. As of that moment, he is no longer simply part of the system, nor is he totally immersed in it, but has become capable of striking an independent attitude toward it. It is this attitude toward the system as a whole that gives him back his sovereignty. And from that point on, he will be able to recognize sovereignty as his most intimate companion. Once the entire Communist economy becomes real, all workers who before had been reduced to mere instruments of (sovereign) others, have become sovereign themselves over all things and all instruments, without having someone above them as their (sovereign) master. In effect, every "all-round" skilled worker can admire in every comrade his own sovereignty as well as the one of universal mankind.

Necessity and *impossibility of modern sovereignty*

This situation would, according to Bataille, "draw as possible to that kind of sovereignty which, linked to the voluntary respect of the sovereignty of others, would go back to the initial sovereignty [*souverainité initiale*] that we must ascribe to the shepherds and hunters of ancient humanity." Bataille immediately adds the following remark: "But the latter, if they respected the sovereignty of others, respected it only, it must be said, as a matter of fact" (8:341; 3:302); so they did not do it with conscious knowledge.

In Communist society, no one is master or sovereign precisely because *everybody* has become one—just as in early, archaic societies. There, nobody was anyone else's sovereign, and therefore everyone could be sovereign. But in those societies the mutual respect toward each other's sovereignty was, as Bataille suggests, not the result of a conscious willing decision, but a situation that de facto happened to be so. In fact, after the detour of its history, sovereignty, which found its way back to man in Communism, was far from being a brute, contingent *factuality*, but was rather a matter of *self-conscious* decision. Indeed, sovereignty by which—denied or acknowledged—modern society is characterized, is the result of a decision and is therefore self-conscious.

Analyzing this self-conscious sovereignty in Hegelian terms, one must notice that here the negative power by which sovereignty was driven and by which it "negated" everyone and everything, has now been applied to itself, to its own negation. It has negated its own negativity and (in this way) become pure positivity. Communism has pretended to demonstrate that this sovereign negativity, by sovereignly negating itself, can re-establish a free, sovereign, and peaceful society—a society without sovereigns oppressing the other people.

The whole question however, is whether this *self-conscious* sovereign decision (whether it is collectively to be sovereign or, which amounts to the same, sovereignly to refuse sovereignty) is indeed possible at all. Will such a decision ever be able to revive the society of "shepherds and hunters" in which the sovereignty of each individual was respected? The only thing that Communism has shown is that hitherto this has *not* been the case: it couldn't offer any guarantees toward a collective mutual respect for one's sovereignty. And for Bataille, the Communist system is not so much just another example, but rather the paradigm, the "truth" about the entire modern (essentially capitalist) economic social policy. Communism is close to its principal goal of "sovereignly eliminating sovereignty" (i.e., renouncing sovereignty as the cause of social inequality and eliminating the waste that undermines economy). At the same time, however, it is this very sovereignty that, in a Communist society, unfolds its most catastrophic guise. First of all, there are those figures like Stalin, who are infinitely more sovereign than the greatest medieval feudal lord ever was—and this in spite of their own claiming to be sovereignty's fiercest adversary, or their promises to make everyone sovereign, which amounts to the same. Worse, however, are the excesses to which the Communist system has given itself, which can be taken as proof of the ineradicability of sovereignty. Waste, a practice that Communism strove to eliminate, now involved masses of its "best" people, with which it fed an insatiable holocaust in its gulags. And even if nobody in this system (Stalin included) could openly act as a sovereign, sovereignty was nevertheless manifested in a terror that was crueler than any political oppression of the past.

In the fate of Communism, we thus face the impasse of modern, self-conscious sovereignty: while trying to eliminate or integrate its negative side (of which it has become aware as being its very essence), this negativity strikes harshly and fatally more than ever. On the one hand, it seems as if consciousness in the long run cannot consciously master the negative powers by which it is driven. On the other hand, we have only this consciousness to solve the problem sovereignty has become for us. Our culture cannot return to an archaic, not yet consciously sovereign society, even if only for the fact that this would be the result of a consciously taken step. Our culture will have to look at that missed, impossible sovereignty as being a failure of its own consciousness, but paradoxically, it will only be able to strike a conscious attitude toward it.

Witnessing the terror Communism itself had fallen into, Bataille leaves no doubt as to this impasse in which our culture became stuck: if our culture will not be able to take sovereignty (as it presents itself in Communism) into account in a lucid way, it will be brought down by it. But at the same time, sovereignty escapes anything like the "taking into account" that self-consciousness is, by definition. This impossibility cannot, however, mitigate the *demand* for modern self-consciousness to take sovereignty into account, says Bataille. Here we have the persistent short-circuit between the explosive impasse and the demand our culture can no longer ignore.

Just as the way out of the impasse cannot circumvent consciousness, only a keen consciousness can provide one. Bataille's entire oeuvre explores the possibility of such a keener consciousness. The seriousness of his attempt appears from the mere fact that he uncompromisingly approaches thought and consciousness from the angle of their inherent impasse.

Conscious Sovereignty

Self-consciousness, it has been said before, has caused sovereignty to escape itself, hence causing alienation and social repression. If this sovereignty returns to itself after its odyssey, it can only do this *self-consciously.* In the quote in which Bataille compares Communist sovereignty with the early sovereignty of "shepherds and hunters" (8:341; 3:302), he suggests that at the end of history, man will have to be the *same* "shepherd and hunter" he was in the beginning, but *lucidly, consciously* so.

Bataille's solution for the impasse of modern sovereignty seems to go toward a kind of lucid "shepherdness." According to Bataille, modern man will have to be lucid enough for himself to see that his perfect self-consciousness is ultimately the *same* as the "factual," probably most "unconscious" self-awareness of the early, primitive shepherds and hunters. Modern man will have to see his self-consciousness mirrored, not in the results of his work (perfect as it may be in comparison with the more primitive work of the shepherds and hunters), but in their very insignificance—an insignificance these results fully share with the things produced by the labor of the ancient shepherds and hunters. He will also have to affirm the insignificance of his work in the *way* that the "primitives" did (i.e., by explicitly destroying his products). To endorse their sovereignty, to affirm that their products were not so much something that they *needed,* than something they had made in sovereign freedom, the "primitives" explicitly consigned them to destruction with their own hands. This was the essence of their sacrificial religion, the expression of the finitude and sovereignty of their economy. But while the early shepherds and hunters acted unconsciously, modern sovereign man has to bring about destruction *in full consciousness.*

Starting from Hegel's *Phenomenology of Spirit* and with the paradigm of sacrificial religion in mind, Bataille pretends he can think through the negative power of self-consciousness more than Hegel did. To Bataille, as to Hegel, self-consciousness will recognize itself and its sovereignty in its infinite negativity, which is the capacity to bring reality "to itself" (this is: to its "concept") by negating itself. But unlike Hegel, Bataille will insist that in the end, this self-consciousness will not be able to sublate the negation, which it essentially "is," exhaustively. The negation that carries reality will in the end recognize itself in a negativity that it cannot include in the functioning of its own economy. On the most fundamental level, negation, which lies at the basis of all functioning (and reality), offers itself to itself as a radically "unemployed negativity."[2] Self-consciousness does not recognize itself so much in the *infinity* as in the *finitude* of its negation: a hard, stubborn negativity that it cannot assume control of. The sovereign negativity that keeps our human self-consciousness going is, according to Bataille, the code of our finitude; therefore, in its radicalism, it cannot come to us as infinite *consciousness,* but as a radical finite *experience.*

It is this "expérience intérieure" of the unemployed negativity that is uncompromisingly affirmed by "sovereign" man. Bataille's sovereignty must therefore not be confused with the subjective, complacent arbitrariness in which man could confidently cherish himself; it is the experience of a subject being confronted with its own radical and intimate finitude, that is, with the fact that it escapes itself precisely in its most intimate self-experience and is therefore traversed by a lethal exteriority. The attitude asserting this intimate exteriority or the radical finitude of the subject is what Bataille designates as "sovereign." It affirms the fact that the subject is not grounded in its own self, that is, in its own negation. This negation is its most intimate self, and at the same time comes from a radical "outside."

Our self-conscious civilization, which thinks of itself as being at "the end of history" or living in "the best of all possible worlds," must confront itself with its own sovereignty or "identity" as coming from a radical outside. In order to recognize our sovereignty in a *sovereign* way, we have to be overtaken by it as if by something *exterior,* coming from the outside. Otherwise we should lose ourselves in it as in something that *transcends* our own limits and (which comes to the same) forces us into deadly excesses. The sacrifice of the ancient "shepherds and hunters" in the Bataillean sense revolves around this experience: sovereign uselessness, light-spirited gratuitousness, and the radically unbound, deadly freedom—all being names for the same "essence" of man. They all appear in the form of a sovereign death, to which one sovereignly surrenders the products of one's labor.

Holocaust versus holocaust

But what then is the difference between this and Stalinist terror? Does sovereignty not overtake man here *from the outside* as well—even clearly and embarrassingly so? Does the sovereign power of negativity, which has given to society its existence and its strength, not reveal itself here in its pure radicalism, in its unconquerable *exteriority?* Is Stalin's terror, are the gulags a modern form of sacrifice? Are we to see this macabre show as our sovereignty and as an affirmation of our finitude?

Bataille's positive answer seems to be as radical as it is untenable: the gulags may indeed be seen as some kind of "sacrifice," but only if we are willing to look at them actively and *consciously,* that is, consciously affirming that this "sacrifice" both escapes our consciousness, and at the same time is closely related to it. Only when we—and with us our entire culture—succeed in this, in "consciously" maintaining this *impossibly conscious* view of the gulags, will we stand a chance to avoid the abomination manifested in the gulag.

However, before going into this problematic position, the following should be made clear: Bataille unequivocally disapproves of any abominations of the sort that took place in Auschwitz and in the gulags. As has been stated, his thought wants to help to make these atrocities avoidable, but Bataille realizes that these atrocities could descend upon us precisely because we pretend to have eliminated such things from our world. As already mentioned, this pretention is based on the denial of sovereignty and of the hard, unsublatable negation active inside our consciousness. Therefore, our consciousness cannot but face these atrocities now. In them, we see something absolutely useless and pointless. But it is in this that we see the essence and the finitude of our own purpose.

Our culture, in a way, has achieved "everything" and has reached "the end of its history" (as Bataille phrases it, referring to Hegel), the end of its consciousness-raising process. Modern man is no longer a subordinate "thing" within the totality of being, but has assumed an attitude *toward* it and now *faces* it sovereignly, both individually and collectively. Therefore, this sovereignty is not reflected in something purposeful, but rather in purposeless and senseless things, in whatever appears not to *need* an aim or a purpose whatsoever, and which is therefore absolutely unacceptable.

It is this kind of radical, abominable, unacceptable pointlessness in which modern man must recognize himself, not by approving it, even less by profiting from it, but by first seeing what these unacceptable atrocities are all about, and then by consciously realizing this himself. He first has to realize that the atrocities, much like his entire economy (in the widest sense of that word, also like the economy of being), are a matter of waste and destruction. Although one might be inclined to think the opposite, the excesses have become unavoidable and even vital to our (accumulative, capitalist) economy, as this economy is defined by the principle of sovereignty, and therefore heads for its transgression. Modern sovereign man will then have to execute this (ontologically based) destruction himself, and *consciously* so: instead of "draining away" excess population into camps *for certain reasons,* man now has to realize a similar thing being totally aware it is radically senseless. He now has to destroy the products of his accumulative economy *without having a reason,* and *sovereignly* consign the product of his labor to death. The result will be that he will no longer have to destroy *people* whom he thinks to be the cause of waste in his economy. He will understand that the reason he had put those people inside camps ("they sabotaged the economy, they assumed sovereign rights, they wasted what belonged to the entire community," etc.) was the very reason of his economy as such, and mainly of its sovereignty.

Bataille's position implies that destruction can only be averted by destruction: the (profane) holocaust of the gulags by a (religious) holocaust, an "unconscious" holocaust by a "conscious" holocaust. The power of negativity that keeps a system or another organism alive will have to burst for the sake of the sovereignty of this power, and lose itself in unrecoverable economic waste. It is precisely man's being sovereign (just like "being" itself) that makes this waste, this "all-consuming fire" (which is the literal meaning of the Greek word *holocaustos*) inevitable. While the one holocaust will kill people *en masse* because they do not seem to suit the ultimate sense that their society has given to man and the universe, the other holocaust will convince these same people of their sovereignty vis-à-vis every sense, by letting them consciously destroy the products of their sense-giving or their labor. The result of this latter holocaust will be that people themselves will not be deprived of their lives, but *endowed* with them, with wasteful, sovereign, finitude-conscious lives.

The claim Bataille brings forward here, a claim that bears upon his entire thought, is a difficult one, to say the least. On one of the last pages of his *Théorie de la Religion* of 1948, the hardness of his reasoning is unequivocal: "It is a matter of endlessly consuming—or destroying—the objects which are produced. This could just as well be done without the least *consciousness*. But it is insofar as clear consciousness prevails, that the objects actually destroyed will not destroy humanity itself" (7:345). In the end, everything is to be consciously destroyed by us, and if we do not destroy it ourselves, we ourselves will be destroyed by it; this is the ultimate consequence of the sovereignty that is the essence of our being.

Sovereignty and Finitude

Since Bataille's oeuvre, we can no longer disregard things like sovereignty and dissipation at work in human society, in politics and in the economy. With these Bataillean terms we are better armed to conceive and to affirm our finitude—an affirmation required by our modernity itself. But *conscious* sovereignty, his "solution" to the modern problem of an economy that is perpetually at its zenith, is, to say the least, a rather strange if not untenable solution. To say that this economy wishes to escape its own finitude by perpetually conquering new domains and sources, without noticing that it is in fact merely seeking new opportunities to allow dissipation (in the form of war or terror), be it under the guise of some motive or ideal—so far, such an analysis is acceptable. But why should it, after becoming aware of this, also start spilling *effectively*? Why is it impossible for a *conscious* human society to be sovereignly free without effectively destroying something? Why can this sovereignty (which we, according to Bataille, should consciously assume, if we don't want to be destroyed by it in the shape of terror or war) not exist without an actual "holocaust" or destruction?

To put this same question more concretely: Why should the sovereign *game* of the (*working*) man be "played" in a conscious, *real* holocaust? Why should a holocaust, consciously "played" to avert an unconscious, *real* holocaust, also itself be effective and *real?* Why should we "really play" dissipation, spilling, and destruction in order to avoid the dissipation, the spilling, and the destruction that threaten to wipe us off the planet by terror, or at least threaten to turn us into amorphous slaves of totalitarian systems?

How can the "realness" of a (sovereign) *game* be thought? This is the problem Bataille is confronted with. In what follows we will see how, to cope with this, he forcefully pushes conscious thought *beyond* its utmost limits. And we will also detect that the "hardness" and the untenability of Bataille's sovereign "solution" to the problem of modern sovereignty is in a certain way due to the interrelation between three basic concepts of his thought: consciousness, game, and reality. Of course, Bataille is strongly aware of the problem of modernity, which permeates his entire thinking to a large extent, but this does not prevent it, at a certain moment, from bouncing off this problem of modernity. Only in viewing the contours of Bataille's thought from this perspective will we be able to understand why he keeps returning to his "solution" while openly admitting its untenability.

Sunny sovereignty

Bataille is able to think the "realness" of the sovereign game because, for him, on the most fundamental level, reality *is* a sovereign game. "Being" itself is playing a lethal game, playing frivolously with all that lives, works, and produces. Bataille may call the sovereignty of that game Nothing, but then this nothingness is about the only thing that can fully claim to exist.

To understand this, our thinking needs the courage to undergo a sort of "Copernican revolution." Just like Copernicus, who abandoned the "limited" terrestrial view of our planetary system in favor of a more "general" solar view, Bataille advocates an abandonment of the limited (*restreint*) view of the "economic" game of being for a view from a more general angle.[3] The first pages of his "Introduction Théorique" in *La part maudite* (1949) shed some light on this turnover. When we observe things in action from their *own* (limited) angle, the frivolous, dangerous, and sovereign game they so often surrender to looks like a senseless act that needlessly endangers their vital power. Seen from *their* angle, their death implies an irreparable loss. Yet, this very death, when observed from a more "general" angle (i.e., from the angle of the infinite transgressive movement with which "being" actually coincides) is all but a loss: it is a necessary element in this being that perpetually transgresses its boundaries. Here, *playing* and (lethally) *putting at stake* are coincidental. From the point of view of the "économie générale" things exist not so much *by* energy, but fundamentally, energy lives *within* everything, and *outlives* everything. From the limited angle, death may be the ultimate sign of man's and the world's deficiency, but from the wider angle it is luxury "pur sang," a luxury that even indicates the most essential element of life. The energy concentrated and accumulated inside a being (and thus giving it its existence), escapes upon the death of this entity and joins the universal free movement of energy that "being" (fundamentally) *is*. The energy will then accumulate inside a newly formed entity, finally escape again and bring about its death.

Bataille's view on "being" appears to be a strongly *energetic* one. Everything that exists—from the tiniest particle of dust, to human consciousness, to the most distant stars—is supposed to be a source brimming over with vital power that is not teleologically tuned to any preset objective, but which (sovereignly) knows its goal inside itself, in its own use (i.e., its own spilling) of energy as such. The structure in which this brimming power is kept, is therefore a transgressive and an excessive one. Everything that exists is already in decomposition, it keeps on going by the same force that will later start the process of decomposition. Every being lives by a power that has given itself away to that being, and the same power makes it unavoidable that this being too, one day, will lethally give itself away. A being is sovereign when it recognizes that every being is actually a pure (and therefore) lethal *gift* and *self-gift*.

It is from this perspective that we must understand Bataille's claim that on the most fundamental level, everything is sovereign since it is "cosmic solar energy": energy originating in energy "itself," that is, in something that exists entirely by giving itself away. Everything *is* solar energy, and is therefore radical self-giving. As individuals, beings store and accumulate that energy for a restricted period and build a temporally limited existence. What keeps these beings alive, however, is (at least when seen from the limited angle) a "death drive": they are driven by an energy that perpetually tries to transgress the accumulated equilibrium and radically give itself away to the pure "giving" that "being" fundamentally *is*. But only from our limited point of view is this principle a *principle of death*. When seen from a wider, "general" angle, this principle is a principle of *life,* if a term like that can still make sense, since on that level, life is the only thing there is. So must we conclude that, strictly speaking, there is no such thing as death? For Bataille, death is merely the event of individual, "personal" life transforming into "impersonal" life (7:41).

This impersonal life, this cosmic energy of being flowing through a person, is larger than what this person needs to keep himself alive. The concept of excessive vital energy implies a radically *finite* concept of man: what keeps him alive is not *his* energy, but an energy that transcends him and that as such could also turn against him. Therefore, he is not necessarily capable of keeping the energy within the limits he wants, and this explains why he is able to live the excesses and commit the atrocities he is too often known for, why his economy is secretly fascinated by waste and excessive luxuries. In all of these excesses, man is confronted with his irreversible finitude: they reveal not only the limits within which his existence has to take place, but also his inability to keep those limits from being transgressed. This last unavoidable transgression confronts man with his finitude in the clearest possible way because he has to fail in this transgression; if he does not, he "really" will get lost in the decomposition he has surrendered his vital energy to.

Therefore, our existence is based on an essentially excessive and (from the limited angle even) destructive energy: "the ground we live on is little other than a field of multiple destructions." If we are not aware of this, "our ignorance only has this uncontestable effect: It causes us to *undergo* what we could *bring about* in our own way, if we understood [elle nous fait *subir* ce que nous pourrions, si nous savions, *opérer* à notre guise (at pleasure)]. It deprives us of the choice of an exudation that might suit us. Above all, it consigns men and their works to catastrophic destructions. For if we do not have the force to destroy the surplus energy ourselves, it cannot be used; and like an unbroken animal that cannot be trained, it is this energy that destroys us; it is we who will have to pay the prize of the inevitable explosion" (7:31; 1:23–24). Our "ground" turns out to be an untamable, violent "animal" that, if not disciplined or tamed, will bite at our own flesh.

Which brings us back to the aforementioned "holocaust versus holocaust" dialectics. We need to gain insight into the sovereign holocaustal character of being as such, and even more so, we must assume the excess and the superfluity of being in "general" by consciously executing "real played" holocausts ourselves. If we ourselves do not "play" *real* holocausts, the holocaust that being itself *is*, will conquer us, bringing catastrophes as witnessed by the gulags, Auschwitz, or the seemingly peaceful cruelty of a "people's dictatorship." The sovereign holocaust that being itself *is*, we ourselves have to be it in a *conscious* way: this is for Bataille the way to affirm the radical finitude of ourselves and of being as such. If we do not do this, the holocaustal sovereignty will wash us away like a wave of blind terror, or at best, we will remain "slaves" forever. With all of the power that our lucidity still possesses, we must affirmatively assume our finitude, for if not, the "adventure of man" might soon belong to the past—this way one could, in a nutshell, resume Bataille's position (and that of his entire intellectual engagement).

The capitalized "nothing" of sovereignty

Bataille's concept of sovereignty therefore confronts us with this task, which should be seen in the context of the typically modern finitude problem. Modernity as such coincides with a radical concept of finitude, and Bataille even endows it with something like an ontological statute: in his eyes, the finitude man has been confronted with in the course of the last three centuries is the one of "being" itself. Being itself is but a permanent transgressive force that lethally goes beyond the limits of every singular "being." However, this implies that the limits of this thing have been created by being itself as well. In order to transgress every limit, it is being itself that creates those limits.

Yet, we should ask now, has the Bataillean reflection approached finitude in a way justified by the *modernity* of this problem? Has it been thought "finitely" enough? Has Bataille been sufficiently aware of the finitude of his *own* thought, when thinking finitude? We are confronted here with the question of the finitude of Bataille's own thinking, and especially of the possibility of thinking the finitude problem in a *transgressive* way, as this is what the Bataillean "Copernican revolution" means: in it, thinking makes the same transgressive movement as the things that are thought of. In the same way that things transgress and lose themselves into a form of existence that is pure excessive energy, thinking must transgress and mortally lose itself in an eccentric, principally "general" view.

Where this transgression confirms its own failure, where this "general" view confirms that it de facto never takes place because it cannot be held, finitude will (also) be thought in a finite way. In this way, a thinking that transgressively attempts to capture finitude also confirms its *own* finitude. In this respect, Bataille's thought is a radical (and therefore a *modern*) finite thought; for him, thinking must go further than it actually can. It has to go beyond every kind of knowledge and aim to reach radical "non-knowledge" (*non-savoir*). And by experiencing the nothingness and the impossibility of this transgression, Bataille's thought is confronted with its own finitude. In a double, essentially tragic movement in which thought transgresses its limits *and* also fails in doing this, the finitude of thought is revealed. It demonstrates the extent to which it is marked by the nothingness that can only find an adequate pendant in a "non-knowledge."

Yet, it is not his concept of non-knowledge as such that has made Bataille a milestone in modern thinking about finitude, but rather his discontentment toward it, which can be read on every page of his oeuvre. This non-knowledge is never employed as a cunning solution by which to evade all problems. Never does it function as that "night in which all cows are black." Rather, it is a concept with which he wants to think the finitude of reality in relation to the finitude of his own thinking.

And yet, in spite of what it asserts itself, this thought seems to "know" of what this non-knowledge still refers to. Somewhere in his rotating about this nothingness, this thought seems to hide a non-expressed insight. Occasionally, complete cosmological explanations are given, which, while not being the kernel of his thought, are yet inseparable from it. Often, it seems as if this non-knowledge is completely based on an ancient metaphysical knowledge. Therefore, it is not uninterest-ing to detect and reflect upon the "cosmological" and "(meta)physical" statements in the Bataillean oeuvre, even if only to do justice to his own demand, which is to think finitude, the finitude of *his* thinking included.

Sovereignty may be a Nothing that is confirmed only by non-knowl-edge, but in many places throughout his oeuvre, Bataille seems to *know* what this nothingness is. He knows that this nothingness is "being" itself. He knows that it is what Hegel called "negation": something per-petually negating itself, and thereby founding a positivity; a positivity, however, that will only be reality as long as negativity will be actively at work in it. He knows—taking a step beyond Hegel—that this negation is more arduous than its ability to sublate itself, and that therefore it is not merely (inner) *Geist*, but harsh exteriority, and (even) biological, energetic materiality. This nothingness is a biological-energetic object-less "being," which, in its sovereign game, runs into limits that it has created itself,[4] and thereby "enwraps" itself into objects that eventually will unwrap again in their excessive, sovereign moment. To this object, death, which happens to nothing but Nothing, means the ultimate life, as it is the ultimate excess.

But doesn't Bataille know too much here? Nota bene: of course he realizes that what he knows is too much, that what he knows is but an "excédent," an excessive product of luxury in which Nothing and death (which is the living life itself) have transgressed themselves. But doesn't he know *too well* that he knows too much? Doesn't he know *too well* that his knowledge is finite, and therefore essentially Nothing? Hasn't he fixed finitude by charting it so? Hasn't his concept of finitude (the nothingness underlying everything) closed the circle again? Hasn't he made death into an—be it ungodly—immortality, which gratuitously and sovereignly hands out mortality?

An antique, closed cosmology

These questions suggest that at least one of the basic schemes underlying Bataille's thought tends toward an *antique, closed* worldview. Being's finitude is also charted by such a worldview, but not in a way conform-ing to modernity and the problems related to the latter. At least, the cosmic-energetic and biophysical schemes in Bataille's oeuvre, which are all pre-Newtonian and therefore premodern, point in that direction.

If we think through the logical consequences of Bataille's "cosmology," we find that outside this cosmos, in which this nothingness unfolds its binding-unbinding activity, there is "nothing" indeed, as everything takes place *in*side of it. Bataille's transgressive, "general" view is limited to the *inside* of the absolute space of nothingness, whereas on the outside there is "nothing." This last "nothing" simply does not exist for Bataille, and therefore the universe, based on his concept of nothingness, is *closed and finite.* This final, closed finitude is precisely a "classic," "antique" finitude, in which the universe was said to rigorously embrace everything, including the *space* in which things, and the universe itself, existed. Therefore, strictly speaking, this cosmos was *nowhere,* because everything, *space* included, took place *within* the cosmos. The outermost arch of heaven was not *in* space (as we moderns spontaneously assume), but it was space, rather, that was situated within the outer star-adorned firmament (as we moderns since Newton cannot even imagine): the firmament was the "end" of all that existed, and as such it was finite. This did not rule out the possibility, however, that everything *inside* could be considered as *in*finite and unlimited: everything connected with everything else and participating in a "primal cause" that was caused only by itself. Within this closed, finite universe it was possible to have an infinite all-embracing outlook without any limit; every limit one confronted was a limit brought about by the limitless "prime cause," which was being as such. Finitude, being its own cause and its own ground, could in this respect be conceived as being at the same time infinite.

Surprisingly, perhaps, Bataille's cosmology could in this light be compared to that of the Stoic Marcus Aurelius. In his thought, too, "being" exists merely by the grace of that which drives it into disintegration. Here too, death means disintegration into elements that are not really lost, but that recombine to form a new "being." Here too, the wisdom of an emperor or a politician lies not in denying this excess (something Bataille accuses Stalin of), but in linking that disintegration to the regularity of being as such; a more "general" view is expected of him as well.

Not that there would be anything Stoical about Bataille's opinions. Therefore, they lack the necessary calmness (the *apatheia*) underlying the worldview of the Stoic. The Stoic does not call his wider, "general" view of things nothingness, but rather uses positive terms like "Soul of the World," "Cosmos," or "Nature." If the Bataillean concept of nothingness is to be linked to a closed (for instance, a Stoic) worldview and

inherits therefore some antique influence, this does not count for the unbearable restless "pathos" that characterized his thinking. This pathos,
anything but Stoic, is extremely *modern,* in the sense of being a "finite
affirmation of finitude." Permanently, this pathos throws his thinking
out of balance and pitilessly tortures every conceptual pattern that could
give a resting point or any other point of certainty to his thought. "Modern," in Bataille's thinking, is not so much the (Hegelian) insight that
the "loss" that rules everything can only be regained with a supreme
effort, but rather the insight that this loss is to be abandoned to its radical chasm (as Bataille's reading of Hegel demonstrates).

"Modern" is a concept of loss indeed, of shortcoming, death, and
finitude. "Modern" is first and foremost the insight that no insight can
understand it completely, that no insight can touch what is lost, dead,
or finite, even if, from a certain point of view, it comes very close to it.
This modern understanding of finitude is displayed by the disarmingly
honest "patheticity" in Bataille's thinking, which uncompromisingly directs (i.e., confuses) his writing. This "patheticity" can be described as
honest because his thought openly dares to get stuck in the impasse of
his experience (i.e., of the experience of his thinking as such). In Bataille's writing we can indeed feel how thinking itself becomes touched
(even physically so) by its own "uncanny" *exteriority.* This "pathetic"
experience of the exteriority of thinking itself is the kernel of what Bataille calls "inner experience" (*expérience intérieure*).

But perhaps Bataille's patheticity is as forceful as it is, simply because
the conceptual patterns he uses are in a certain way too easy, capable
as they are to give at any time the solution to all his questions. The
antique (meta)physical schemes he uses can easily make of his concept
of nothingness, which is made to affirm finitude, that which explains
everything and thus "sublates" finitude into infinity. Thinking within
terms inherited from a closed worldview threatens to place finitude in
a world in which this nothingness would be everything. So, the moment Bataille's writing "feels" the easiness of his antique schemes and
is almost forced to solve his question of finitude, it seems he has to let
its impossibility formally interpose. Every time, death threatens, *not* to
threaten, but to be a smooth and easy "solution." The lethal *insolubility*
that Bataille wants to demonstrate, threatens to become enfeebled by
the "easy" death. Only a pathetically invoked unsublatability of death

(and here he can rely only on the pathos of the *inner experience*) seems to be able to ensure the finitude of his reflection, that is, to deliver it to the typically modern restlessness with regard to the concept of finitude.

Bataille's Newtonian shortfall

It might not be totally indefensible to argue that Bataille's understanding of finitude depends largely on his honest "patheticity" and that he therefore does a certain injustice to the specifically modern character of this problem. The reason may be found in an obstacle that Bataille's thought seems to have circumvented—more specifically, the obstacle of the "Kantian caesura," which we prefer to link to modernity. In this respect, Bataille seems not to have taken a particular stand regarding Kantian thought or—which in this context comes to almost the same— to Newtonian physics. From this perspective it might be arguable that Bataille—surprisingly, and in spite of the indications to the contrary —did *not* think through profoundly enough, things like "death" and "Nothing."

In Bataille's conceptual schemes, it is unthinkable that things are dead, *without life,* that they are an indifferent neutral "mass," as Newtonian physics teaches. Things may be marked by death, their vital energy may be integrally oriented toward it, but for Bataille this is only thinkable because death is not merely death, but rather a closed cosmos of nothingness, within which, from the viewpoint of the "économie générale," nothing can be lost. From the Bataillean viewpoint, the neutral, bloodless death attributed by Newton to things without the least degree of "patheticity" is an absolute incongruity or a totally insane "skandalon."

The difference between the two visions of (the death of) things can best be explained by way of the problem of the death of God, to which both "thinkers of death" react in clearly distinct manners. The perspective of God's death will enable us to have a look at the kernel of the two physical systems (antique Bataillean physics, and modern Newtonian physics).

In *La Souveraineté* Bataille states in a footnote: "The place left by the absence of God (if we prefer, by the death of God) is enormous" (8:274; 3:441). For Bataille, modern man must affirm the tragedy of God's death by keeping open and empty this "immense place," by making this tragedy into an (objectless) "object" of non-knowledge, to put it in his own terms. Within his "cosmology," this infinite open place will become the place or the "space" *tout court,* which will be modeled after an antique, closed model of finitude.

God is dead, indeed, and the infinite universe is not closed anymore in (and by) the infinity of God. So, with God's death, the infinite has become simply the infinite "place," the limitless "space." But for Bataille this space nevertheless *"closes" in its own limitlessness itself.* For him, the whole of being remains *within* the very limits of this infinity. After God's death, being remains closed within (and by) the infinity of death itself. So we see how, in its infinity, "death" itself has—so to speak— survived even God. *Within* this infinite space, but precisely because it somewhere does still have a limit where it resists the vital power of being that is "pressing" at it, death will be able to play its excessive games, and maintain life, of which it is the basic principle.

Bataille thus accomplishes a regressive movement with regard to the Christian *creationist* vision of being. Christianity had broken up the finite world of antiquity with the idea that being as such had a "sovereign" origin *outside* of what was held to be "being." From a classical Greek philosophical point of view, Christianity was doing something quite absurd: it founded "being" in a place where until then one could only (unreasonably) speak of non-being, in a "space" where there was only pure, nonexistent nothing. Strangely enough, this vision survived, among other reasons because this "nothing" was mitigated in its severe and incongruous negativity by being seen as something "more than being," and by attributing this "hyperbolic" ontological character to God. Christianity taught that the all-embracing cosmos turned out not to be "everything"; outside of it there was an infinite "nothing," in which the Infinite One dwelled. The feeling of infinity did not depart from internal closeness of being itself any longer, but from an exterior infinity *within* which there was "being." If, in the past, the cosmos was based only on itself, henceforth it was to be based on the Infinite One who had created (ex nihilo) the cosmos while, in essence, not being part of it.

When this infinite God died, the infinite space he left behind did not disappear along with him, but did henceforth, as *radically open* infinity, define man's finitude. Henceforth everything that *is,* is in a space that does not necessarily coincide with "being," nor does it go back to its "exterior creator," but literally loses itself in *indefinite* infinity. Everything that is, exists in an infinite "space" devoid of any raison d'être. Since God's death, that is since the beginning of modernity, it is this kind of "cold" abysmal infinity that has determined the being of things. If in the past these were determined by an infinitely distant God who would touch their soul and "give" them their existence, this God now ceased to be, and so did the soul, which was embedded in his existence. Things are only embedded in an empty, exterior, and unbounded space. Things have turned into dead mass, entirely defined by their exteriority. Whatever it is that moves them, it has nothing to do with their inner "essence," but only with mechanical laws directed at the exterior protocol of their movements. The rest—their inner essence—is dead to the new knowledge, simply dead, and (scientifically) not worth thinking of.

Sensitive as he was to the dramatic situation that thought fell to after it was forced to give up its hold on the inner essence, Kant turned out to be the first to affirm that traumatic caesura with "the things themselves." In his attempt to radically think *modern* finitude, he was the first to succeed in investigating the conditions of a thought that has given up the claim to be able to know "das Ding an sich." According to Kant, the infinity of the space previously occupied by God could never be conquered by knowledge, and thus, in its endlessness, it characterizes knowledge as something finite. While human knowledge will indeed be finite in the sense that it will never live up to its final end (i.e., *das Ding an sich*), this virtually unlimited knowledge will nevertheless be radically finite: the ultimate knowledge will escape and remain absent from every known object. This absence (of *das Ding an sich*, that is, of a rational and free raison d'être, formerly known as God) makes the knowledge both its infinity and, on a more fundamental level, its finitude. So, the typically modern finitude is installed with Kant. Man is virtually able to know everything, and as such he feels himself capable of (technically) doing everything, but only *because* of the radical finite status of that infinite knowledge: the real *essence*, the *real* thing to know can never be known or controlled.

Like no other, Bataille is aware of this dramatic and even traumatic aspect of modern infinity, and tries to affirm this infinity (or the "totality," as he often calls it) in its radical finitude. By writing closely to the skin of his brute "experience" of thinking itself, he confronts the reader with the modern finitude-problem in a very sharp way. Where, for example, he reports to us on the way in which his thought takes an infinite (i.e., transgressive) position only so as to frightfully experience the transgressive and failing character of it, he is effectively demonstrating a radical modern understanding of finitude. This character is threatened, however, when he wants to trace this "inner experience" back to his bioenergetic cosmology, or rather, to his cosmic-biologic reading of Hegel's negation. It is as if he wants to "close" again the open universe left by God's death, albeit a "closure" in infinity itself. It is as if he wants to give his experience of finitude an ontological foundation: the fear of infinity (being the basic experience of modern finitude) would be in "harmony" with the terrifying character of being itself—whereas perhaps the frightening side of our limited experience of being is only really radical if it simply lacks any relation to being itself. The possibility that this conceptualization may temper (if not neutralize) the very terrifying aspect of his inner experience prompts him to invoke its fear and its impossibility in a formal way. This formal invocation often seems to be the ultimate reason for the "pathos" of Bataille's writing.

Translated from the Dutch by G. Daniël Bügel.

Notes

1   References to Georges Bataille's *Oeuvres completes,* vols. 1–12 (Paris: Gallimard, 1970–88) are given parenthetically in the text by volume and page number. Volumes most often quoted are 7 (*La part maudite*) and 8 (*La Souverainité*). Volume and page numbers given after a semicolon reference the English translation; quotes are from Bataille, *The Accursed Share,* vol. 1 (New York: Zone Books, 1988) and Bataille, *The Accursed Share,* vols. 2 and 3 (New York: Zone Books, 1993). All other translations are mine.

2   Georges Bataille, *Theory of Religion* (New York: Zone Books, 1989), 103–4.

3   "Changing from the perspectives of a *restrictive* economy to those of a *general* economy actually accomplishes a Copernican transformation: a reversal of thinking—and of ethics" (7:33; 1:25).

4   Bataille works out his "biochemical energetics" in the second part of his "Introduction Théorique" of *La part maudite.* Life (which to Bataille is the same as "being") is thought according to the laws of pressure (*pression*). Once "life" (i.e., the vital energy) has reached certain limits, it will come under high pressure and, transgressive as it is, burst out to start new life (7:36–37).

From "Cogito" to Its Negative Representation

In a brilliant interpretation of Ridley Scott's movie *Blade Runner,* Slavoj Žižek has shown that the plot of this film is, at various points, a reprise of the problematic developed in Descartes's *Meditations.*[1]

The movie, as we know, deals with an imminent future where, among the earth's population, there are a number of artificial beings ("replicants") who, resembling humans and even having artificial childhood memories (although they were assembled as adult machines), are misperceived, and misperceive themselves, as human beings. But, since they are capable of high intellectual performance, they themselves have their doubts, as in Descartes's second meditation, about the authenticity of their memories as well as their whole (human) subjectivity.[2] So, once again, a point has to be found that escapes this universal doubt. Žižek writes: "Therein consists the implicit philosophical lesson of *Blade Runner* attested to by numerous allusions to the Cartesian *cogito* (like when the replicant-character played by Darryl Hannah ironically points out 'I think, therefore I am'): where is the *cogito,* the point of my self-consciousness, when everything that I actually am is an artifact—not only my body, my eyes, but even my most intimate memories and fantasies?"[3] The Cartesian answer can be explained, as Žižek shows, by applying a conceptual tool that has been developed by Jacques Lacan:[4] "It is here that we again encounter the Lacanian distinction between the subject of enunciation and the subject of the enunciated: everything that I positively am, every enunciated content I can point at and say 'that's *me*,' is not 'I'; I am only the void that remains, the empty distance toward every content."[5] Under the condition of universal doubt, every possible content must appear questionable. But there is one level that evades this doubt: the level from which the doubt originates. The agency that doubts is not identical with anything that can be submitted to the doubt. What thinks, is not identical with anything that is being thought.

This finding, which Descartes experienced as a certain relief, can also be regarded as something quite alarming for the subject: one point is beyond the subject's power of doubting; there is a dimension that always escapes his/her theoretical grasp (although it persistently signalizes its existence precisely in the failed attempt to grasp it). This alarming side of the Cartesian discovery has been underlined by Lacan. Lacan showed the radicality of the Cartesian result by emphasizing that due to its generality it also applied for a special case: what thinks, is not identical with what is being thought—even if what is being thought is the thinking subject itself.[6]

This was important especially in the case of utterances that seemed to contain the position from where they were enunciated (such as "I think" or "I lie").[7] Following Descartes radically, Lacan made clear that the position where the utterance was enunciated from was never identical with anything contained within this utterance. The enunciating instance, the "subject of enunciation," was not to be identified with the "subject of the enunciated," the subject that figured within the content of the utterance.

This Lacanian consequence would, at first sight, seem quite disappointing for the replicants and their specific concern, since it gives a simple, negative answer to the question of where my true, unfeigned subjectivity could be situated (i.e., where my "cogito" is): it is somewhere outside the field of anything I can speak about. A certainty for the subject who doubts and thinks, the cogito is a problem of representation for the subject who speaks.

But at the same time, the Lacanian distinction between the two levels of speech (the level of the enunciated content and the level of enunciation) allows us to understand the functioning of a possible solution—since, by this distinction, Lacan showed how the subject in his/her speech constantly announces his/her elusive dimension without even wanting or noticing it. The subject of the unconscious was, according to Lacan, to be found in every discourse on the level of its enunciation.[8] This means that the mechanism by which the unconscious manifests itself, according to Lacan, should also provide the key to the replicant problem: if there existed a way of communicating in an utterance not only its enunciated content (i.e., what is being said) but also the level of enunciation (the position from where it is being said), then this would be a possibility of how someone could signalize that there is something else in him or her than just his/her possibly faked presence of body and (contents of) mind.

As Žižek shows, the replicants find such a solution for their problem (a solution that gives the film its moving, tragic dimension). They seem to have one paradoxical possibility of signalizing that they are not replicants but human beings: by affirming the opposite, by saying "I am a replicant." Precisely the negation of the status they want to achieve seems to provide them with this status. Žižek writes: "it is only when, at the level of the enunciated content, I assume my replicant-status, that, at the level of enunciation, I become a truly human subject. 'I am a replicant' is the statement of the subject in its purest."[9] The paradoxical mechanism that produces the opposite meaning of the enunciated proposition is what Sigmund Freud called *Verneinung* (negation). As Freud noted, utterances like "You ask me who this person in my dream might be. It is *not* the mother," must be immediately understood in the opposite sense: "So it is the mother."[10]

The linguistic feature that enabled Freud to perform such an interpretation and saved him from succumbing to arbitrariness consists in the *split* between the two levels of speech in such a proposition. On the level of the enunciated, on the level of *what is being said*, everything seems OK; there is nothing strange or irritating for the analysand's (or anyone else's) consciousness in it. But what is strange is the fact *that this is being said at all*. On the level of enunciation the proposition "It is not the mother" is highly irritating, it gives rise to the question: If nobody ever posed the hypothesis of the mother, why does it have to be explicitly negated? If everything is just OK, why does this have to be emphasized?

A special relationship between the two levels of speech is established in this case. If the content of the proposition builds a first message, then there lies a second message in the fact that the first message is being sent. The sending of the message is another message. And the second message contradicts the first one. This split, this contradiction between what is being said and what is being signalized by saying it, conveys the level of enunciation (and its difference from the level of the enunciated). In negation this elusive dimension of speech is brought to its (negative) representation.[11]

The means by which this is being done is a displacement of the communicative situation: the situation that seemed to build the frame of communication is transferred to its explicit content, "perverted" into a remarkable fact. Negation "redoubles" tautologically what we considered unnecessary to mention, the unspoken presuppositions of our utterances: it affirms what seemed to stand on its own, it assures us of something that seemed beyond any doubt, it denies something that no one thought to state, it forbids what was considered to be impossible, it answers something that seemed beyond question.[12]

Precisely by affirming these presuppositions explicitly, negation puts them into question. It confronts us with our own presuppositions "in the wrong place" as it were; it makes us ask ourselves: If what was supposed to be a presupposition figures as an explicit statement—then, what are the presuppositions of this statement? If what was considered to be the "common sense," the background of our talk, figures in its foreground, as a "particular sense," then, what is the real background, the founding common sense of our communication? By its ironic means, negation signalizes for us a description of this background different from that which we considered it to be.

The same mechanism seems to be known by the replicants. It seems to give them a chance to prove—by saying that they are replicants— that they are something else. Žižek concludes in his interpretation: "In short, the implicit thesis of *Blade Runner* is that replicants are pure subjects precisely insofar as they testify that every positive, substantial content, inclusive of the most intimate fantasies, is not 'their own' but already implanted. In this precise sense, subject is by definition nostalgic, a subject of loss. Let us recall how, in *Blade Runner*, Rachel silently starts to cry when Deckard proves to her that she is a replicant. The silent grief over the loss of her 'humanity,' the infinite longing to be or to become human again, although she knows this will never happen; or, conversely, the eternal gnawing doubt over whether I am truly human or just an android—it is these very undecided, intermediate states which make me human."[13] If we leave aside the question of what this finding means for the replicants and instead look at what it implies for psychoanalytical theory, we can enumerate a number of consequences. There are a series of propositions that must be supported by Lacanian theory. These are: (1) that there is a primacy of negation over positive representation: negation can express something that cannot be told in a direct, positive expression; (2) that what negation tells is necessarily true; (3) that (in general) there exist things that can only be represented negatively, by negation; (4) that (in particular) there exists, represented by negation, a true, empty subjectivity beyond "full," imaginary subjectivity. From the last point follows an important consequence for the Lacanian theory of ideology: the thesis that this empty subjectivity has to be regarded as the cause of ideological effects for which a theory of the imaginary alone cannot account.

This is the argument developed by Lacanian theorists in opposition to Louis Althusser's psychoanalytical theory of ideology. Althusser, it was argued by Mladen Dolar and Slavoj Žižek, linked ideology, by conceptualizing it as a process of interpellation, to the sphere of mere imaginary subjectivity. But to give a full account of the whole domain of ideology, a "beyond of interpellation,"[14] a second subjectivity, a "subject before subjectivization"[15] had to be thought. Since interpellation never seems to succeed totally, the subject seems to remain at a certain distance toward his/her "meaningful" identity given to him/her by interpellation, and precisely this "meaningless" remainder should be regarded as a condition of the subject's submission to the "meaningless" command of the ideological rituals and apparatuses.[16]

Since these consequences of the replicant reprise of the "cogito" do not only concern androids and problems of other planets but—with regard to the question of subjectivity—address crucial questions of social life and its theory, they seem to merit close examination.[17] It seems, furthermore, that a precise answer to the Lacanian theses can be found in Louis Althusser's writings. A certain negativism in Lacan has been criticized by the Spinozean wing of French antihumanist philosophy: while Deleuze and Guattari have developed their criticism in relation to the concept of the "lack,"[18] Althusser seems to have done the same with some implications of the Lacanian concept of negation.

Slavoj Žižek also refers to Althusser in his interpretation of *Blade Runner* and uses this reference to support his argument. But it might be possible to develop from this reference an alternative model of the Althusserian position, which would not only reestablish a different image of the theory of this widely forgotten philosopher but also render visible the cornerstones of a totally different theory of negation as well as of empty subjectivity.

Negation, the Empty Subject, and the Theory of Ideology

The split and the truth of its message

In his analysis of the philosophical mechanisms at work in *Blade Runner*, Slavoj Žižek refers to a conceptual figure developed in the theory of the French philosopher Louis Althusser. At first sight it seems that Althusser, with this figure, had described precisely the same logic as is practiced by the replicants. So the comparison would show further support for the Lacanian position on the part of Althusser. Žižek writes: "it is only when, at the level of the enunciated content, I assume my replicant-status, that, at the level of enunciation, I become a truly human subject. 'I am a replicant' is the statement of the subject in its purest— the same as in Althusser's theory of ideology where the statement 'I am in ideology' is the only way for me to truly avoid the vicious circle of ideology (or the Spinozean version of it: the awareness that nothing can ever escape the grasp of necessity is the only way for us to be truly free)." [19] It is true, in his essay "Ideology and Ideological State Apparatuses" Althusser writes: "ideology never says, 'I am ideological'. It is necessary to be outside ideology, i.e. in scientific knowledge, to be able to say: I am in ideology (a quite exceptional case) or (the general case): I was in ideology." [20] But it seems that this remark is in a way too short, that it does not fully correspond to Althusser's position on this problem. On the one hand, of course, this remark is correct, as far as it says that science does not destroy ideology when it breaks with it. Ideology persists in a conflictual coexistence with the new science. Therefore even the scientist, after breaking with an ideological illusion on the level of his science, cannot fully escape ideology on the level of the rest of his social existence (for example, the very scientist becomes susceptible to an ideology of science, a "spontaneous philosophy"). So science (the scientist) must never say: "I am outside ideology."

Yet on the other hand, Althusser's remark could lead one to a wrong conclusion. It could be concluded (and Žižek's passage seems to suggest it) that the proposition "I am in ideology" were an unquestionable, doubtless mark of science or scientificality—or even the only possible way to achieve scientificality. However, the *Verneinung* (the split between the level of the enunciated and the level of enunciation), the negation that characterizes such remarks as "I am in ideology" is not always reliable. On the contrary, there is an ideology that is based precisely on propositions like this; there exists an ideology that consists in saying things like "I am in ideology."

For Althusser, this structure might even be the basic feature of ideology as such. He has, however, noticed such cases and criticized them. This can be seen for example in his remark on certain anti-intellectual (i.e., vitalist, empiricist, and pragmatist) philosophical positions: "No doubt this proclamation of the exalted status of the superabundance of 'life' and 'concreteness', of the superiority of the world's imagination and the green leaves of action over the poverty of grey theory, contains a serious lesson in intellectual modesty, healthy for the right (presumptuous and dogmatic) ears."[21] What Althusser examines here is, once again, a negation. Propositions like "My knowledge is abstract" (or "I am in abstraction") are characterized by a split between the level of the enunciated content and the level of its enunciation. This split can be heard by a good ear ("à bon entendeur salut"), capable of "symptomatic reading."[22] It can be heard that, on the level of enunciation, the proposition says the contrary. The utterance "My knowledge is abstract" must be understood as saying: "My knowledge is concrete—so concrete that I know if it is abstract."

But to hear this split does not mean in this case to conclude that the speaker must have a position of enunciation outside the limits of his knowledge, which are described and regretted on the level of the enunciated content. The enunciation of the proposition "My knowledge is abstract" does not necessarily testify to the fact that the speaker has overcome this very abstraction of his knowledge. The split between the two levels of speech is not identical with a split between two levels of knowledge, with a *coupure épistémologique*.[23]

As Althusser notices, the split between the two levels of speech in this case only symbolizes such a *coupure*, it only pretends that the speaker has been able to transgress the abstraction of knowledge he admits. But in this case it is a wrong pretension, an unjustified claim ("présomptueux et dogmatique"). The modesty of the enunciated is not so modest on the level of enunciation; and it is presumptuous, because the position of enunciation to which the enunciated alludes is imaginary.

This means that we can, even on the level of enunciation, tell something other than the truth: somebody who knows about the mechanisms of negation can instrumentalize them as a code of communication. He or she can use negation to tell a lie. For example, the proposition "I am a replicant" would not provide a reliable criterion for recognizing human beings. This criterion would not pass Turing's test (which tries to see if a criterion that we have found for the difference between man and machine can be formalized and implanted into the software of the machine). Also, a real replicant can, as a part of his software, be programmed to show the gesture of doubting his human nature.

Negation and cunning negation

As far as psychoanalytical theory is concerned, we have therefore to make a distinction between (1) the question of whether a proposition like "I am in ideology" is a negation; and (2) the question of whether what this proposition denies is true. Only in Freud's special cases of negation ("It was *not* my mother") does the second fact seem to be implied by the first, because the speaker does not know the first, that is, he does not know that what he says is a negation. Recognizing the fact that there is a hidden message is therefore the same as recognizing the hidden message's truth.

Now there seems to be a simple criterion for discerning between doubtless, unconscious negation and its conscious, dubitable use: in unconscious negation (such as "It is not the mother") the subject says, on the level of the enunciated content, something pleasant for him/her. He/she fully identifies with this content, and the fact that its enunciation conveys a second message, is extremely unpleasant for the subject. He/she does not want to have it; he/she is driven to drown it out precisely by enunciating it.[24]

In the case of the conscious use of negation the situation is totally different: the subject enunciates a content that is unpleasant for him/her, often under the form of a self-accusation (for example "I am a replicant"). He/she does not identify with this content but with the level of enunciation that is meant to call the content into question. By negation the speaker depicts himself/herself as something beyond this content and identifies with this "transcendent" position.

The structure of this "cunning" type of negation was also described by Freud. A subject acquainted with some principles of psychoanalytical theory would, for example, avoid saying "It was not the mother" and say instead "I think it is the mother. But no, that cannot be true— otherwise I could not know it." The cunning negator only enunciates the first part and leaves the second sentence up to the listener.[25]

As can be seen, for psychoanalytical theory negation is a code, a way of producing meaning. This meaning is not necessarily unconscious. Since it is also possible that somebody uses the code of negation consciously to transmit a certain message, the question of truth arises exactly as in every other production of meaning. We could therefore say: everything that negation says—even what it says on the level of its enunciation—belongs to its enunciated content. Only the fact that it is a negation remains on the level of enunciation. Everything that can be falsified or verified is a part of the constative level of the enunciated— not of the performative level of enunciation, where the question of truth does not play any role.

Thus negation is one way of representation among others. It is not a privileged way of representation. What is expressed by negation can just as well be said in a positive expression.[26] And an expression by negation is not necessarily more true than an ordinary, positive expression.

Transgression by explicit immanence

Negation is therefore not an apt mode for representing something that is constitutively absent. Negation cannot be regarded as the only possible testimony of something that can only have a negative status (for example, the status of man, or a position outside ideology, etc.). For the same reason, negation is not the instrument for the only possible transgression of a totally closed space. It is not a performative way to transgress something that by definition cannot be transgressed (the status of a replicant; the sphere of ideology, the abstraction of knowledge; i.e., the sphere described on the constative level of the enunciated).

Once again, we could use here Althusser's opposition between (Hegelian) contradiction and (Freudian) overdetermination.[27] Negation is overdetermined, it is not contradictory. It solves the problem of how to tell something under the condition that it should not be told directly. But it does not solve the problem of how to make something true whose truth cannot appear or be told directly.[28] Negation represents an absence, but it is not the presence of the absent itself. (The contradiction that appears in negation is a mode of representation, it is not what contradiction in Hegelian tradition is supposed to be: a feature belonging to the *Sache selbst*.)

Negation cannot let such a thing appear, and, according to Althusser, such a thing does not exist. This might be explained by a difference between the Althusserian (psychoanalytical, Spinozean) ontology—or rather, topology—and the Hegelian one. The Hegelian solution that Slavoj Žižek proposed for the replicant problem can be resumed by the formula: *transgression by explicit immanence*. This presupposes topologically that the only transgression of certain spaces is a negative transgression; that the only beyond of a closed space is an empty beyond. What limits the positive has, according to this, to be characterized as something negative. Althusser, on the contrary, in his interpretation of psychoanalytical theory seems to follow the Spinozean principle that something can only be limited by something else that is of the same nature.[29] Therefore, for Althusser and Spinoza, the solution of a problem of transgression can never consist only in the "empty gesture" of a negation. If we want to transgress a space we must arrive at another space. The transgression, as well as the space where we arrive by this transgression, must have a positive nature. (Whereas a space that cannot be transgressed at all, cannot be transgressed by negation either.)

The closed spaces of android and human misery

This can be seen, for example, in Spinoza's critical objection against an attitude of Pascal. Pascal had proposed a (Hegelian) dialectical solution for the problem of human greatness. Since, for Pascal, human misery is a closed space, human greatness can only be achieved and testified negatively. And, as in Hegelianism, this negative gesture is regarded as a mark of distinction between man and nature:

> Man's greatness comes from knowing he is wretched: a tree does not know it is wretched.
>
> Thus it is wretched to know that one is wretched, but there is greatness in knowing one is wretched.[30]

Spinoza seems to reply directly to this in a passage of his *Ethics:* "He who succeeds in hitting off the weakness of the human mind more eloquently or more acutely than his fellows, is looked upon as a seer."[31] For Spinoza, the Pascalian solution is nothing but an example of "presumptuous modesty." Human greatness, which is for Spinoza the same as human freedom, cannot at all be achieved or reliably testified by its denial. (Nor is this negative gesture, as well as real freedom, a mark of distinction between humanity and nature.) To be free means, for Spinoza, to arrive at a greater power of producing effects that result only from one's own nature. To recognize that we are not free is therefore only useful as a positive knowledge, not as an empty admission without knowledge. It only helps if it means to see that what we considered to be our own effects are in fact not wholly our own—and if this is a first step to produce different effects that really are our own.

The same seems to apply for Althusser. For example, to know that we are in ideology means to be within the space of a certain positive, scientific knowledge—a space also with a positive existence, materialized in an apparatus of thought ("appareil de pensée").[32] Therefore we should try a different reading of Althusser's passage in "Ideology and Ideological State Apparatuses." If, as Althusser writes, "It is necessary to be outside ideology, i.e. in scientific knowledge, to be able to say: I am in ideology," this does not mean that everybody who says "I am in ideology" is, by proof of this enunciation, within science. On the contrary, it means that only under a certain condition we are allowed to say that we are in ideology. Only if we are within science we can say such a thing without lying or being presumptuously modest. Only under the condition that we have arrived at the positive space of science, are we legitimated to say that we are in ideology. But then this sentence expresses a positive knowledge. It can therefore be followed by other sentences that explain this statement (for example, the sentences in Althusser's essay on ideology). It is not the last and only possible sentence on this topic. And it is not a negation anymore.

With regard to this, the Pascalian gesture of negation has to be seen as an overdetermined gesture in another sense: it is not only overdetermined in that it transports two contradictory meanings on its two levels of speech. It is also overdetermined on the level of enunciation itself. Because on this level it pretends a transgression, it signalizes the wish to transgress the closed sphere of human misery. But at the same time it shows that it does not really want to transgress this sphere. It wants to maintain the certainty that there is no real space beyond; it expresses the fear that the space beyond might not be empty.

Therefore, Althusser would regard the Pascalian attitude as imaginary: it is an imaginary transgression, and even the wish of transgression within it is imaginary. The dialectical concept of transgression by explicit immanence is a concept of ideological integration. (We might remember here Althusser's remark on Hegel as "(unknowingly) an admirable 'theoretician' of ideology.")[33]

Religious ideology and the shadow of its doubt

This means that, according to Althusser, ideological integration sometimes works precisely by virtue of this gesture of imaginary transgression. We can be totally integrated by ideology only if ideology itself gives us the means to transgress it in an imaginary way. Therefore, ideology seems sometimes to need a gesture of negation for it to function.[34]

This is not only the case in the quoted examples of pragmatism, empiricism, etcetera, where the negation (which pretends to criticize the limits of theoretical knowledge) has the role of blocking every positive attempt toward a theoretical concretization. The same can also be seen, for example, in the Kierkegaardian figure of the "true Christian believer." Žižek refers to this figure as follows: "we, finite mortals, are condemned to 'believe that we believe'; we can never be certain that we actually believe. This position of eternal doubt, this awareness that our belief is forever condemned to remain a hazardous wager, is the only way for us to be true Christian believers: those who go beyond the threshold of uncertainty, preposterously assuming that they really do believe, are not believers at all but arrogant sinners."[35] According to Kierkegaard, a true Christian can only be the one who says "I doubt whether I really am a Christian."

In this case, it seems probable that Althusser would completely agree with the result of the Kierkegaardian analysis: negation is necessary in order to be a true Christian (i.e., in Althusserian terms, to be fully subjectivized by Christian ideology). But Althusser's reasons would be completely different from Kierkegaard's. According to Althusser, to be a true Christian does not work by negation, because, as Kierkegaard postulates, such a being could only have a negative existence (an "intermediate state"), only negation being able to testify to this existence— without any possibility of lie or error for this negative testimony. For Althusser, such a gesture of negation would be, as a pure negation, a lie. A pure negation, or a pure doubt without any positive reason, would only pretend that there exists a reason, a beyond of the closed space of non-Christianity. It would only make up a semblance of an "intermediate state," being in fact nothing but the present state's empty gestures (or, as Hegel would have said, "ein trockenes Versichern").

So, this negation would, at first sight, be only an imaginary transgression of non-Christianity; a presumptuous modesty, necessary for total integration into the closed space of nonauthentic Christianity. But we must not forget that this result includes a basic Christian presupposition: the idea that non-Christianity builds a closed space and that its beyond can only have a negative status; that true Christianity can only be an "intermediate state" and not, as it might appear to non-Christians, an enormous positivity materialized in a powerful apparatus at work in perfectly visible rituals.

For Althusser, the pronouncement of this presupposition in terms of a presumptuously modest doubt, is a crucial feature of (true) Christianity, of Christian ideology as such. This presupposition testifies to the basic Christian metaphysical attitude: the devaluation of the positive, in the name of a nonpositive viewpoint. The suggestion that behind the utterance "I doubt whether I am a true Christian" there lurks a true Christian, is a lie. But this lie is constitutive of Christianity: you are only a true Christian if you have learned to perform this ritual of negation.[36] Therefore, this gesture of negation really shows that one is a true Christian: *not because what it denies were necessarily true, but because the gesture of negation is real.* The importance of the denial does not lie on its constative level; it lies on its performative level. What it says does not have to be true, but it must be said. The denial must be performed as a part of this ideology's customs.

The Christian devaluation of the positive concerns in this case, of course, the positive of Christian ideology itself (e.g., the materiality of its rituals), because the utterance "I doubt whether I am a true Christian" does not have its Kierkegaardian negation-power if it is spoken by someone who, for example, sits praying in a mosque. Negation can only make a difference between "true" Christianity and something that already looks very much like Christianity, let us call it "machine-Christianity" (or between man and something that looks very much like man, the perfect "homme-machine").[37]

Negation only works in the case wherein everything looks as if the speaker were already a true Christian—if he/she participates in the Christian rituals. Then this proposition assumes its distinctive ideological value. It says then: "I look like a Christian and I behave like a Christian. But this is not the reason why I really am a Christian."

What denial says, on its constative level, is wrong. Its "truth" lies in its performative level: performing this denial is itself the "surplus" (over ideology's materiality) that denial pretends to speak about. We could therefore say that the Christian religion must always be structured like René Magritte's well-known painting "Ceci n'est pas une pipe," which shows something that looks very much like a pipe and an inscription that says that it is not a pipe. In the case of religion we have something that looks very much like religious belief (going to the church, kneeling down, praying, etc.) and an additional remark saying that "this is not it" —and it is really not "it," since it lacks one thing: precisely this remark.

By metaphysically devaluing the materiality of Christian ideology, negation fulfills the function of "internalizing" this ideology, according to the attempts of internalization (*Verinnerlichung*) proper to Protestantism and its "purification" of Christianity. But we must probably say that this Protestant attitude is a necessary part of all Christianity, a "supplement" that can never be taken away even from the most orthodox, "machinelike" forms of Catholicism. It marks a constitutive point of Christian ideology, since it is the necessary ideological reversal between the ideology's rituals and the consciousness of the subjects subjected to these rituals. The theoretical misrecognition of the importance of the rituals (accompanied by full practical recognition), expressed by ritual negation, is a crucial feature of this ideology—and maybe characteristic, as Althusser regarded it, for all kinds of ideology.

The zero-degree of interpellation: the subject and its empty double

This seems important also with regard to the question of subjectivity, that is, to the question of whether the split between the two levels of speech is an apt instrument for transgressing the sphere of imaginary subjectivity—toward a "true" subjectivity of the unconscious, a subjectivity beyond subjectivization and interpellation (the questions that seem to return again and again, troubling Lacanians and Althusserians). In a footnote to *Tarrying with the Negative*, Žižek writes: "Therein consists the anti-Althusserian gist of Lacan: subject qua $ is not an effect of interpellation, of the recognition in an ideological call; it rather stands for the very gesture of calling into question the identity conferred on me by way of interpellation." [38] For Althusser, precisely this "gesture of calling into question the identity conferred on me by way of interpellation" is a necessary part of interpellation. This gesture is what Althusser calls "effet-sujet." [39] It is an imaginary transgression of imaginary subjectivity. It pretends the autonomy of the subject toward the very ideology by which it became subject. This corresponds to the imaginary subject's ideological feeling that it has always already been a subject—that it has been a subject even before achieving its imaginary subjectivity.

As we have seen, the empty subject is only produced by "cunning," conscious use of negation: the "self-accusation type" of negation where the subject makes his/her utterance only in order to be identified with the level of its enunciation (i.e., a negation that can lie). By such a negation I, as it were, "throw myself out of the universe of my dubitable ideological identity given to me by my image" and rise above it as a pure gaze. Yet, although apparently nothing but a gaze, this new identity is nevertheless imaginary, not symbolic. It is still an image: since by the enunciation of my negation I testify the fact that I *want to be seen* in this position of the gaze.

The ideological nature of this feeling, of course, lies in its function of internalizing ideology, metaphysically devaluing the importance of the ideological materiality—for ideology itself, as well as for the identity of the ideological subjects. Ideology even has to provide the subjects with such a feature in order to enable them to "transgress" their ideology: it has to interpellate them as something "beyond ideology," "beyond identity."[40] This "interpellation beyond interpellation" is a commonplace of numerous ideologies, such as the "Generation X"-movement or French existentialism (ideologies, as we know, that, although allegedly beyond interpellation, identity, and the materiality of ideology, always possess a very distinctive materiality—i.e., of fashion design and mores, such as frequenting certain bars, coffeehouses, or semipublic events); but the same applies for a less programmatic, cynical, liberalist pragmatism: in this case the absence of identity can itself be perceived as an identity— as such a rigid identity, that it again has to be imaginarily transgressed. The transgression, then, can assume the form of a more colorful identity, for example, an urban tribalism or romantic motorcycling as a pastime. Thus even "full" identity itself can take over the role of the necessary beyond that allows the subjects to live their "effet-sujet," their independence from the "empty" identity that their own ideology seems to confer upon them.

We could say that, analogous to every society's structure, which, as Althusser has pointed out, always consists of at least two modes of production,[41] the ideological superstructure also always consists of at least two modes of identity. This seems important to me with regard to the reply that Slavoj Žižek has given to my argument (as it was developed in an earlier, private communication). Žižek writes: "In order to provide a Lacanian answer to this criticism, it is necessary to introduce the distinction between subject qua pure void of self-relating negativity ($\$$) and the phantasmic content which fills out this void (the 'stuff of the I', as Lacan puts it). That is to say: the very aim of the psychoanalytic process is, of course, to induce the subject to renounce the 'secret treasure' which forms the kernel of his phantasmic identity. . . . However, the subject prior to interpellation-subjectivization is not this imaginary phantasmic depth which allegedly precedes the process of interpellation, but the very void which remains once the phantasmic space is emptied of its content."[42] From an Althusserian position, again, I would answer that in ideology we do not only have to do with some phantasmatic or imaginary content (which fills the void of "true subjectivity");

ideology is as well the appearance of a void that seems to be something totally different from any ideological content. Klaus Heinrich has demonstrated this by analyzing two famous "subjects beyond interpellation," two classical "nobodies" or "men without qualities": the cases of Homerian Odysseus (who, as we know, tricks the giant Polyphemus by telling him that his name is Nobody) and of Bertolt Brecht's Herrn Keuner (which alludes to German "keiner" = nobody). Heinrich shows that their "non-identity" is precisely an imaginary mode of identity: "The early, heroic nobody-characters . . . could still enjoy their non-liability as a gliding. They opposed, as the subtle beings, the crustaceans, the bourgeois, who seemed obdurate and blocked in their identity. . . . Today's nobody-characters want to be a void: really a nothing. But . . . precisely the void, the negative, is liable."[43] Ideology does not have an outside: the void is still an identity, and a "zero-interpellation," an "interpellation beyond interpellation," is still an interpellation. Herein might lie the reason why Althusser, as opposed to Lacan, refused to accept the notion of "true subjectivity" as a theoretical concept.

But if there is a "true subject," then it cannot always be found with the theoretical instrument of the distinction between the level of the enunciated and the level of enunciation. What is hidden on the level of enunciation is sometimes nothing but, again, the very subject—the imaginary subject that we hoped to transgress by leaving the level of the enunciated.

Two consequences could be drawn from this for a psychoanalytical theory of ideology: first, that theory must try not to share the self-understanding of its object[44]—theory should refrain from believing in the forms of ideology's imaginary self-transgression (which produce illusionary subject-positions beyond ideology). And, second: any primacy of negation over positive representation must be regarded as one of the suggestions of ideology's self-understanding. To evade this suggestion means to follow Louis Althusser in his Spinozean serenity: to regard the object strictly as a theoretical object—as a "plan d'immanence," a wholly positive whole.

Notes

This article is based on a letter to Slavoj Žižek dating from March 26, 1995. Slavoj Žižek referred to this letter in *The Indivisible Remainder: An Essay on Schelling and Related Matters* (London: Verso, 1996), 165–66.

1   Cf. Slavoj Žižek, *Tarrying with the Negative: Kant, Hegel and the Critique of Ideology* (Durham: Duke University Press, 1993), 9–11.

2   The question of whether a proof of the existence of one's subjectivity (which Descartes produces) is at the same time a proof of one's human nature (which the replicants strive for) will be left aside here. The common denominator of the two questions is the search for something that lies beyond dubitable phenomenality.

3   Žižek, *Tarrying,* 40.

4   Cf. Jacques Lacan, *The Four Fundamental Concepts of Psycho-Analysis,* trans. Alan Sheridan (New York: Norton, 1981), 35.

5   Žižek, *Tarrying,* 40.

6   Cf. Jacques Lacan, *Écrits: A Selection,* trans. Alan Sheridan (New York: Norton, 1977), 165.

7   Cf. Lacan, *Four Fundamental,* 138–40.

8   Cf. Jacques Lacan, "Position of the Unconscious," in *Reading Seminar XI,* ed. Richard Feldstein, Bruce Fink, and Maire Jaanus (Albany: SUNY Press, 1995), 263–64.

9   Žižek, *Tarrying,* 41.

10 Cf. Sigmund Freud, "Negation," in *General Psychological Theory* (New York: Collier, 1963), 213.

11 By interpreting the problem of negation (for example, in the case of the famous "ne explétif" [cf. Lacan, *Écrits,* 298]) in terms of "enunciated/enunciation," Jacques Lacan has contributed an important clarification to psychoanalytical theory. Because Freud's own words (especially his use of the term "symbol of negation [*Verneinungssymbol*]" [cf. Freud, "Negation," 214]) could suggest that his theory relied on the old Aristotelian distinction between positive and negative judgments ("kataphasis" and "apophasis," [cf. Aristotle, *De interpretatione,* 5]). A negation would, according to this reading, be discernible by a word like "not." But there are a lot of negations that do not contain a "not." And there are, by the same token, a lot of propositions that, although containing a "not," are not negations.

Lacan's new conceptualization made clear that the key feature of negation had to be found elsewhere: in the split between the two levels of speech. Precisely the same position had been developed by Ludwig Wittgenstein in his considerations *On Certainty.* For example, if somebody uttered to a friend during their conversation a proposition like "I have all the time known that you are N. N.," this proposition, although its content could not be objected to, would become (on the level of enunciation) extremely unclear: it would not be understandable why it was uttered at all. The "background" of the message was "missing," as Wittgenstein noted: it was not clear why the situation should make such an utterance necessary. Assuring the friend of something that was beyond any possible doubt immediately signalized the contrary: that there existed some reason for such a doubt, a necessity for such an assurance. The indubitable foreground of the message negated the indubitability of its background. Therefore, in Wittgenstein's understanding, doubting, as well as affirming certainty, was an operation between these two levels of speech, "foreground" and "background," or, in Lacan's terms, between the level of the enunciated and that of enunciation (cf. Ludwig Wittgenstein, *On Certainty* [New York: Harper and Row, 1972], 461, 464).

For Wittgenstein, as for Lacan, it was clear that if there were negation involved, it had to be found in the relationship between these two levels. Therefore, the proposition itself could be entirely positive, without any "no" or "not." Negation could have the form of propositions like "I know that this is a hand" or "I knew all the time that you are N. N."

The fact that Freud himself did not rely on the Aristotelian concept of negation, can be seen *à l'état pratique* in his analysis of various forms of negation at work in paranoia: in his reading of Schreber's memoirs (cf. Sigmund Freud, "Psychoanalytic Notes Upon an Autobiographical Account of Paranoia," in *Three Case Histories* [New York: Collier, 1970], 165–68), he shows that a negation can have a purely positive form like "He hates me" (instead of "I hate him") or "She loves that man" (instead of "I love him").

The logical criticism of the Aristotelian concept of negation had been performed, only a few years before Freud's "Negation," by Gottlob Frege ("Die Verneinung," in *Logische Untersuchungen* [Göttingen: Vandenhoek & Ruprecht, 1966], 54–71), and by Ludwig Wittgenstein, in his *Tractatus logico-philosophicus* (proposition 4.0621).

12   The role of answers without questions in theoretical discourses has specifically been investigated by Louis Althusser in his theory of "symptomatic reading." Althusser regarded a certain type of these answers as the "negation," the tacit presence, of a new theoretical problematic within an old theoretical field (cf. Louis Althusser and Etienne Balibar, *Reading Capital* [London: NLB, 1977], 25–28). I have elaborated on this point, which marks a new invention of Althusser in breaking with a certain heritage of Bachelardian epistemology, in my book *Althusser — The Silence in the Text* (Munich: W. Fink Verlag, forthcoming).

13   Žižek, *Tarrying,* 41.

14   Mladen Dolar, "Beyond Interpellation," *Qui parle* 6, no. 2 (spring/summer 1993): 75–96.

15   Cf. Slavoj Žižek, *The Sublime Object of Ideology* (London: Verso, 1989), 43–47.

16   Cf. ibid., 43: *"this leftover, far from hindering the full submission of the subject to the ideological command, is the very condition of it:* it is precisely this non-integrated surplus of senseless traumatism which confers on the Law its unconditional authority."

17   Of course, the question of negation is also crucial for several other philosophical fields. It appears for example within aesthetics, where the themes of "negative representation" and the "sublime" have been reintroduced into discussion recently by J.-F. Lyotard.

18   Cf. Gilles Deleuze and Félix Guattari, trans. Robert Hurley, Mark Seem, and Helen R. Lane, *Anti-Oedipus: Capitalism and Schizophrenia* (Minneapolis: University of Minnesota Press, 1983).

19   Žižek, *Tarrying,* 41.

20   Louis Althusser, "Ideology and Ideological State Apparatuses," in *Essays on Ideology,* (London: Verso, 1984), 49.

21   Althusser and Balibar, *Reading Capital,* 117.

22   For this Althusserian concept, see ibid., 25–28.

23   Cf. ibid., 44–46; Louis Althusser, *For Marx* (London: Verso, 1969), 33; Etienne Bali-
     bar, "Le concept de 'coupure épistémologique' de Gaston Bachelard à Louis Althus-
     ser," in *Écrits pour Althusser* (Paris: Éd. la Découverte, 1991), 9–57.

24   This applies also to the examples of "absolute certainty" given by G. E. Moore: Witt-
     genstein's discovery, namely that the utterance of a pleasant certainty like "I know
     that this is my hand" has to be read as a negation, is hardly pleasant for Moore.

25   Freud would probably have claimed that, contrary to ordinary negations, negations
     of this type, on the level of their enunciated content, *always* tell the truth: they try
     to "lie by telling the truth." Analogous to the Lemberg-Krakau joke (cf. Sigmund
     Freud, *Jokes and Their Relation to the Unconscious* [New York: Norton, 1989], 137–
     38), his answer might have been: "If you tell me it is the mother, you want me to
     believe that it is somebody else. But now I know that it is the mother. So why do you
     lie?" ("If you tell me you are a replicant . . . etc."). Also Lacan's solution of the liar-
     paradox was to interpret it as a "cunning" negation ("If you tell me you lie . . ."); cf.
     Lacan, *Four Fundamental,* 138–39.

26   Negation is a matter of censorship. This means that something is not permitted to
     be expressed directly, on the level of the enunciated, without using the split between
     the two levels as a sign. But this prohibition implies that a positive expression is pos-
     sible. Censorship does not forbid the impossible.

27   Cf. Althusser, *For Marx,* 101–2.

28   The idea of such a negation, however, describes an interesting form of a performa-
     tive utterance: different from ordinary performative utterances like "I thank you,"
     "You are husband and wife," etc., which make true what they speak of, a performa-
     tive utterance by negation would *make true what it does not speak of.*

29   Cf. Spinoza, *Ethics,* part 1, def. 2.

30   Blaise Pascal, *Pensées* (Harmondsworth, England: Penguin, 1966), 114 (p. 59).

31   Spinoza, *Ethics,* part 3, introduction, in *On the Improvement of the Understanding,
     The Ethics, Correspondence* (New York: Dover, n.d.), 128.

32   Cf. Althusser and Balibar, *Reading Capital,* 41. The reason why this space, although
     positive, cannot limit the positive space of ideology is that they belong to different
     types of positivity, which produce different specific effects. Ideology is not a lie or an
     error—which would be the precise opposite of scientific truth (and disappear when
     it arises). There is no common space that includes the both of them. A limitation of
     theoretical ideology only takes place within the space of science.

33   Cf. Althusser, "Ideology," 55 n. 22.

34   The thesis that "ideology *has no outside* (for itself)" (cf. Althusser, "Ideology," 49)
     should be understood as an explanation of this fact: this thesis should not be read
     as an admittance that ideology can only be transgressed negatively; on the contrary,
     it should be read in the following sense: negation (such as "I am in ideology") is an
     integral part of ideology, since it produces an imaginary outside of ideology. Nega-
     tion is the imaginary way out that leads us right back into ideology.

35 Žižek, *Tarrying*, 247 n. 53.

36 I saw this ritual very clearly when, shortly after the so-called "reunification" between West and East Germany, dissident intellectuals from the former GDR were invited by Austrian television to discuss guilt and heroism at the time under "Stasi" surveillance. Members of Protestant dissident groups especially astonished and irritated the Austrian leading the discussion when, instead of attacking the present representatives of the former repressive state's apparatuses, they repeatedly banged their hands against their chests, making very loud noises on the hidden TV-microphones, and said: "Everyone of us is so guilty." This extreme (Protestant as well as suppression-specific) language game of defeating each other by humiliating oneself in presumptions of modesty was surprising and quite difficult to understand for a spectator not acquainted with the situation.

37 Negation only "christianizes" the Christians (which might remind us of Pascal's remark on the proofs of God: they only convince the already convinced). The same applies for the replicant problem: the proposition "I doubt whether I am a human being" would have nothing but a comical effect if it were uttered, for example, by the character played by Arnold Schwarzenegger in *The Terminator,* after being transformed into a robotlike machine.

38 Žižek, *Tarrying*, 254 n. 39.

39 Cf. Louis Althusser, *Écrits sur la psychanalyse* (Paris: Stock/IMEC, 1993), 131. To give a very rough model, we could say that in Althusser's theory of ideology there are only two "spheres": the social structure and the imaginary of the subjects' self-understanding. These two spheres can be identified with the "symbolic" and the "imaginary" in Lacan. But Lacan posits a third sphere: the Real (with a series of concepts belonging to this sphere, such as the lack of the Other, the subject of the signifier, the phantasmatic, etc.). The reason why, for Althusser, there is no choice between these two paradigms and why he refuses to accept the position of a third sphere seems to be the fact that with this notion, science would begin affirming the subject's imaginary self-understanding (for example, it would regard the subject's imaginary distance toward its identity as a real distance). Science, then, becomes susceptible to the suspicion that it might be nothing but a "rationalization" (in the Freudian sense) of ideology. And as long as this suspicion can be maintained, there is no possibility for truth in science's propositions. The field is not open, it is conflict-ridden—in other words: in this situation, within science, the philosophical, polemical aspect dominates over the scientific aspect. Science cannot simply "say what it wants" (for example, pose a new hypothesis). As long as "the stick is bent" by ideology, science must direct all its efforts at bending it back (cf. Louis Althusser, *Philosophy and the Spontaneous Philosophy of the Scientists* [London: Verso, 1990], 210).

40 The effect of such an interpellation of the subject as a pure void could be called a "screen-psychosis." This apparently "psychotic" layer covers the subject's ordinary, "full" identity—which, as we know, is always "neurotic," i.e., the result of an over-identification.

41 Cf. Louis Althusser, *Écrits philosophiques et politiques*, (Paris: Stock/IMEC, 1995), 2:421.

42 Cf. Žižek, *Indivisible Remainder*, 166.

43 Klaus Heinrich, *Versuch über die Schwierigkeit nein zu sagen* (Frankfurt: Suhrkamp, 1964), 56; translation mine.

44 Cf. Althusser, *Écrits sur la psychanalyse*, 234: "Regle d'or du matérialisme: *ne pas juger de l'être par sa conscience de soi!*"

9

The Cartesian Subject versus the Cartesian Theater

Slavoj Žižek

In his attacks on bourgeois ideology, Lenin liked to emphasize the need for a thorough knowledge of one's enemies: one can sometimes learn a lot from them, since, in an ideological struggle, the enemy often perceives what is truly at stake in the struggle more accurately than those closer to us. Therein resides the interest, for those who consider themselves close to "postmodernism" or "deconstructionism," of the emerging school of German and American followers of Dieter Henrich: the basic project of this school is to counteract the different versions of today's "decenterment" or "deconstruction" of the subject by way of a return to the notion of subjectivity in the sense of German Idealism.[1] It would be easy to demonstrate how their critical reading of "deconstructionists" (under this designation, they usually throw together, in a rather indiscriminate way, Heidegger, Lacan, Foucault, Derrida, Rorty) often misses the mark;[2] however, far more productive than to engage in such attempts to score points, is to focus on the central position of this school, which undoubtedly is of substantial theoretical interest: their endeavor to prove that the notion of the subject as it was elaborated in German Idealism, in no way precludes the subject's "decenterment" (i.e., the rejection of the principle of subjectivity as the ultimate metaphysical foundation). What the "deconstructionist" hasty dismissal of self-consciousness in German Idealism fails to take note of is precisely this paradoxical complicity of the two aspects of self-consciousness: the dimension of subjectivity is irreducible, the subject's self-acquaintance is always already presupposed in all our acts, the gap between the subject's immediate self-experience and the mechanisms of its objective genesis is constitutive, which is why one cannot reduce the subject to an effect of some underlying objective process. However, the unavoidability of this principle of subjectivity in no way compels us to accept subjectivity as the ultimate metaphysical foundation—the very notion of subject, when its consequences are thought out, propels us to posit the subject's embeddedness in some pre-reflective nonsubjective Ground (the "Absolute"). For that reason, Henrich's school focuses on those often neglected authors who, within German Idealism, elaborated the contours of a possible "alternative history" to the official story of the Absolute Idealist Foundationalism culminating in Hegel: Hölderlin, Novalis, Schelling. . . .[3] The crucial difference between Hegel and Schelling concerns precisely the subject's "decenterment": Hegel was well aware that the constitutive gesture of subjectivity is a violent reversal of the preceding "natural" substantial balance—the "subject" is some subordinated moment of the presupposed substantial totality that retroactively "posits its own presuppositions" (i.e., elevates itself into the Master of its own Ground). For Hegel, this reversal is the necessary path of dialectical progress in which "Substance becomes Subject," while for Schelling, this violent reversal by means of which the Subject subordinates the Ground of its being to itself, is the original *hubris,* the source and the very definition of Evil: the ethical goal is precisely to reestablish the lost balance by way of renouncing this *hubris*—the subject should humbly accept its "decenterment" and ecstatically submit to the pre-subjective Absolute. . . .

Instead of engaging in a direct dialogue with Henrich's school, it seems more promising to confront it with contemporary endeavors by cognitive sciences to provide an empirical/evolutionary account of the emergence of consciousness. The representative example here is Daniel Dennett's *Consciousness Explained,* a work that, precisely, wants to accomplish what the authors of *The Modern Subject* consider a priori impossible: the genesis of consciousness, of the self-conscious subject, out of the biological evolutionary process. Although Dennett's propositions, regarding the dispersed multitude of narratives fighting for hegemony within the human mind and the lack of any agent coordinating this pandemonium, often sound close to deconstruction (he himself quotes the ironic definition of "semiotic materialism" from David Lodge's *Nice*

Work), the temptation to be avoided is precisely the hasty conclusion that Dennett is a kind of deconstructionist wolf in the sheep's clothing of empirical science: there is a gap that forever separates Dennett's scientific evolutionary explanation, which combines cognitive science, neurology, and artificial intelligence research, from the deconstructionist "metatranscendental" probing into the conditions of (im)possibility of the philosophical discourse.

The basic premise of Dennett's "*hetero*phenomenology" is that subjective experience is *the theorist's* (interpreter's) *symbolic fiction*, his *supposition*, not the domain of phenomena directly accessible to the subject: the universe of subjective experience is reconstructed in exactly the same way we reconstruct the universe of a novel from reading its text. In a first approach, this seems innocent enough, self-evident even: of course we do not have direct access to another person's mind, of course we have to reconstruct an individual's self-experience from his external gestures, expressions and, above all, words. . . . However, Dennett's point is much more radical, he pushes the parallel to the extreme. In a novel, the universe we reconstruct is full of "holes," not fully constituted; for example, when Conan Doyle describes the flat of Sherlock Holmes, it is in a way meaningless to ask how many books were there exactly on the shelves—the writer simply did not have in his mind an exact idea of it. And, for Dennett, it is the same with another person's experience in "reality": what one should *not* do is to suppose that, deep in another's psyche, there is a full self-experience of which we only get fragments. *Even the appearances cannot be saved.*

This central point of Dennett can be nicely rendered if one contrasts it with two standard positions that are usually opposed as incompatible, but are effectively solidary: first-person phenomenalism and third-person behavioral operationalism. On the one hand, the idea that, even if our mind *is* merely a software in our brains, nobody can take from us the full first-person experience of reality; on the other hand, the idea that, in order to understand the mind, we should limit ourselves to third-person observations that can be objectively verified and not accept any first-person accounts. Dennett undermines this opposition by what he calls "first-person operationalism": the gap is to be introduced into my very first-person experience, the gap between content and its registration, between represented time and the time of representation. A nice proto-

Lacanian point of Dennett (and the key to his heterophenomenology) is this insistence on the distinction, in homology with space, between the time of representation and the representation of time: they are not the same, that is, the loop of flashback is discernible even in our most immediate temporal experience—the succession of events ABCDEF . . . is represented in our consciousness so that it begins with E, then goes back to ABCD, and, finally, returns to F, which in reality directly follows E. So even in our most direct temporal self-experience, a gap akin to that between signifier and signified is already at work: even here, one cannot "save the phenomena," since what we (mis)perceive as directly experienced representation of time (the phenomenal succession ABCDEF . . .) is already a "mediated" construct from a different time of representation (E/ABCD/F . . .). "First-person operationalism" thus emphasizes how, even in our "direct (self-)experience," there is a gap between content (the narrative inscribed into our memory) and the "operational" level of how the subject constructed this content, where we always have a series of rewritings and tinkerings: "introspection provides us—the subject as well as the 'outside' experimenter—only with the content of representation, not with the features of the representational medium itself."[4] In this precise sense, the subject is his own fiction: the content of his own self-experience is a narrativization in which memory traces already intervene. So when Dennett makes " 'writing it down' in memory criterial for consciousness; that is *what it is* for the 'given' to be 'taken'— to be taken one way rather than another," and claims that "there is no reality of conscious experience independent of the effects of various vehicles of content on subsequent action (and, hence, on memory),"[5] we should be careful not to miss the point: what counts for the concerned subject himself is the way an event is "written down," memorized— memory is constitutive of my "direct experience" itself, that is, "direct experience" is what I *memorize* as my direct experience. Or, to put it in Hegelian terms (which would undoubtedly appall Dennett): immediacy itself is mediated, it is a product of the mediation of traces. One can also put this in terms of the relationship between direct experience and judgment on it: Dennett's point is that there is no "direct experience" prior to judgement—what I (re)construct (write down) as my experience is already supported by judgmental decisions. For this reason, the whole problem of "filling in the gaps" is a false problem since there are no gaps to be filled in. Let us take the classic example of our reading a text that contains a lot of printing mistakes: most of the mistakes pass unnoticed; since, in our reading, we are guided by an active attitude of recognizing patterns, we, for the most part, simply read the text as if there were no mistakes. The usual phenomenological account of this would be that, due to my active attitude of recognizing ideal patterns, I "fill in the gaps" and automatically, even prior to my conscious perception, reconstitute the correct spelling, so that it appears to me that I read the correct text, without mistakes. What if, however, the actual procedure is different?—driven by the attitude of actively searching for known patterns, I quickly scan a text (our actual perception is much more discontinuous and fragmentary than it may appear), and this combination of an active attitude of searching and fragmented perception leads my mind directly to the conlcusion that, for example, the word I just read is "conclusion," not "conlcusion," as it was actually written? There are no gaps to be filled in here, since there is no moment of perceptual experience prior to the conclusion (i.e., judgment) that the word I've just read is "conclusion": again, my active attitude drives me directly to the conclusion. This (somewhat simplified) example also renders clear Dennett's point that the opposition between (what he calls) "Stalinesque" and "Orwellian" interpretation is irrelevant: it is wrong to ask if I first, for a brief moment, perceive the word the way it is actually written ("conlcusion") and then, after a brief lapse of time, under the pressure of my search for recognizable patterns, change it into "conclusion" (the "Orwellian" brainwashing, which convinces the subject who first sees five fingers, that he actually sees four fingers), or if there is no actual perception of the misspelled word, so that the corrective misreading occurs already prior to my act of (conscious) perception (the "Stalinesque" pre-perceptual manipulation in which there is no moment of adequate perception of "conlcusion," since all I am ever aware of are already falsified memory traces, i.e., the theater of consciousness is like the courtroom stage in Stalinist show trials). Therein resides Dennett's key point: there is no limit that separates what goes on "before" our direct "live experience" (the pre-perceptual, pre-conscious processes), from what goes on "after" (the memory inscription, reporting, etc., on our experience), no It (a direct moment of experience) where the presubjective processes are magically transformed into the event of sense, into the subjective experience of sense, to which then refer later acts of reporting, memorizing it, etcetera. It is, on the contrary, the very act of judgment, the conclusion that "it is so," which makes us perceive the previous pre-subjective confusion as the consistent experience: "We don't *first* apprehend our experience in the Cartesian Theatre and *then,* on the basis of that acquired knowledge, have the ability to frame reports to express. . . . The emergence of the expression is precisely what creates or fixes the content of the higher-order thought expressed. There need be no *additional* episodic 'thought.' The higher-order state literally depends on—causally depends on—the expression of the speech act."[6]

The perfect example of this point, of course, is a situation in which I become aware of a "deep" attitude of mine, when, in a totally unexpected way, without any premeditation, I simply blurt something out. Dennett himself refers to the famous passage from one of Bertrand Russell's letters to Lady Ottoline in which he recalls the circumstances of his declaration of love to her: "I did not know I loved you till I heard myself telling you so—for one instant I thought 'Good God, what have I said?' and then I knew it was the truth."[7] For Dennett, this is not an exceptional feature but the basic mechanism that generates meaning: a word or a phrase forces itself upon us, and thereby imposes a semblance of narrative order on our confused experience; there is no preexisting "deep awareness of it" expressed in this phrase—it is, on the contrary, this very phrase that *organizes* our experience into a "deep awareness." . . . In literature, an outstanding example is provided by the very last lines of Patricia Highsmith's *Strangers on a Train:* in contrast to Hitchcock's film version, Guy *does* also kill Bruno's wife, and, at the novel's end, police detectives who have been closely monitoring him for some time, finally approach him in order to take him in for questioning. Guy, who has been preparing for this moment for a long time and has memorized a detailed alibi, reacts with a confessionary gesture of surrender that takes even him by surprise: "Guy tried to speak, and said something entirely different from what he had intended. 'Take me.'"[8] Again, Dennett's point would be that it is wrong to "substantialize" the attitude expressed in Guy's last words, as if, "deep in himself," he was all the time aware of his guilt and nourished a desire to be arrested and punished for it. There was, of course, a confessional "disposition" in Guy, but it was competing with other dispositions, ambiguous, not clearly defined, and it won over due to a concrete contingent constellation; not unlike Kieslowski's early *Blind Chance* (1981), which deals with three different outcomes of a man running for a train: he catches it and becomes a Communist official; he misses it and becomes a dissident; there is no train and he settles down to a mundane life. This notion of a mere chance that can determine the outcome of a man's life was unacceptable to Communists as well as to their opposition (it deprives dissident attitude of its deep moral foundation).[9] The point is that in each of the three cases, the contingency that gave the "spin" to his life would be "repressed," that is, the hero would construct his life story as a narrative leading to its final result (a dissident, an ordinary man, a Communist apparatchik) with a "deep necessity." Is this not what Lacan referred to as the *futur antérieur* of the unconscious that "will have been"?

The title of chapter 8 of *Consciousness Explained* ("How Words Do Things with Us") makes the point clear by means of a reversal of Austin's *How to Do Things with Words*: our symbolic universe is a pandemonium of competing forces (words, phrases, syntactic figures . . .), a universe of tinkering and opportunistic enlisting (i.e., of the exploitation of contingent opportunities). Dennett quotes Lincoln's famous line "You can fool all the people some of the time, and some of the people all the time, but you cannot fool all the people all of the time," drawing attention to its logical ambiguity: does it mean that there are some people who can always be fooled, or that on every occasion, someone or other is bound to be fooled? His point[10] is that it is wrong to ask "What did Lincoln really mean?"—probably, Lincoln himself was not aware of the ambiguity. He simply wanted to make a witty point, and the phrase "imposed itself on him" because "it sounded good." Here we have an exemplary case of how, when the subject has a vague intention-to-signify and is "looking for the right expression" (as we usually put it), the influence goes both ways: it is not only that, among the multitude of contenders, the best expression wins, but some expression might impose itself that changes more or less considerably the very intention-to-signify . . . is this not what Lacan referred to as the "efficiency of the signifier"?[11]

Dennett thus conceives of the human mind as a multitude of vaguely coordinated "softwares": programs created by evolution to solve some particular problem, and which, later, take over other functions. The structure of the human mind is that of overdetermination: in it, we find neither isolated particular organs with clearly defined functions, nor a universal Master-Self coordinating between them, but a permanently shifting "improvised" coordination—some particular program (not always the same) can temporarily assume the coordinating function (i.e., some specialists can be temporarily recruited as generalists). The human mind is thus a pandemonium of competing forces: words impose themselves, want to be spoken, so that we often say something without knowing in advance what we wanted to say. The function of language is thus ultimately *parasitic*: not only do words and phrases seem to impose themselves on us, trying to gain the upper hand, fighting for hegemony, but the very fundamental relationship between language and human beings who use it can be reversed—it could be argued that not only do human beings use language to reproduce themselves, multiply their power and knowledge, etcetera, but also, at perhaps a more fundamental level, language itself uses human beings to replicate and expand itself, to gain new wealth of meanings, etcetera (following Dawkins, Dennett calls the smallest unit of the symbolic reproduction a "meme"). What really happens when, for example, a man sacrifices his material well-being, his life even, for some cause, for "an idea" (say, for his religious belief)? One cannot reduce this "idea" to a shorthand for the well-being of other human beings: this man literally sacrificed himself for an "idea," he gave precedence to the strengthening of this "meme" over his own life. So it is not sufficient to say that men use ideas as means of communication among themselves, as mental patterns to better organize their lives and cope with dangerous situations, and so on—in a way, ideas themselves use men as the expendable means of their proliferation. (In Hegelian terms, this shift is, of course, the shift from individuals to their social substance, as the Ground that reduces them to its accidents.)

The first, obvious result of this account is that it allows no place for the philosophical subject, the Cartesian *cogito* or transcendental self-consciousness, nor for (what appears to be) its opposite, the Freudian unconscious as the hidden agency that effectively "pulls the strings" of our psychic life: what they both presuppose is a unified agent (the subject, the unconscious), which controls and directs the course of events, and Dennett's point is, precisely, that there is *no* such agent.[12] Dennett's account of the spontaneous, "mechanistic" emergence of a narrative out of the encounter between the subject's attitude (interest, "thrust") and a series of ultimately contingent responses/signals from the real,[13] intends to get rid of the unconscious as the hidden narrative master staging and controlling everything behind the scenes, and to show how a narrative can emerge out of opportunistic tinkering (*bricolage*). His example is that of a party game in which the dupe is told that while he is out of the room, one member of the assembled party will relate to all others a recent dream. When the dupe returns to the room, he can ask anyone in the room questions, the answers to which have to be a simple "Yes!" or "No!"—the point of the game is for the dupe to guess from the contours of the dream the identity of the dreamer. However, once the dupe is out of the room, the rest of the party agrees that there will simply be no dream: they will answer the dupe's questions following some simple rule unrelated to their content (say, if the last letter is from the first half of the alphabet, the answer should be "Yes!," otherwise "No!"), with the proviso of non-contradiction. What thus often emerges is a ludicrous and obscene narrative to which *there is no author:* the closest to the author is the dupe himself, who provides the general thrust by means of the direction implied by his questions, while the rest is the result of a pure contingency. Dennett's point is that not only dreams, but even the narratives that form the cobweb of our daily existence, emerge in this way, by means of opportunistic tinkering and contingent encounters. . . . Although this explanation involves a model materialist procedure, accounting for the appearance of a coherent and purposeful totality of sense from contingent encounters between two heterogeneous levels (the subject's cognitive thrust; signals from reality), one is nonetheless tempted to counter it with an argument homologous to Kant's rejection of the empiricist claim that the entire content of our mind comes from sensual experience: the problem that Dennett does not resolve is that of the very *form* of narrative—where does the subject's capacity to organize its contingent experience into the *form* of narrative (or to recognize in a series of events the form of narrative) come from? Everything can be explained this way except the narrative form itself, which, in a way, *must already be here.* One is tempted to say that this silently presupposed form is Dennett's unconscious, an invisible structure he is unaware of, operative in the phenomena he describes.[14]

Are we then back at the Kantian idealist position of a formal a priori as the condition of possibility for the organization of our contingent experiences into a coherent narrative? At this point, it is crucial to take into account one of the fundamental lessons of psychoanalytic theory: a form that precedes content is always an index of some traumatic "primordially repressed" content. This lesson holds especially for the formalism encountered in art: as it was emphasized by Fredric Jameson, the desperate formalist attempt to distinguish the formal structure from any positive content, is the unfailing index of the violent repression of some traumatic content—the last trace of this content is the frozen form itself. This notion of autonomous form as the index of some repressed traumatic content applies specifically to the narrative form—this brings us to Jameson's other thesis, according to which, *narrative as such is ideological*, the elementary form of ideology: it is not only that some narratives are "false," based upon the exclusion of traumatic events and the patching-up of the gaps left over by these exclusions—the answer to the question "Why do we tell stories?" is that the *narrative as such* emerges in order to resolve some fundamental antagonism by way of rearranging its terms into a temporal succession. It is thus the very *form* of narrative that bears witness to some repressed antagonism.[15]

So, back to Dennett: the fact that "we are all storytellers" has to be grounded in an act of "primordial repression." Where, in Dennett, do we find traces of the absence of this repression (to use the somewhat outdated jargon)? Dennett draws a convincing and insightful parallel between an animal's physical environs and human environs; not only human artifacts (clothes, houses, tools), but also the "virtual" environs of the discursive cobweb: "Stripped of [the 'web of discourses'], an individual human being is as incomplete as a bird without feathers, a turtle without its shell."[16] A naked man is the same nonsense as a shaved ape: without language (and tools and . . .), man is a crippled animal—it is this lack that is supplemented by symbolic institutions and tools, so that the point made obvious today, in popular culture figures like Robocop (man is simultaneously super-animal and crippled), holds from the very beginning. The problem here is: how do we pass from "natural" to "symbolic" environs? The unexplained presupposition of the narrative form in Dennett bears witness to the fact that this passage is not direct, that one cannot account for it within a continuous evolutionary narrative: something has to intervene between the two, a kind of "vanishing mediator," which is neither Nature nor Culture—this in-between is silently presupposed and jumped over by Dennett. Again, we are not idealists: this in-between is not the spark of *logos* magically conferred on *Homo sapiens,* enabling him to form his supplementary virtual symbolic environs, but precisely something that, although it is also no longer nature, is not yet *logos,* and has to be "repressed" by *logos*—the Freudian name for this in-between, of course, is death drive. With regard to this in-between, it is interesting to note how philosophical narratives of the "birth of man" are always compelled to presuppose such a moment in human (pre)history when (what will become) man, is no longer a mere animal and simultaneously not yet a "being of language," bound by symbolic Law; a moment of thoroughly "perverted," "denaturalized," "derailed" nature that is not yet culture. In his anthropological writings, Kant emphasized that the human animal needs disciplinary pressure in order to tame an uncanny "unruliness" that seems to be inherent to human nature—a wild, unconstrained propensity to insist stubbornly on one's own will, cost what it may. It is on account of this "unruliness" that the human animal needs a Master to discipline him: discipline targets this "unruliness," not the animal nature in man. In Hegel's *Lectures on Philosophy of History,* a similar role is played by the reference to "negroes": significantly, Hegel deals with "negroes" before history proper (which starts with ancient China), in the section entitled "The Natural Context or the Geographical Basis of World History": "negroes" stand there for the human spirit in its "state of nature," they are described as a kind of perverted, monstrous child, simultaneously naive and extremely corrupted, that is, living in the prelapsarian state of innocence, and, precisely as such, the most cruel barbarians; part of nature and yet thoroughly denaturalized; ruthlessly manipulating nature through primitive sorcery, yet simultaneously terrified by the raging natural forces; mindlessly brave cowards. . . .[17] *This in-between is the "repressed" of the narrative form* (in this case, of Hegel's "large narrative" of world-historical succession of spiritual forms): not nature as such, but the very break with nature that is (later) supplemented by the virtual universe of narratives.

And, it is on account of this in-between that the subject cannot be reduced to the Self as a "center of narrative gravity." Where, then, do we find traces of this in-between in philosophy? In the Cartesian *cogito.* For a systematic deployment of this dimension, one has to wait for the advent of German Idealism. The basic insight of Schelling, whereby, prior to its assertion as the medium of the rational Word, the subject is the "infinite lack of being [*unendliche Mangel an Sein*]," the violent gesture of contraction that negates every being outside itself, also forms the core of Hegel's notion of madness: when Hegel determines madness to be a withdrawal from the actual world, the closing of the soul into itself, its "contraction," the cutting-off of its links with external reality, he all too quickly conceives of this withdrawal as a "regression" to the level of the "animal soul" still embedded in its natural environs and determined by the rhythm of nature (night and day, etc.). Does this withdrawal, on the contrary, not designate the severing of the links with the *Umwelt,* the end of the subject's immersion into its immediate natural environs, and is it, as such, not the founding gesture of "humanization"? Was this withdrawal-into-self not accomplished by Descartes in his universal doubt and reduction to *cogito,* which, as Derrida pointed out in his "Cogito and the History of Madness,"[18] also involves a passage through the moment of radical madness? Are we thus not back at the well-known and often-quoted passage from *Jenaer Realphilosophie,* where Hegel characterizes the experience of pure Self, of the contraction-into-self of the subject, as the "night of the world," the eclipse of (constituted) reality?:

> The human being is this night, this empty nothing, that contains everything in its simplicity—an unending wealth of many representations, images, of which none belongs to him—or which are not present. This night, the inner of nature, that exists here—pure self—in phantasmagorical representations, is night all around it, in which here shoots a bloody head—there another white ghastly apparition, suddenly here before it, and just so disappears. One catches sight of this night when one looks human beings in the eye—into a night that becomes awful.[19]

And the symbolic order, the universe of the Word, *logos,* can only emerge from the experience of this abyss. As Hegel puts it, this inwardness of the pure self "must enter also into existence, become an object, oppose itself to this innerness to be external; return to being. This is language as name-giving power. . . . Through the name the object as individual entity is born out of the I."[20] What we must be careful not to miss here, is how Hegel's break with the Enlightenment tradition can be discerned in the reversal of the very metaphor for the subject: the subject is no longer the Light of Reason opposed to the nontransparent, impenetrable Stuff (of Nature, Tradition . . .); his very kernel, the gesture that opens up the space for the Light of Logos, is absolute negativity, the "night of the world," the point of utter madness in which fantasmatic apparitions of "partial objects" err around. Consequently, there is no subjectivity without this gesture of withdrawal; which is why Hegel is fully justified in inverting the standard question of how the fall-regression into madness is possible: the true question is rather how the subject is able to climb out of madness and to reach "normalcy." That is to say, the withdrawal-into-self, the cutting-off of the links to the environs, is followed by the construction of a symbolic universe that the subject projects onto reality as a kind of substitute-formation, destined to recompense us for the loss of the immediate, pre-symbolic real. However, as Freud himself asserted in his analysis of Daniel Paul Schreber's paranoia, the manufacturing of a substitute-formation that recompenses the subject for the loss of reality, is the most succinct definition of the paranoiac construction as an attempt to cure the subject of the disintegration of his universe. In short, the ontological necessity of "madness" resides in the fact that it is not possible to pass directly from the purely "animal soul," immersed in its natural environs, to "normal" subjectivity, dwelling in its symbolic virtual environs—the "vanishing mediator" between the two is the "mad" gesture of radical withdrawal from reality, which opens up the space for its symbolic (re)constitution.[21]

So, back to Dennett again: we may seem to have erred far from his evolutionary-scientific problematic, and well into the murky waters of metaphysical speculation. Here, however, a reference to *psychoanalytic* experience becomes crucial. Does Hegel's brief description—"here shoots a bloody head, there another white ghastly apparition"—not fit perfectly with Lacan's notion of the "dismembered body [*le corps morcelé*]"? What Hegel calls the "night of the world" (the fantasmatic, pre-symbolic domain of partial drives), is an undeniable component of the subject's most radical self-experience, exemplified, among others, by Hieronymous Bosch's celebrated paintings. In a way, the entire psychoanalytic experience focuses on the traces of the traumatic passage from this "night of the world" into our "daily" universe of *logos*. The tension between the narrative form and the "death drive," as the withdrawal-into-self constitutive of the subject, is thus the missing link that has to be presupposed if we are to account for the passage from "natural" to "symbolic" environs. Within the symbolic space itself, this vanishing point of the "withdrawal-into-self" is operative in the guise of what Lacan calls the "subject of the enunciation," as opposed to the "subject of the enunciated" (the subject's symbolic and/or imaginary identifications). The moment Descartes interprets *cogito* as *res cogitans,* he, of course, conflates the two; the reduction of the subject to what Dennett calls the "Cartesian Theater" (the stage of self-awareness in which we immediately experience phenomena, the place where the objective neuronal, etc., bodily mechanisms "magically" produce the effect of phenomenal [self-]experience) is another version of this conflation, of the reduction of the subject of enunciation to the subject of the enunciated. However, what about the Kantian rereading of *cogito* as the pure point of self-consciousness, which does not designate any actual self-awareness, but rather functions as a kind of logical fiction, as the point of virtual self-awareness that is *as such* already actual (i.e., operative)?: I could have become self-conscious of each of my mental acts if I had chosen to probe into them, and the awareness of this possibility already determines the way I actually behave. For Kant, consciousness is always already self-consciousness, but *not* in the sense that, whenever I am aware of the content of my thoughts, I am simultaneously aware of myself being aware of this content—this is not only patently untrue, but also, if this were the case, we would be caught in the vicious cycle of infinite regression (am I also conscious of my being conscious of my object-directed consciousness? etc.). In his concise account of the status of Kantian self-consciousness, Robert Pippin[22] emphasized that Kantian self-consciousness points toward the fact that our consciousness of objects is "implicitly reflexive" (Pippin also speaks of "implicit awareness" or "potential awareness"): when I assert (or desire or imagine or reject . . .) X, I always already implicitly "take myself" as the one who is asserting (or desiring or . . .) X. Perhaps the best example is that of "spontaneously" following a rule (as when one engages in speech activity): when I speak a language, I am, of course, not actively conscious of the rules I follow—my active focusing on these rules would prevent me from fluently speaking this language; but, I am nonetheless implicitly aware that I am speaking a language, and thus, following rules. In this sense, self-consciousness is not an additional reflexive turn of the gaze from the object one is conscious of upon oneself, but is constitutive of "direct" consciousness itself: "to be conscious of X" *means that* I "take myself" to be related to X (i.e., that my relation toward X is minimally reflective). This reflexivity is not only not to be opposed to pre-reflexive spontaneity (in the standard sense of the contrast between being directly immersed in an activity and maintaining a reflexive distance toward it: in the ethical domain, for example, the contrast between spontaneously doing one's duty, since "it is part of my nature, I cannot do it otherwise," and doing my duty after a tortuous self-examination), but the two are strictly synonymous. The Kantian notion of "spontaneity" means precisely that I, the subject, am not directly determined by (external or internal) causes: causes motivate me only insofar as I reflexively accept them as motifs (i.e., insofar as I accept to be determined by them). In the domain of ethics, this self-consciousness qua reflexivity is discernible in the guise of the so-called "incorporation thesis": when, in my acts, I succumb to a temptation, I am never justified in saying "What can I do, I am made like this, it's my nature, I cannot resist it!"—"spontaneity" qua reflexivity means precisely that this very passive succumbing to a temptation already involves a previous active acceptance of such a passive position toward the temptation.[23] In this sense, self-consciousness means that every immediacy is always already mediated: when I directly immerse myself in an activity, this immersion is always grounded in an implicit act of immersing oneself; when I follow my most brutal instincts and "behave as an animal," I still remain the one who *decided* to behave in that way, however deeply repressed this decision may be.[24]

Self-consciousness is thus, in a way, even less than a software program, it is a pure logical function, even symbolic fiction or presupposition (the point conceded to Dennett), which is nonetheless necessary for the functioning of the subject in "reality": there is no subject who, in the full presence of self-awareness, reflects and decides—it is just that, in the way I effectively act, a reflective attitude of deciding is always already presupposed. We encounter here again the difference between subject and Self: the Self, of course, is a mere "center of narrative gravity," while the subject is the void itself filled in by the ever-changing centers of narrative gravity. Kant thus wholly endorses the famous Humean rejection of the notion of substantial Self, that is, his claim that, no matter how attentively he probes introspectively into the content of his mind, he always encounters some particular, determinate idea, never his Self as such:[25] of course, there is no Self in the sense of a particular substantial representation above and beyond other such representations. No stable substantial content guarantees the unity of the subject; any such content would involve an infinite regress, since it would mean that the Self is in a way "a part of himself," as if the subject can encounter, within himself, a part that is "his Self." Consequently, Kant also accepts the claim that the subject is not directly accessible to himself: the introspective perceptions of my inner life are no closer to the noumenal dimension than the perceptions of external reality, that is, for Kant, it is not legitimate to posit the direct coincidence of the observer and the observed. This coincidence is *not* what Kantian self-consciousness ("transcendental apperception") is about: to postulate such an identity would mean, precisely, to commit the "paralogism of pure reason."

Dennett is at his best when he viciously demolishes the standard philosophical game of "let us imagine that . . ." (let us imagine a zombie who acts and speaks exactly like a human, i.e., whose behavior is indistinguishable from a human, and who is nonetheless *not* a human, but merely a mindless machine following a built-in program . . .) and of drawing conclusions from such counterfactual mental experiments (about the a priori impossibility of artificial intelligence, of a biological foundation of mind, etc.): his counter-question is simply, "Can you *really* imagine it?" The Kantian self-consciousness involves a similar gap: although one can imagine self-consciousness accompanying all the acts of our mind, for structural reasons, this potentiality can never be fully actualized, and it is this very intermediate status that defines self-consciousness. For that reason, one should counter the mystique of "self-acquaintance" as the primordial, unsurpassable fact, with the claim that self-consciousness emerges precisely because there is no direct "self-awareness" or "self-acquaintance" of the subject: the Kantian self-consciousness is an empty logical presupposition that fills in the gap of the impossibility of direct "self-awareness" (Kant himself makes this point quite clearly when he emphasizes how the subject is inaccessible to himself, not only in its noumenal dimension—I cannot ever get to know what I am for a Thing—but even phenomenally: the representation of "I" is necessarily empty). Henrich himself makes this point in his own way, when he actualizes the crucial Kantian distinction between "subject" and "person": the "person" is the psychophysical individual, a living being with a place among all mundane things, part of the common life-world; while the "subject" is the point of self-consciousness that does not coincide with any specific feature of the world—it is rather the void of the One, to which every thinkable and experienceable content should be related, insofar as it is thinkable and experienceable.[26] What one should do in order to accomplish the crucial passage from the subject of self-acquaintance to the subject of the unconscious, is simply to "de-psychologize" the former, to erase all traces of "actual self-experience" and to purify it into a pure logical function (or, rather, presupposition) of an X, to whom attitudes are attributed; the Lacanian "subject of the unconscious" is thus not the pre-discursive reservoir of affects and drives, but its exact opposite: a pure logical construct, devoid of any experiential content and as such beyond reach for our self-experience.

The Kantian self-consciousness is thus *more* than my fragmentary and shifting awareness of the states of my mind, and *less* than a direct insight into "what I am myself," into my substantial identity: it is a logical fiction, a nonsubstantial point of reference, which has to be added in order to stand for "that which" has an attitude, desires, makes judgments, and so on. To put it in Dennett's terms: for Kant, self-consciousness is not only not hindered by the absence of the Cartesian Theater—quite on the contrary, it emerges as an empty logical function *because* there is no Cartesian Theater, no direct phenomenal self-acquaintance of the subject. There is subject *qua $* insofar as (and because) there is no direct *Selbst-Vertrautheit,* insofar as (and because) the subject is not directly accessible to himself, because (as Kant put it) I cannot ever know what I am in my noumenal dimension, as the "Thing that thinks." One is thus tempted to reverse the standard Manfred Frank gesture of concluding (from the failure of reflection, of the self-reflective grounding of the subject's identity in the recognition of "himself" in his other), that there must be a previous direct self-acquaintance: what if *failure comes first,* what if "subject" is nothing but the void, the gap, opened up by the failure of reflection? What if all the figures of positive self-acquaintance are just so many secondary "fillers" of this primordial gap? Every recognition of the subject, in an image or a signifying trait (in short: every identification), already betrays its core; every jubilant "That's me!" already contains the seed of "That's *not* me!" However, what if, far from consisting in some substantial kernel of identity, inaccessible to reflective recuperation, the subject (as distinct from substance) emerges in this very movement of the failure of identification?

The point here is that one should take Lacan's term "subject of the signifier" literally: there is, of course, no substantial signified content that guarantees the unity of the I; at this level, the subject is multiple, dispersed—its unity is guaranteed only by the self-referential symbolic act, that is, "I" is a purely performative entity, it is the one who *says* "I." Therein resides the mystery of the subject's "self-positing," rendered thematic by Fichte: of course, when I say "I," I do not create any new content, I merely designate myself, the person who is uttering the phrase. This self-designation nonetheless gives rise to ("posits") an X that is *not* the "real" flesh-and-blood person uttering it, but, precisely and merely, the pure void of self-referential designation (the Lacanian "subject of the enunciation"): "I" am not directly my body or even the content of my mind; "I" am rather that X which *has* all these features as its properties. The Lacanian subject is thus the "subject of the signifier," not in the sense of being reducible to one of the signifiers in the signifying chain ("I" is not directly the signifier *I*, since, in this case, a computer or another machine writing "I" would be a subject), but in a much more precise sense: when I say "I" (i.e., when I designate "myself" as "I") this very act of signifying adds something to the "real flesh-and-blood entity" (inclusive of the content of its mental states, desires, attitudes) thus designated, and the subject is that X which is added to the designated content by means of the act of its self-referential designation. It is therefore misleading to say that the unity of the I is "a mere fiction" beneath which there is the multitude of inconsistent mental processes: the point is that this fiction gives rise to "effects in the real," that it acts as a necessary presupposition to a series of "real" acts.

It is significant how, in his brief account of the evolutionary emergence of self-consciousness, Dennett basically relies on G. H. Mead's famous account on how Self emerges from social interaction (from acts of imagining how I appear to another subject and from "internalizing" the other's view: in my "conscience," I perform imaginatively, in "silent inner speech," the possible reproaches that others may voice against my

acts, etc.). Here, however, one should again invoke the difference between subject and person: Henrich was quite justified in pointing out
how this dialectic of self-reflection as internalized social interaction, can
only account for my Self or "personhood," for the features that constitute my "self-image" (my imaginary and/or symbolic identifications),
not for the emergence of the subject itself qua $.

To recapitulate: the Kantian self-consciousness is a purely logical
function that signals only that every content of my consciousness is
already minimally mediated/reflected: as we have already pointed out,
when I desire X, I can never say "I am simply like that, I cannot help
desiring X, it's part of my nature," since, I always *desire to desire X,* that
is, I reflectively accept my desire for X—all reasons that motivate me to
act, exert their causal power only insofar as I "posit" or accept them as
reasons. . . . Unexpectedly, this already brings us close to the psychoanalytic problematic; that is to say, one would think that "implicit reflexivity" is limited to conscious activity and is, as such, precisely that which
our unconscious acts lack—when I act unconsciously, I act as if I follow
a blind compulsion, as if I am submitted to a pseudonatural causality.
However, according to Lacan, "implicit reflexivity" is not only "also"
discernible in the unconscious, it is precisely that which, at its most radical, *is unconscious.* Let us recall the typical attitude of a hysterical subject
who complains how he is exploited, manipulated, victimized by others,
reduced to an object of exchange—Lacan's answer to this is that this
subjective position of a passive victim of circumstances is never simply
imposed from outside onto the subject but has to be at least minimally
endorsed by him. The subject, of course, is not aware of his active participation in his own victimization—this, precisely, is the "unconscious"
truth of the subject's conscious experience of being a mere passive victim of circumstances. One can see now in what precise psychoanalytical
context Lacan's apparently nonsensical thesis is grounded, according to
which, the Cartesian *cogito* (or, rather, the Kantian self-consciousness)
is the very subject of the unconscious: for Lacan, "subject of the unconscious," the subject to be attributed to the Freudian unconscious, is
precisely this empty point of self-relating, not a subject bursting with
a wealth of libidinal forces and fantasies. This paradoxical identity of
self-consciousness (in the precise sense that this term acquires in German Idealism) with the subject of the unconscious becomes clear in

the problematic of radical Evil, from Kant to Schelling: faced with the enigma of how it is that we hold an evil person responsible for his deeds (although it is clear to us that the propensity to Evil is part of this person's "nature," i.e., that he cannot but "follow his nature" and accomplish his deeds with an absolute necessity), Kant and Schelling postulate a nonphenomenal, transcendental, atemporal act of primordial choice, by means of which, each of us, prior to his temporal bodily existence, chooses his eternal character.[27] Within our temporal phenomenal existence, this act of choice is experienced as an imposed necessity, which means that the subject, in his phenomenal self-awareness, is not conscious of the free choice that grounds his character (his ethical "nature") —that is to say, *this act is radically unconscious* (the conclusion explicitly drawn by Schelling). We encounter here again the subject as the void of pure reflectivity, as that X to which one can attribute (as his free decision) what, in our phenomenal self-awareness, one experiences as part of our inherited or otherwise imposed nature. The conclusion to be drawn is thus, again, that *self-consciousness itself is radically unconscious.*[28]

The (Lacanian) subject of the unconscious is thus neither the standard (anti-)philosophical subject of self-awareness, nor the dispersed multitude of fluxes that explode the subject's unity: this opposition between the "unified" subject of self-awareness and the dispersed pre-subjective multitude is false, it relies on the exclusion of the subject qua $, the "vanishing mediator" between the two.[29] Dennett is right in emphasizing how our conscious awareness is fragmentary, partial, discontinuous: one never encounters "Self" as a determinate representation in and of our mind. However, is not the conclusion to be drawn from this, that the unity of the subject, that which makes him a One, is unconscious? Again, this subject is not some positive content, inaccessible to our conscious awareness, but a pure logical function: when the subject conceives himself as One—as that One, to which acts, attitudes, etcetera, are attributed (or, rather, imputed)—this "One" has no positive content that would guarantee its consistency—its unity is purely logical and performative (i.e., the only content of this One is the operation of assuming as "mine," a multitude of acts, attitudes, etc.). One is thus tempted to claim that, while, as the title of his book suggests, Dennett may well succeed in explaining consciousness, what he does not explain, what awaits to be explained, is the unconscious, namely the Freudian unconscious, which is neither the pre-subjective ("objective") neuronal apparatus, the material vehicle of my mind, nor the subject's fragmentary self-awareness.

Where, then, is the place for the Freudian unconscious? Again, Dennett is right in undermining the phenomenological attempt to "save the phenomena," that is, in demonstrating how what we take to be our direct phenomenal (self-)experience is a later construct, based on a mixture of discontinuous perceptions, judgments, etcetera. In short, Dennett demonstrates the reflective status of our phenomenal self-awareness: it is not only that phenomena point toward a hidden transphenomenal essence; phenomena themselves are mediated (i.e., the phenomenal experience itself appears [is materialized-operationalized] in a multitude of its particular phenomenal vehicles, gestures, etc.). Therefore, what a multitude of actual phenomena (fragmentary phenomenal experiences) point toward, is the phenomenon itself, the construct of a continuous "stream of consciousness," a theater, a screen in our mind in which the mind directly perceives itself. In order to demonstrate the senselessness of the philosophical insistence on our direct (self-)experience, after we have demonstrated how this direct experience never effectively occurs in our consciousness, Dennett claims that, in order to "save phenomena," one would have to introduce the "bizarre category of the objectively subjective—the way things actually, objectively seem to you even if they don't seem that way to you."[30] That is to say, one would have to distinguish between our actual phenomenal (self-)experience (which is a fragmentary and inconsistent mixture of perceptions, judgments, etc.) and the true phenomenal self-experience, which, precisely, is never given to us in direct experience. While Dennett thus evokes this hypothesis of the "objectively subjective" only to reject it as a senseless, self-defeating paradox, one is tempted to conceive this level of the "objectively subjective" as the very locus of the unconscious: does the Freudian unconscious not designate precisely the way things appear to us without our ever being directly aware of them?[31] And, is the subject of the unconscious not precisely that X to which these ("objectively subjective") modes of appearance, inaccessible to our conscious awareness, are attributed/imputed (or, rather, *have to be* attributed/imputed)? In this sense, as Lacan points out, the subject of the unconscious is not a given but an ethical supposition, i.e., there *has to be* an X to whom the "objectively subjective" unconscious phenomena are attributed. This complicity between the pure subject of the signifier ($) and the "objectively subjective" unconscious allows us to save both, the unconscious as well as the *cogito*, by proving that, far from excluding each other, they effectively presuppose each other—as Lacan put it, the Cartesian *cogito* is the subject of the unconscious.

There is, however, a final misunderstanding to be dispelled here: the attribution of the "objectively subjective" fantasy to the *cogito* does not mean that, beneath the everyday subject that we are in our conscious lives, one has to presuppose another, "deeper" subject who is able to experience directly the unconscious fantasies inaccessible to our conscious Self. What one should insist on, in contrast to such a misreading, is the insurmountable gap between the empty subject ($) and the wealth of fantasies: for a priori topological reasons, they can never directly meet, since they are located at the opposite surfaces of the Möbius band. The dimension of fantasy is constitutive of the subject (i.e., there is no subject without fantasy)—this constitutive link between subject and fantasy, however, does *not* mean that we are dealing with a subject the moment an entity displays signs of "inner life" (i.e., of a fantasmatic self-experience that cannot be reduced to external behavior). What characterizes human subjectivity proper is rather the gap that separates the two: the fact that fantasy, at its most elementary, becomes inaccessible to the subject—it is this inaccessibility which makes the subject "empty" ($). We thus obtain a relationship that totally subverts the standard notion of the subject of phenomenal (self-)experience (i.e., of the subject who directly experiences himself, his "inner states"): an "impossible" relationship between the *empty, nonphenomenal subject* and the *phenomenon that remains inaccessible to the subject*—the very relation registered by Lacan's formula of fantasy, $\$ \lozenge a$.

Among today's cognitive scientists, the preferred model for the emergence of (self-)consciousness is that of the multiple parallel networks whose interaction is not dominated by any central controller: the microcosm of interacting agents spontaneously gives rise to a global pattern that sets the context of interaction without being embodied in any particular agent (the subject's "true Self"). Cognitive scientists repeat again and again how our mind does not possess a centralized control structure that runs top-down, executing designs in a linear way: our mind is rather a *bricolage* of multiple agents who collaborate bottom-up (i.e., whose organization is shifting, "opportunistic," robust, adaptive, flexible . . .). However, how do we get from here to (self-)consciousness? That is to say, (self-)consciousness is *not* the pattern that "spontaneously" emerges from the interaction of multiple agents, but, rather, its exact obverse or a kind of negative: it is, in its primordial dimension, the experience of some malfunctioning, of some perturbation, in this spontaneous pattern or organization. (Self-)consciousness (the "thick moment" of consciousness, the awareness that I am now-here-alive)[32] is originally passive: in clear contrast to the notion according to which self-awareness originates in the subject's active relationship toward its environs, and is the constitutive moment of our activity of realizing a determinate goal, what originally I am "aware of" is that I am *not* in control, that my design misfired, that things just drift by. A computer that merely executes its program in a top-down way, *for that very reason* "does not think," is not conscious of itself.

One is thus tempted to apply here the dialectical reversal of epistemological obstacle into a positive ontological condition: what if the "enigma of consciousness," its inexplicable character, contains its own solution? What if all we have to do is to transpose the gap that renders consciousness (as the object of our study) "inexplicable," *into consciousness itself*? What if consciousness (or self-awareness) occurs only insofar as it appears to itself as an inexplicable emergence, that is, only insofar as it misrecognizes its own causes, the network that generates it? What if the ultimate paradox of consciousness is that consciousness—the very organ of "awareness"—can only occur insofar as it is *unaware* of its own conditions? However, this solution is still ambiguous: the obstacle remains epistemological, we merely transposed it into consciousness itself. What we thus obtain is the position of Kant who, in a mysterious subchapter of his *Critique of Practical Reason* entitled "Of the Wise Adaptation of Man's Cognitive Faculties to His Practical Vocation," endeavored to answer the question of what would happen to us if we were to gain access to the noumenal domain, to Things in themselves:

> instead of the conflict which now the moral disposition has to wage with inclinations and in which, after some defeats, moral strength of mind may be gradually won, God and eternity in their awful maj-

esty would stand unceasingly before our eyes. . . . Thus most actions conforming to the law would be done from fear, few would be done from hope, none from duty. The moral worth of actions, on which alone the worth of the person and even of the world depends in the eyes of supreme wisdom, would not exist at all. The conduct of man, so long as his nature remained as it is now, would be changed into mere mechanism, where, as in a puppet show, everything would gesticulate well but no life would be found in the figures.[33]

So, for Kant, the direct access to the noumenal domain would deprive us of the very "spontaneity" that forms the kernel of transcendental freedom: it would turn us into lifeless automata, or, to put it in today's terms, into computers, into "thinking machines."

Is, however, this conclusion really unavoidable? Is the status of consciousness basically that of freedom in a system of radical determinism? Are we free only insofar as we misrecognize the causes that determine us? In order to save us from this predicament, we should again displace the epistemological obstacle into a positive ontological condition. That is to say, the mistake of the identification of (self-)consciousness with misrecognition, with an epistemological obstacle, is that it stealthily (re)introduces the standard, premodern, "cosmological" notion of reality as a positive order of being: in such a fully constituted positive "chain of being," there is, of course, no place for the subject, so the dimension of subjectivity can only be conceived of as something that is strictly codependent with the epistemological misrecognition of the true positivity of being. Consequently, the only way effectively to account for the status of (self-) consciousness is to assert *the ontological incompleteness of "reality" itself*: there is "reality" only insofar as there is an ontological gap, a crack, in its very heart (i.e., a traumatic excess, a foreign body that cannot be integrated into it). This brings us back to the notion of the "night of the world": in this momentary suspension of the positive order of reality, we confront the ontological gap on account of which "reality" is never a complete, self-enclosed, positive order of being. It is only this experience of the psychotic withdrawal from reality, of the absolute self-contraction, that accounts for the mysterious "fact" of transcendental freedom, that is to say, for a (self-)consciousness that is effectively "spontaneous," whose spontaneity is not an effect of misrecognition of some "objective" process.

Notes

1 See, as a representative recent volume, *The Modern Subject: Conceptions of the Self in Classical German Philosophy,* ed. Karl Ameriks and Dieter Sturma (Albany: SUNY Press, 1995).

2 When, for example, Manfred Frank, the key representative of this movement, argues, against Lacan, that one cannot ground the subject in his identification with his mirror image (according to Frank, such an account "reifies" the subject, reduces him to an object of mirror-identification, and thus simply misses the proper dimension of subjectivity), one can only stare at this line of argumentation: as if Lacan's main point is not the distinction between the *ego (moi)*, which is explicitly determined by Lacan as an object grounded in mirror-identification, and the *subject* of the signifier.

3 The first great result of this school was thus to elucidate the passage from Kant to Fichte: this passage is not a direct one, i.e., Fichte is not the only "logical" radicalization of Kant—the first reactions to Kant's transcendental turn point toward the overcoming of idealist foundationalism and delineate the necessity to presuppose a pre-subjective and pre-reflective Ground as the ontological (pre)condition of the transcendental subject. Another interesting feature of this school is its antihistoricist turn: it is almost unique among "Continental" philosophical orientations in its rehabilitation of standard "ahistorical" philosophical argumentation—the reason why it often finds common language with analytical philosophy.

4 Daniel C. Dennett, *Consciousness Explained* (New York: Little, Brown and Company, 1991), 354.

5 Ibid., 132.

6 Ibid., 315.

7 Quoted in R. W. Clark, *The Life of Bertrand Russell* (London: Weidenfeld and Nicolson, 1975), 176.

8 Patricia Highsmith, *Strangers on a Train* (Harmondsworth, England: Penguin, 1982), 256.

9 One finds a similar anecdote in *Journey into Fear,* Eric Ambler's classic spy thriller: one of its heroes starts to advocate socialism in dinner talks just to embarrass and annoy his rich wife; however, step by step, he is taken in by his own socialist arguments, so he finishes as an authentic socialist. . . . Crucial here is the structure of overdetermination: a fundamental ethical decision can be triggered by some marginal contingent intrusion, and this reliance on contingency makes the fundamental decision no less "authentic." At a somewhat different level, one encounters the same structure of overdetermination in the two *Forrest Gump* novels: the hero has repeated brushes with history and unknowingly influences world-historical events (when, in the Watergate Hotel, he notices some burglars in a room opposite the courtyard, he calls guards; when playing football near the Berlin wall, he throws the ball across the wall and thereby sets in motion the chain of events that leads to its demolition . . .)— this idea of the totally contingent intervention of an idiot who triggers some well-known turnabout is definitely close to the materialist notion of history.

10 Dennett, *Consciousness Explained,* 244.

11 One is tempted to claim that, especially in his refined description of the temporality of (self-)perception, Dennett provides a version of the Derridean *différance:* the subject's most direct experience of a "now" is the result of a double temporary move, forward and backward—on the one hand, our perception is, of course, always minimally delayed in regard to what it perceives; on the other hand, it, as it were, tries to restore the balance (canceling the delay of perception) by automatically moving back the represented time with regard to the time of representation—to put it in somewhat simplified terms, I experience the content of my experience as taking place slightly earlier than the actual time of my experiencing, in order to compensate for the delay of my perception.

12 With regard to this precise point, Lacan fully agrees with Dennett: the Freudian unconscious is not another, hidden Controller, the ego's puppet-master, a shadowy double of the ego who effectively pulls its strings, but a pandemonium of inconsistent tendencies that endeavor to exploit contingent opportunities in order to articulate themselves.

13 Dennett, *Consciousness Explained,* 10–16.

14 The same goes for art as a social form: as Lacan emphasizes, the standard psychoanalytic explanation of art as the "sublimation" of illicit impulses—by way of formulating these impulses in a socially acceptable way and thus charming the public, art provides the artist with the satisfactions he was originally craving for and renounced when he became an artist (glory, women, power, money . . .)—silently presupposes that "the already established function of poet exists on the outside": "What needs to be justified is not simply the secondary benefits that individuals might derive from their works, but the originary possibility of a function like the poetic function in the form of a structure within a social consensus" (Jacques Lacan, *The Ethics of Psychoanalysis,* trans. Dennis Porter [London: Routledge, 1992], 145). Even the "transgressive" or "subversive" position of the artist as a marginal outcast (i.e., even the artist's very exclusion from society) already involves a "social consensus" that maintains open this space from which the artist can exert his attraction on the public.

15 In the domain of philosophy, it was F. W. J. Schelling who first articulated this connection between narrativization and primordial "repression": the emergence of the narrative space with its logic of temporal succession involves the repression of the vortex of "eternal" drives into the primordial, "absolute" Past (i.e., the original gesture of differentiation between Past and Present). See chapter 1 of Slavoj Žižek, *The Indivisible Remainder* (London: Verso, 1996).

16 Dennett, *Consciousness Explained,* 416.

17 See G. W. F. Hegel, *Lectures On the Philosophy of World History, Introduction: Reason in History* (Cambridge: Cambridge University Press, 1975), 176–90.

18 See Jacques Derrida, "Cogito and the History of Madness," in *Writing and Difference,* trans. Alan Bass (Chicago: University of Chicago Press, 1978), 31–63.

19 Quoted in Donald Phillip Verene, *Hegel's Recollection* (Albany: SUNY Press, 1985), 7–8.

20 Quoted in ibid., 8.

21 At its most radical, the German Idealist problematic of the "absolute negativity" thus involves a reversal of Austin's *How to Do Things with Words:* the true enigma is not "how can words act, how can they have an effect in the real?" but the opposite one, "how to do words with things" (i.e., how can the surface of meaning, the symbolic universe, emerge from the density of "things," of the Real, in the first place?).

22 See Robert Pippin, *Hegel's Idealism: The Satisfactions of Self-Consciousness* (Cambridge, Mass.: Cambridge University Press, 1989), 19–24.

23 As for the "incorporation thesis", see Henry E. Allison, *Kant's Theory of Freedom* (Cambridge: Cambridge University Press, 1990), and also chapter 4 of Slavoj Žižek, *Tarrying with the Negative* (Durham: Duke University Press, 1993).

24 It is crucial to see how Hegel's *Phenomenology of Spirit* in its entirety relies on this "implicit reflexivity": already at its very starting point, in the dialectic of "sensible certainty," the subject can (and has to) move beyond the direct fixation on a sensible "this," "now," or "here," because he is not simply transfixed on a "this," but simultaneously *takes himself as the one who is transfixed on a "this"*—only in this way, can he *compare* the two aspects of the relationship, the in-itself and his relationship to it, and become aware of the inconsistency of his position.

25 "For my part, when I enter most intimately into what I call *myself,* I always stumble on some particular perception or other, of heat or cold, light or shade, love or hatred, pain or pleasure. I never can catch *myself* at any time without a perception, and never can observe anything but the perception" (David Hume, *Treatise on Human Nature* [Oxford: Oxford University Press, 1978], 252).

26 See Dieter Henrich, *Fluchtlinien* (Frankfurt: Suhrkamp, 1982). (Incidentally, Henrich uses the same term as Gilles Deleuze, who also constantly refers to the *lignes de fuite.*)

27 For a detailed explanation of this notion of atemporal choice of one's character, see chapter 1 of Slavoj Žižek, *The Indivisible Remainder* (London: Verso, 1996).

28 It was already Fichte who was compelled to assume this paradox and to acknowledge that self-consciousness's primordial, absolute act of self-positing is never accessible to human consciousness.

29 We can see in what, precisely, consists the gap that separates Lacan (who is here much closer to Kant and Hegel) from the immediacy of the subjective "self-awareness" or "self-acquaintance" on which Henrich and his followers (especially Manfred Frank) insist: for Lacan, to designate this "implicite reflexivity," which constitutes the core of subjectivity as "self-acquaintance," already goes too far in the direction of phenomenology, and thus obfuscates the radically nonphenomenological status of the subject as pure logical presupposition, a priori inaccessible to any direct introspective insight. Frank rehearses the same argument against Idealist reflectivity as against Lacan: one cannot ground the subject's identity in an act of reflective self-recognition, since in order for me to recognize myself in an other (say, my mirror image), I must already be minimally acquainted with who I am—to be able to exclaim in front of a mirror "That's me!" I must have an idea of who this "me" is. Lacan's answer to this is that two levels are to be distinguished here. The identification with a mirror image is the identification with an object that effectively cannot ground the dimension of

subjectivity; for that reason, this identification is alienating and performative: in the very act of recognizing myself as that image, I performatively posit that image as "me"—prior to it, I was nothing, I simply had no content. Who, then, is the "me" that recognizes itself as that image? The point is that this "nothing," previous to imaginary recognition, is not a pure absence, but the subject itself, i.e., the void of self-relating negativity, the substanceless X to which attitudes, desires, etc., are attributed—I cannot be "acquainted" with it precisely because its status is thoroughly nonphenomenological. Any act of "self-acquaintance" thus already relies on a combination (or overlapping) of two radically heterogeneous levels, the pure subject of the signifier and an object of imaginary identification.

30   Dennett, *Consciousness Explained,* 132.

31   The standard phenomenalist reproach to the materialist description of the mind, involves the so-called Tibetan Prayer Wheel paradox: one can imagine a machine whose external behavior would imitate perfectly that of a human being, giving intelligent answers, making jokes, etc., but this machine would nonetheless remain a mere machine, since, it would not effectively understand the meaning of its (speech and other) acts, but just mechanically accomplish them. What is always missing in such a description is the mysterious X that makes these acts conscious-intentional acts. . . . From the Lacanian perspective, one is tempted to invert the problem and to claim that the true enigma rather consists in the fact that *there is no consciousness without the Tibetan Prayer Wheel effect:* if I am to experience myself as conscious and engage in intentional acts, there must be, on some "other scene," a (symbolic) machine functioning like the Tibetan Prayer Wheel (i.e., following its path blindly, but nonetheless producing symbolic effects).

32   See Nicholas Humphrey, "The Thick Moment," in *The Third Culture,* ed. John Brockman (New York: Touchstone, 1996).

33   Immanuel Kant, *Critique of Practical Reason* (New York: Macmillan, 1956), 152–53.

Notes on Contributors

Miran Božovič, Professor of Modern Philosophy at the University of Ljubljana (Slovenia), is the editor of Jeremy Bentham, *The Panopticon Writings* (1995).

Mladen Dolar, Professor of Social Philosophy at the University of Ljubljana (Slovenia), is the author of *The Bone in the Spirit: A Lacanian Reading of Hegel's 'Phenomenology of Spirit'* (1998).

Alain Grosrichard, Professor of French literature at the University of Geneva (Switzerland), is the author of *The Structure of Seraglio: The Fantasy of Oriental Despotism in 18th Century Europe* (1997).

Marc de Kessel, Professor of Philosophy at the University of Ghent (Belgium), is the author of numerous essays on philosophy and psychoanalysis (in Dutch).

Robert Pfaller, Professor of Aesthetics at the Hochschule für Kunst, Linz (Austria), is the author of *Althusser—Das Schweigen in der Text* (1997).

Renata Salecl, Researcher at the Institute of Criminology, University of Ljubljana (Slovenia), is the author of *The Spoils of Freedom: Psychoanalysis and Feminism After the Fall of Socialism* (1994).

Slavoj Žižek, Senior Researcher at the Institute for Social Sciences, University of Ljubljana (Slovenia), is the author of *The Indivisible Remainder: An Essay on Schelling and Related Matters* (1996) and *The Plague of Fantasies* (1997).

Alenka Zupančič, Researcher at the Institute of Philosophy, Slovene Academy of Sciences, Ljubljana (Slovenia), is the author of *Die Ethik des Realen: Kant mit Lacan* (1995).

Index

terror: Stalinist terror in Bataille, 210–212
Todorov, Tzvetan, 177

Unconscious, the, 3, 30–31; versus the Id, 31

Vernant, Jean-Pierre, 176

Wagner, Richard: *Parsifal,* 99, 105–106
Welles, Orson, 92–100; allegory in, 92; *Chimes at Midnight,* 97–98; split subjectivity in, 95–96
will: in Kant, 59
Wittgenstein, Ludwig, 83

Library of Congress Cataloging-in-Publication Data
Cogito and the unconscious / edited by Slavoj Žižek.
p.   cm. — (SIC ; 2)
Includes bibliographical references and index.
ISBN 0-8223-2083-5 (hardcover : alk. paper).
— ISBN 0-8223-2097-5 (pbk. : alk. paper)
1. Psychoanalysis and philosophy.   2. Lacan, Jacques.
I. Žižek, Slavoj.   II. Series: SIC (Durham, N.C.) ; 2.
BF175.4.P45C64   1998   150.19′5—dc21   97-35189 CIP